Patterns of Legislative Politics

*Roll-Call Voting in Latin America and
the United States*

SCOTT MORGENSTERN

Duke University

CAMBRIDGE
UNIVERSITY PRESS

PUBLISHED BY THE PRESS SYNDICATE OF THE UNIVERSITY OF CAMBRIDGE
The Pitt Building, Trumpington Street, Cambridge, United Kingdom

CAMBRIDGE UNIVERSITY PRESS
The Edinburgh Building, Cambridge CB2 2RU, UK
40 West 20th Street, New York, NY 10011-4211, USA
477 Williamstown Road, Port Melbourne, VIC 3207, Australia
Ruiz de Alarcón 13, 28014 Madrid, Spain
Dock House, The Waterfront, Cape Town 8001, South Africa

http://www.cambridge.org

First published 2004

Printed in the United States of America

Typeface Sabon 10/12 pt.   *System* LATEX 2_ε [TB]

A catalog record for this book is available from the British Library.

Library of Congress Cataloging in Publication Data
Morgenstern, Scott.
   Patterns of legislative politics : roll-call voting in Latin America and the United States /
Scott Morgenstern.
      p.   cm.
Includes bibliographical references and index.
ISBN 0-521-82056-1 (hardback)
1. Legislative bodies – Southern Cone of South America – Voting. 2. United States.
Congress – Voting. I. Title.
JL1863M67   2003
328.3'75–dc21
                                                                          2003043027

ISBN 0 521 82056 1 hardback

10039 6711 X

Patterns of Legislative Politics

Using the United States as a basis of comparison, this book makes extensive use of roll-call data to explore patterns of legislative politics in Argentina, Brazil, Chile, and Uruguay. The patterns are defined by the extent to which parties, factions, delegations, or alliances – what the author collectively terms "legislative agents" – are unified in their voting and hence are collectively identifiable to voters as being responsible for policy decisions. Then, to develop an indicator of the second central pattern, the book examines the propensity of the legislative agents to form policy coalitions with one another. It shows that agents in Chile and to some extent Uruguay are more coalitional than in Argentina and Brazil, but there is evidence that the agents work with one another in these latter countries as well. The U.S. parties have exhibited an important shift, moving from low levels of unity and frequent bipartisanship toward considerably higher levels of unity and more frequent polarization. In explaining the patterns, the book considers the effects of the electoral system, legislators' ideology, cabinet membership, and other variables.

Scott Morgenstern is assistant professor of Political Science at Duke University and has been a visiting scholar at CIDE in Mexico, the Universidad de la Republica in Uruguay, and the Instituto Interuniversitario de Estudios de Iberoamérica y Portugal in Spain. He is coeditor of *Legislative Politics in Latin America*, and his articles have appeared in the *Journal of Politics, Party Politics, Comparative Politics*, and *Legislative Studies Quarterly*. His work has also appeared in several collected volumes and in journals in Argentina, Spain, Mexico, and Uruguay.

Contents

Tables and Figures

FIGURES

Preface and Acknowledgments

Legislatures house multiple individuals, most of whom are grouped into factions, parties, and coalitions. The patterns of legislative politics, then, are a product of the interactions among group members and among the groups. This book is an exploration of these interactions in Argentina, Brazil, Chile, and Uruguay, using the United States for a point of reference. The four Latin American countries share important commonalities in terms of geography and politics but are also clearly distinguishable for their political histories and institutions. All four countries suffered democratic breakdowns between 1964 and 1973 and only returned to democracy in the 1980s. Since then all have faced important threats to their democracies, ranging from a rising left in Uruguay, the removal of a president in Brazil, Pinochet's move from life-senator to foreign captive and accused murderer in Chile, and Argentina's economic collapse and the resignation of its elected and successor presidents. Though these and other pressures have led the countries to debate and implement important institutional reforms, they have not led to democratic breakdown.

In the past, students of Latin American politics have been forced to focus on the upheavals, military interludes, and democratic transitions. Since democracy seems to have implanted itself, there is a new value and interest in following the traditions of studies of the United States or European democracies and studying how prosaic issues affect legislative dynamics, representation, and coalition formation. This book follows this course, offering a comparative view of the unity of legislative groups – which is tied to representation – and the policy coalitions that form among them.

Producing a comparative statistical study implies important tradeoffs. On the one hand, the explicit comparisons allow better tests of the hypotheses than single-country studies. On the other, the amount of detail for each case must be limited for the comparison, and the statistical tests (and data collection efforts!) face new challenges. I have tried to balance these two sides by providing both country-focused and comparative descriptions and statistics.

In some places the results are not entirely satisfactory, but the results are suggestive enough to validate the hypotheses and encourage further study.

In order to facilitate the comparisons and hypothesis testing, this study relies on an intensive analysis of legislative roll-call votes. Roll-call data provide a unique opportunity to compare and contrast general patterns of policy making in the legislatures. Studies of particular policies would surely turn up new and perhaps more nuanced explanations of legislators' behavior, but they would do so at the expense of generalizability. Roll-call data, in contrast, allow direct comparisons among countries (and over time), and they have the added advantage of providing a view of the common patterns of legislative politics. These general patterns provide indicators relevant to representation of voters and the degree of accommodation or polarization inherent in the legislature, issues that are important in this continual, albeit troubled, era of democratic politics. These larger issues, and their links to the sustainability or quality of democracy, motivated this study.

This book has been in the making for a long time and has undergone several complete overhauls. The important idea about "agent systems" began its life while I was working on my dissertation, and I must thank Gary Cox for helping me to develop the terminology. I also want to acknowledge his critical but constructive commentary and indefatigable help in completing my dissertation, as well as his unending support since that time. Paul Drake and Matthew Shugart were also very helpful with the dissertation and its aftermath, and their influence is carried forth into this book. From the dissertation, I also salvaged my collection of the Uruguayan roll-call and interview data, as well as the ideas about nomination control. In working to expand that work into a comparative framework I discovered, however, that the dissertation placed too much emphasis on electoral systems and nomination control and ignored the role of legislators' electoral interests and ideology in explaining voting patterns. This book, therefore, builds on, but to an important extent contradicts, my dissertation.

The dissertation research, however, is still the basis from which this book grew, and I must thank Jorge Lanzaro, Gerardo Caetano, and the Instituto of Ciencia Política who hosted me during my year in Uruguay and facilitated my learning about the complex world of Uruguayan politics. Oscar Bottinelli was also instrumental in Uruguay for his help with several data sources. Daniel Buquet, Juan Andrés Moraes, and Daniel Chasquetti have been invaluable sources of information, and with the help of David Altman, they initiated me into the arcane Uruguayan culture.

The data collection and analysis for the rest of the book were completed during my time at Duke and my year of leave spent at the University of Salamanca. Conversations with John Aldrich, Jonathan Hartlyn, and Herbert Kitschelt were particularly helpful in developing the theoretical ideas, and Barry Ames, Octavio Amorim Neto, John Carey, Mark Jones,

John Londregan, and Peter Siavelis have all been extremely forthcoming with data, description, and explanations. I am sure, however, they all will be glad that I will now have fewer reasons to pelt them with requests for information. David Samuels offered some very helpful comments on a late draft of the manuscript, as well as help at other times. Kirk Hawkins has also been quite important, as the paper we wrote together on cohesion helped me to reach a more thorough understanding of that concept. Instead of a simple answer, Richard Potthoff answered my plea for help with what I first thought was a simple question about "national effects" with a detailed analysis that pushed my discussion much further than would have been possible without his help and interest. (We also developed a stand-alone paper based on his analysis.) At Duke, Lynn Van Scoyoc's SAS programming made possible the first round of the comparative analysis. Finally, Allan Kornberg's early work on legislatures inspired my interest in the subject, and his support at Duke has been invaluable.

Next, this book would not have been possible without the work and generosity of Manuel Alcantara at the University of Salamanca. Alcantara's surveys of Latin American legislators and party elites will be a valued source of information for years to come, and Alcantara should be commended for both arming the comprehensive project and allowing full access to scholars. Of course, I must also thank him for hosting me and helping to locate funding for my year in Spain, which allowed me to complete this book.

My final institutional debts are to the numerous groups that helped fund my research endeavors. My initial research in Uruguay was financed, in part, by the Center of Iberian and Latin American Studies at the University of California, San Diego. Several successive research trips were financed by diverse funds at Duke. A trip to Chile was supported by a Faculty Travel Grant administered by Duke's Latin American Studies Center, which also supported my year in Spain. All Latin Americanists at Duke owe Natalie Hartman a great debt for her work in securing funds for the Center and administering the many programs. The year in Spain was also supported by a grant from the Spanish Ministry of Education, Duke's Arts and Science Research Council, the Center for European Studies, and the Trent Foundation.

Finally, while I haven't missed many of the kids' soccer practices or school functions, I thank my immediate and extended family for putting up with computers on vacations, international moves, and occasional screams of frustration.

Party, Faction, and Coalition Names and Abbreviations

Argentina

Partido Justicialista — Justicialist Party; Peronists (PJ)

Unión Cívica Radical — Radical Civic Union (UCR)

Brazil

Partido Democrático Social — Democratic Social Party (PDS)

Partido Democrático Trabalhista — Democratic Labor Party (PDT)

Partido da Frente Liberal — Party of the Liberal Front (PFL)

Partido Liberal — Liberal Party (PL)

Partido do Movimento Democrático Brasileiro — Party of the Brazilian Democratic Movement (PMDB)

Partido Progressista Brasileiro — Brazilian Progressive Party (PPB)

Partido da Social Democracia Brasileira — Party of Brazilian Social Democracy (PSDB)

Partido dos Trabalhadores — Workers' Party (PT)

Partido Trabalhista Brasileiro — Brazilian Labor Party (PTB)

Chile

Concertación de Partidos por la Democracia — Concertation of Parties for Democracy

   Partido Demócrata Cristiano — Christian Democrats (DC)

   Partido por la Democracia — Party for Democracy (PPD)

   Partido Socialista — Socialist Party (PS)

   Partido Radical Social Demócrata — Radical Social Democratic Party (PRSD)

Alianza por Chile* — Alliance for Chile (Right)

   Renovación Nacional — National Renovation (RN)

   Unión Demócrata Independiente — Independent Democratic Union (UDI)

* Note that the rightist alliance has gone under several different names.

Uruguay

Partido Colorado	Red Party (PC)
Batllismo, Lista 15	Batllism List 15 (B15)
Batllismo Unido	Unified Batllism (BU)
Cruzada 94	Crusade 94 (C94)
Corriente Batllista Independiente	Independent Batllist Faction (CBI)
Foro Batllista	Batllism Forum (FORO)
Unión Colorada y Batllista	Red and Batllism Union (UCB)
Partido Nacional/Blanco	National/White Party (PN)
Adelante con Fe	Ahead with Faith (ACF)
Consejo Nacional Herrerista	Herrerist National Council (CNH)
Movimiento Nacional de Rocha	National Movement of Rocha (MNR)
Herrerismo	Herreraists (HERR)
Renovación y Victoria	Renovation and Victory (RyV)
Frente Amplio	Broad Front (FA)
Nuevo Espacio	New Space (NE)
Partido de Gobierno del Pueblo	Party of the People's Government (PPG)

1

Patterns of Legislative Politics

Identifiability and Flexibility

Democracy is not to be found *in* the parties but *between* the parties.
(Schattschneider, 1942, p. 60)

An effective party system requires, first, that the parties are able to bring forth programs to which they commit themselves and, second, that the parties possess sufficient internal cohesion to carry out these programs. In such a system, the party program becomes the work program of the party, so recognized by the party leaders in and out of the government, by the party body as a whole, and by the public.
(American Political Science Association, Committee on Political Parties, 1950, p. 10)

Immoderate and ideological politics is conducive to sheer paralysis or to a disorderly sequence of ill-calculated reforms that end in failure.
(Sartori, 1976, p. 140)

Shackled with dominant presidents and frequent interruptions by military governments, the legislatures have been generally overshadowed in discussions of Latin American politics. These institutions, however, are the cornerstones of democracy. When open, they provide arenas for debates, representation of societal interests, oversight of governmental processes, a source from which to recruit political leadership, a place in which to form political coalitions, as well as a legal institution in which the represented interests can debate and reach decisions on policy directions. Theoretically they, along with the executive, also provide citizens a target at which to address their wrath if government direction or performance run askance.

Aside from Cuba, the legislatures throughout Latin America have been open for some time. Most Latin American legislators still face daunting presidents, but many have not recoiled from their responsibilities, acting forcefully

1

to reform policies, oversee corrupt practices, and serve their constituents. Clearly others have, instead, bowed to executive demands, sought private gains, or served pork to clients. Either way, however, the region's legislatures are clearly central to politics, policy, and democracy.

Though it is common to talk about the role of legislatures, it is the legislators who inhabit the institutions and the interactions among them that define the patterns of legislative politics. The issues involved in this definition are complex, but they can be grouped into two general themes. The first is the shape and structure of the groups that the legislators form and the relation of these collective structures to representative democracy. The second is the propensity of those groups to compromise and work with one another in approving policy decisions.

IDENTIFIABILITY AND DEMOCRACY

Legislatures are the institutional cornerstone of democracy because they embody the principles of representative government. In a representative democracy, voters choose delegates to a law-making body and hold those delegates responsible for their actions. Burke (1774) taught that these responsible delegates could take either of two paths to serve their constituents: acting as a reflection of their constituents' *desires* or taking independent discretionary yet fiduciary action to serve those same constituents' *interests*. Regardless of the path, however, constituents were able to judge their representatives every few years and either reward them with another term or replace them.

In practice, delegates in most representative democracies have formed into groups, generally labeled parties, factions, and coalitions. The theory of representative government, therefore, focuses on the *collective* responsibility and accountability of these groups, rather than on the *individual* accountability of isolated elected officials. A key assumption of the model of "responsible party government" is that voters can identify which groups are responsible for political decisions and target their votes toward those groups. In the simplest Westminster version of the model, two parties compete by promulgating clear and divergent platforms containing their promises and plans for governance. Then, whichever party wins faithfully implements its platform by utilizing its unified majority in parliament.

Under this model the parties are responsible in two senses. First, there is no doubt about which party is responsible for the actions of the government; thus, the governing party can be held fully accountable for its actions. As the voters can identify "who dunnit," I will label this notion of responsibility *identifiability*. Second, because there is so little uncertainty in allocating blame and credit, each governing party faithfully implements its platform. To do otherwise would incur sure electoral retribution for breaking a promise made to voters.

Not all legislatures, however, provide voters equal opportunities for assessing credit or blame. Schattschneider (1942; 1960), whom I quoted to open this chapter, was particularly concerned that parties in the United States did not follow this prescription, which he saw as critical to the development of responsible party government. His Committee on Political Parties railed against the parties' incoherent platforms and insufficient internal unity to carry out their programs. In short, the parties lacked identifiability. Without the ability to really tell which group of politicians controls government policy, voters can hardly hold anyone accountable for poor performance; this inability to mete out electoral pain in turn leaves politicians without an electoral incentive to be faithful to any promises made. Identifiability, thus, is a necessary condition for faithfulness or responsibility.

Though fear of the voters' sword helps ensure a responsible government, not all swords are sharp and not all voters can find (identify) their targets. As discussed in Chapter 3, some balloting systems identify just a candidate or a party, while others direct voters to coalitions or factions. The ability to identify a group on the ballot redounds to the voters' ability to hold accountable those groups that they may have identified as responsible.

On top of the problem of where voters can direct their votes, Powell (1999) argues that without a unified majority party the "clarity of responsibility" suffers (pp. 11–12). Following Olson (1993), there should also be concern about individual politicians who seek only short-term plunder instead of long careers in elected office, since these politicians will have little fear of electoral retribution. Long-term banditry does not worry Olson because he found that kings and presidents (and by implication legislators) could maximize their plunder (which includes power and prestige in addition to gold and silver) by protecting their citizens and ensuring their economic success. In previous epochs this meant that warlords and kings worked to maintain their positions by protecting their subjects from "roving bandits" who had no interest in the welfare (and hence tax base) of the community. In modern democracies, representatives who want to maximize their plunder (for selfish or altruistic ends) must work to maintain their electoral popularity.

However, as I note in Chapter 4, not all elected representatives can become stationary bandits (due to term limits), and others willingly leave their offices (or fail to seek reelection). These representatives, therefore, need not be responsive to voters.

Democracy can help mitigate this problem because the factions, parties, or coalitions to which the bandits belong do generally seek political survival. That is, if voters can attribute responsibility to these electorally motivated groups, then the democratic ideal of voter demands and government response can survive even if individual legislators are beyond the reach of voters. Short-term bandits in the legislature are most dangerous, then, when the groups to which they adhere lack unity and hence collective accountability.

Collective accountability does not ensure that an empowered group will abstain from providing particularistic goods and focus solely on legislation affecting the nation as a whole. Olson's argument, however, is that stationary bandits have a strong incentive to provide public goods, such as beneficial economic policy, in order to survive political competition. Bandits who fail to do so will see their resource base fall, and they will be unable to provide for their clients. Further, the opposition can promote new policies and claim that they will be able to provide more pork as the result of the larger resource base that they will generate. This argument counters several game-theoretic perspectives that suggest that voters always have an incentive to choose representatives that promise pork over policy. My goal here is not to enter into that debate in detail but instead to suggest that whether voters are choosing pork or policy (or more likely a combination of the two), retrospective choices require voters to identify the group of legislators responsible for the current state of affairs. The converse of this statement is perhaps stronger: where voters cannot identify a group responsible for current conditions, policy pronouncements should play a lesser role in voters' decisions. This level of accountability works best when there is an identifiable and coherent majority, and it becomes progressively more problematic as the number of groups increases and the unity of those groups decreases. It also assumes that where legislators act independently of parties or other groups, their impact on policy or their claim on the national budget is necessarily less than where they act in concert with others. This leads us back to the conclusion that for national policy to enter into the voters' calculus when considering their choice for legislative representation, voters must be able to identify coherent groups of legislators.

Voters can identify the collective intention and will of legislative groups when the members of those groups act in concert – repeatedly and predictably. When the groups act as such, the voters, as well as lobbyists, the executive, or other groups can view the group as a legislative *agent*. As defined more carefully in Chapter 2, an agent is the subordinate in a hierarchical relationship with a principal (here the voters). To have agency also implies the ability to take concerted action, and thus I apply the term to those groups of legislators – often factions, parties, or coalitions – who make collective decisions and act as a coherent body. I also apply the term "agent system" to the totality of these groups, in order to avoid a singular focus on parties that the common term, party system, connotes.

Publicly available roll-call votes provide a concrete gauge for the degree to which groups of legislators act in harmony. Patterns of roll-call voting thus indicate whether voters can reasonably attribute successes or failures to a group (such as a party or faction) or whether individual legislators should be the focus of the voters' attention. In most cases, individual voters will not calculate their representatives' unity scores, but daily political dialogue will contain information about the behavior of representatives and the groups that they form. Roll call data thus give the researcher a tool to capture an impression of legislators' actions that voters absorb from the media, social organizations, and general conversations. These data also provide the press and watchdog groups with specific information that they can feed to voters. Thus, while voters may not directly access and analyze roll-call data before making their voting choices, the data are a good proxy for the information that voters do use in identifying and judging their agents.

This book makes extensive use of roll-call data from Argentina, Brazil, Chile, Uruguay, and the United States and applies it first to the relation between voters and accountable legislative agents in these countries. With respect to these five countries, Chapter 3 addresses the two aspects of the accountability of a party, faction, or coalition: the identifiability of groups as collective actors and the ability of the voters to identify those actors on the ballot. The chapter first details these countries' electoral systems to analyze the latter issue, concluding that voters can target parties and provincial or state delegations in Argentina and Brazil, coalitions and parties in Chile, and parties and factions in Uruguay. Then after a historical review to show the continuing political relevance of these same groups, I analyze the roll-call voting data to explore the regularity with which the groups behave as collective actors. The chapter shows that although the frequency with which these groups achieve high levels of unity varies significantly both among and within the countries, all display enough unity, at least on a limited set of issues, to allow voters to consider them collectively responsible agents.

Roll-call data would be unnecessary in exploring legislative behavior in canonical Westminster systems, as the political parties vote as unitary blocs. Indeed, unity rates of some parties are so great that roll-call votes would not reveal underlying tendencies. In the countries that are the main focus of this book, however, the degree of voting unity – and hence the array of potentially responsible agents – is far more diverse. In the United States, voters are aided in attributing blame by the two-party system, but the average level of unity of those parties is much less than most of the agents representing the voters in our other four countries. Of the other countries considered here, only in Argentina have there been two primary and unified political parties, and that system seems to be breaking down. In Chile there are two long-lasting and relatively unified alliances, but the data show that coalition politics has not subsumed the parties' identities.[1] In Uruguay there are well-organized factions, which as the voting unity attests, act independently of the parties. Finally, Brazil lacks durable coalitions, and most parties are not highly unified. All of the parties, however, do unite on an important subset of issues, and several do exhibit quite high degrees of overall unity. There is also evidence that the party delegations from some states are good candidates

---

[1] Generally I use the terms "coalition" and "alliance" interchangeably. Chapter 6, however, gives a specific definition to the term "policy coalitions."

for agency. In sum, while there are many distinct patterns, the roll-call data make clear whether parties or sub- or supraparty actors consistently act as coherent and hence identifiable groups.

The data also allow tests for the sources of voting unity. The explanation I develop in Chapters 4 and 5 revolves around two broad themes: leaders' ability to *discipline* the rank-and-file and the common beliefs and interests among groups of legislators that drive *cohesion*. I argue that because electoral systems determine whether elected legislators owe debts to leaders for nominating them as candidates, they are central to explaining a leader's disciplinary power. But, because the electoral system has a blanket affect on all parties, factions, and coalitions in a given country, that variable cannot explain the important differences among groups within a single country. More importantly, leadership powers are only one of the many factors that can influence legislators' voting patterns. These patterns are also driven by the legislators' ideology, their electoral goals, and other interests. This classification of variables leads me to refer generally to the voting *unity* of a party, faction, or coalition, while I reserve the terms "discipline" and "cohesion" for explanations of the specific sources of that unity.

FLEXIBILITY AND DEMOCRACY

Democracy implies majority rule, but sustainable democracy requires compromise. Identifiability and responsibility, therefore, are insufficient to ensure the continuance of democratic governance. Where mass actors have stood their ground too firmly, rulers have turned to nonpeaceful dispute resolution. Where democratically chosen rulers have failed to calm these situations, the military has often stepped in, ending democracy. Democracy also fails where leaders of social movements, the armed forces, labor and business groups, and political parties fail to work with one another. The converse is also true: pacts and negotiations fortify democracies.

In order to gain viability and win adherence, such pacts – whether formal or informal – require ratification by politicians. If the politicians are left out, then the compromisers will continually worry about new laws that will abrogate their deals. Further, since legislatures are supposed to represent society and provide a forum for debating and resolving conflicts, legislative compromise holds a privileged place among all the negotiating spaces that must take place to ensure democratic continuity. In short, pacts must be sealed by legislators.

Therefore, in addition to an investigation of identifiable legislative agents, this book considers the patterns of compromises among these agents in a region where questions of democratic survival or consolidation are most pertinent. As noted previously, with the exception of Cuba, freely elected presidents and legislatures currently rule all of Latin America. But, this is a quite recent picture. Only about ten years ago we would have included

Mexico, Paraguay, Chile, and Peru alongside Cuba, and going back about twenty years we would have had only a small handful of democratic states (Colombia, Venezuela, and Costa Rica). The region as a whole, in short, is still struggling to consolidate democratic governance.

The legislators in this region on whom compromise and democratic sustainability depend do not have a great track record. Their poor public standing is unsurprising given that they have been marred by charges of corruption, failure to represent their constituents, clientelism, and obsession with the porkbarrel. Further, their predecessors have been blamed for gridlocking the political system – albeit at a time when they have also been charged with such weakness that they helped foster domineering presidencies.[2]

Often with references to the breakdown of Chilean democracy in 1973, the propensity of legislatures toward obstreperousness has generated great concern. Many authors – including Sartori (1976), Valenzuela (1978; 1994), Pasquino (1990), Shugart and Carey (1992), Coppedge (1994), Mainwaring and Scully (1995), Pridham (1995), and Przeworski (1995) – discuss specific aspects of parties, party systems, or other legislative groups that help ensure against democratic breakdown. Among others, these authors cite the importance of the number of parties in a system, the level of party institutionalization, the degree of polarization among the parties, and internal party fragmentation as important factors in determining the sustainability of a democratic system. Though it is seldom an explicit argument, these discussions frequently revolve around the importance of identifiability or accountability. The concern with polarization and interbranch stalemate, however, is more pronounced. Perhaps most prominently Sartori argued that "Polarized multipartism . . . [is] characterized by centrifugal drives, irresponsible opposition, and unfair competition." As a result, it is "hardly a viable system" (1976, p. 140). Linz (1990; 1994) and Mainwaring (1993) add that multipartism is especially problematic when combined with presidentialism.

Many examples illustrate the danger of rigid politics and the benefits of compromise. Smith's studies (1969; 1974) of Argentina in the first half of the twentieth century show not only that increased levels of polarization were evident in rising levels of party-line voting (i.e., identifiability) in Argentina, but that these changes also presaged the fall of democracy. Similarly, the failure of Chilean President Balmaceda and his supporters in the Congress to reach a compromise with the congressional majority over the budget and executive powers generally led to civil war in that country at the end of the nineteenth century. More recently, Chile's 1973 democratic downfall was precipitated by the lack of compromise between the president

---

[2] Linz (1990; 1994) argues that multiparty legislatures are a danger because they can generate executive–legislative stalemate but paradoxically adds that presidentialism creates winner-take-all (i.e., very strong) presidents.

and his leftist supporters on the one side and the center and rightist groups on the other; Brazil's downfall in 1964 was caused by a president unwilling to work through the newly imposed limitations of his powers that would have necessitated coalition building; and Argentina's falls in 1966 and 1973 were the result of wide-scale disputes between the parties, the military, and the classes.

Outside of the Southern Cone is the example of Colombia, where long and intense interparty civil wars were left behind when the two main parties formed the Frente Nacional in 1958. Similarly, the foundational pact in Venezuela, also signed in 1958, is credited with allowing that country to develop a democracy that has now survived for over forty years. Spain, which has completed one of the world's most successful transitions and consolidations, offers another important example. In addition to the well-known deals at the time of democracy's foundation in the 1970s (Tezanos, Cotarelo, and de Blas, 1989; Linz and Stepan, 1996), parties have continued to make important compromises and seek consensus on what they term "organic laws," but which we might term rules of the game. Though the Spanish parties divide and fight each other over economic and social issues, interviews and a review of parliamentary records confirm that the parties seek consensus when debating organic laws that deal with issues such as the electoral system or the banking system.[3] This spirit of inclusion, it seems, keeps the parties who are currently out of government within the democratic game.

These examples of successful compromises suggest that not all multi-agent systems are doomed to failure. Leaving aside the question about electoral fraud, Sartori and Linz's arguments are based on the assumption that extremists will not follow the model of a loyal opposition, which would oppose some – but not all – legislation and attack policy choices without threatening the political system. Linz (1994) and Foweraker (1998) also discuss this issue, with a concern about the willingness of highly ideological and disciplined parties (agents) to join coalitions.

These concerns imply that democracy requires that identifiability be complemented with *flexibility*, the willingness of politicians and political groups to compromise in order to avoid stalemates. Clearly, if the agents are so highly ideological (and identifiable) that they resist compromise, polarization can threaten democracy.

This issue was not lost to Sartori, who discusses it with reference to the Italian Communist Party (PCI). His fear was of parties (agents) that formed part of the "permanent opposition" because such groups had little stake in the system. He found, however, that even though the PCI was never considered a potential coalition partner in the government, they were "semi-responsible." This he attributes to his finding that "no bill is even submitted to parliament without being previously bargained with the PCI" (p. 142).

---

[3] Interviews conducted with Spanish legislators in the summer of 1998.

There is some question about the importance of many of these bills, and he notes that most of the interparty cooperation occurs in closed-door sessions. Still, the fact that the PCI was at least partially integrated into the process favored democratic stability. In Sartori's words, "the centripetal convergence that may be said to exist among Communist and bourgeois party leaders at the invisible levels goes to explain how the Italian polity [has] enjoy[ed] the longest record of survival of the [polarized pluralist] type" (p. 145).

Most Latin American democracies are teeming with parties (as well as factions and coalitions), thus apparently running the risk of generating polarized and irresponsible groups of legislators. Among the Southern Cone cases, the Argentines appear to have the fewest number of parties, but their two longstanding parties (the Radicals and the Peronists) are actually amalgams of different provincial parties. Further, the two parties have not monopolized the vote or the legislature, as together they garnered an average of only about 70 percent of the vote for the elections of 1991, 1993, and 1995. Since that time the Radicals have merged with others, and new alliances have gained prominence. Uruguay's longstanding two-party system devolved into a three-party system just before the dictatorship, and a fourth party has been growing since the mid-1990s. This number, as alluded to earlier, hides a multitude of significant factions. Next, Chile has maintained five primary parties in the legislature, and the Brazilian legislature has housed even more. This relatively large number of significant parties and other legislative groups is also evident in much of the rest of Latin America.

Brazil's Workers' Party (PT), Uruguay's Broad Front (Frente Amplio), and Chile's Independent Democratic Union (UDI) are in potentially similar situations to the Italian Communists. These three strong electoral parties have been on the ideological fringe and could have pushed the countries toward polarization.[4] The UDI, for example, is closely tied to the Pinochet regime, and its reaction to his arrest in England in 1998 could have led the country into crisis. After relatively short protests including a walkout from the legislature, however, the party members returned to their posts and have voiced their opinions without threatening the democratic institutions. On the opposite end of the spectrum, Uruguay's Frente Amplio has members who were imprisoned, exiled, and tortured during the military government. They opposed the amnesty of the military leaders in 1986 but accepted their defeat without mobilizing their forces.

In sum, unlike earlier periods, these legislative groups today have been more open to pragmatism and bargaining than their polarized forerunners. For the countries under study in this book, the roll-call data displayed in Chapter 6 show that even the relatively extremist agents in the Southern Cone are frequent winners in the legislative arena. These agents commonly

---

[4] The political moderation and ideological position of the Frente Amplio and the UDI are discussed in later chapters.

vote with the center on the winning side of issues, and, on occasion, even vote with their polar opposites.

Though pragmatism is an important trait of the systems, politics still determines the coalitions of agents that come together in support of new legislation. Chapter 6 therefore also considers how cabinet membership, electoral alliances, ideology, and electoral cycles affect which groups form "policy coalitions" on the legislative floor.

THE OBJECTS OF STUDY: LEGISLATURES AND LEGISLATIVE ACTORS

Instead of presidents and parties, this book focuses on legislatures and legislative agents. Because the former are often (at best) in the shadow of the president and the latter is an important shift in terminology, it is necessary to validate the importance of the Latin American legislatures and justify the reason for developing the new terminology. It is also necessary to explain the book's focus on the United States and Latin America's Southern Cone.

The Choice of Cases

This book explores legislative politics in Argentina, Brazil, Chile, and Uruguay in the 1990s, using the United States for a comparative perspective. In addition to the intercountry focus, the book also undertakes comparisons among the most prominent parties, factions, and coalitions within these countries. As a result, the study is both case-oriented and comparative. By working neither within a strict case study or large-n framework, the study necessarily loses some attention to detail and some degree of broad applicability (Ragin, 1987). The advantage of this mixed approach, however, is that it allows a detailed, if not complete, exploration of each case, as well as an orientation to variables that focuses attention on the applicability of the theories and findings to a wider set of cases.

The Southern Cone cases were not chosen randomly but were included for both practical and theoretical reasons. As King, Keohane, and Verba (1994) teach, testing the validity of comparisons requires choosing cases that exhibit a range of values on the key independent variables but that are similar in terms of other possibly confounding factors. Though it is not difficult to find cases that fulfill the first necessity, all comparative studies open themselves to challenges about untreated variables and assumed similarities. My defense of the comparison is based on the countries' similarities on two key variables.

First, the four Latin American countries are geographically proximal with similar political histories. These countries share an unfortunate recent past, all having suffered dictatorial rule for extended periods of time. The Brazilian dictators were the first to arrive (in 1964), but in 1967 Argentina's troubled democracy fell for six years and then again in 1976. In Chile and Uruguay the military shut down the legislatures and other democratic institutions in 1973. All four countries then regained their democracies between 1983 and 1989, and though they continue to face economic and political challenges, few analysts expect a return of the dictators. In sum, these four countries have similar political histories, and it is useful to study the role of legislatures in countries that are all struggling to consolidate recently reformed democracies.

Second, the United States and the other countries are comparable for their employment of presidential forms of government. While there are important differences in the amount of influence that presidents have in legislative affairs, the legislatures in presidential systems – at least relative to parliamentary backbenches – are relatively independent of the executive.

Though other variables also come into play, the main variables on which this book focuses are electoral rules, federalism, the ideological beliefs of legislators, and cabinet membership. The five countries exhibit great differences on these issues. First, the systems vary in terms of whether voters can target their choices to factions, parties, or coalitions, and this, I argue in Chapter 3, is related to the varying agent systems. Further, as will also be detailed in Chapter 3, the electoral systems range from those that put a premium on the legislator's personal qualities (in the United States and Brazil) to those that privilege party leaders (in Argentina). The electoral rules also vary in terms of the degree of control over candidate nominations that they offer to leaders, which I argue is a primary source of a faction's, party's, or coalition's discipline.

Related to the electoral rules is federalism. This variable is generally measured in terms of economic or political independence, and my focus here is on the latter. In continuing the focus on the control of candidate nominations, I discuss the role of federal versus state or provincial leaders in drawing up candidate lists, which varies from significant in Argentina and Brazil to inconsequential in Uruguay and Chile. I also develop a statistical model to discuss the electoral ties between the legislators in different districts. These variables, as well as the geographic concentration of an agent's legislators, are related to the voting unity of different agents.

Based on these theoretical grounds alone, other cases could fit into the analysis. These particular cases, however, had the practical advantage of available legislative roll-call voting data. Such data are not widely available with regard to Latin America, but I have been able to gather them for lower houses of each of these five countries, as well as the Chilean Senate. In spite of some important limitations that I discuss later, roll-call data clearly reveal patterns of legislative politics that allow intracountry comparisons among agents and across time and intercountry comparisons among agent systems and legislatures.

Legislatures in Latin America

At least since the 1920s concerns with government efficiency have led to a continual increase in executive powers in Latin America. A characterization of the region's legislatures as weak, however, is oversimplified because even in the eras of populism or decree-wielding presidents, legislatures have maintained significant roles in the policy process and the functioning or breakdown of democracy.

The Chilean and Uruguayan legislatures have long stood apart from their Latin American counterparts in comparative discussions of legislative power. The Chilean legislature's reputation as a central actor dates at least to 1891 when the legislature defeated the executive in a civil war. The Chilean legislature maintained its reputation, thus earning, along with Uruguay's, placement in Mezey's (1979) box for legislatures with "strong" policy-making power, though lacking societal support. Others in Latin America (when not closed by the military) were considered to have modest power as well as weak societal support. For other legislatures, Packenham's (1970) study of the Brazilian legislature – one that he studied while it was under the control of the dictatorship – seemed to become the archetype. In that study he argued that the legislature did not have a policy role per se, instead it was an arena for spouting discontent, filtering information, and legitimating the political regime.

This situation has changed. Though there is a current debate about the degree to which the Brazilian Congress' role is constructive, all agree that the Brazilian president cannot ignore it. Ames's (2002) study is instructive. After coding each executive policy proposal for the period 1990–8, the author concluded that few proposals go through the Brazilian Congress unscathed, many executive bills are bottled up or tabled, and strong congressional opposition discourages the president from formally initiating some bills.

Even the Argentine Congress, which faced the strongest of populist leaders in earlier times (Perón 1946–55, 1973–4) and the quintessential delegative democrat for ten years (Menem 1989–99), has not been absent from the policy arena.[5] Smith's (1969, 1974) studies of the prebureaucratic authoritarian period show the explosion of political debates in the legislature. His study of Argentine politics in the 1930s, as portrayed through his analysis of the beef industry, depicts the Senate as leading the debate about presumed imperialistic practices by the packing houses. It is also telling that an ex-presidential candidate, Lisandro de la Torre, used his seat in the Senate to pursue his political agenda. The vituperative debate reached such levels that it ended

---

[5] O'Donnell (1994) describes a delegative democracy as a situation in which the president assumes such power as to render other democratic institutions all but meaningless. In these cases, the legislature becomes more of a "nuisance" than an important democratic player.

TABLE 1.1. *Vetoes in Argentina: 1983–1995*

	Total vetoes	Partial vetoes	Totals
Alfonsín	37	12	49
Menem	49	60	109

Sources: Alfonsín data are from Jones (2002) and from Mustapic and Ferretti (1995); Menem data are culled from Molinelli (1995).

with a murder on the Senate floor (Smith, 1969, p. 183). Smith goes on to say that the conduct of this debate led to a decline in the legislature's stature, effectiveness, and activity, thereby also discrediting democratic politics generally. Still, this example is important for highlighting the key role that the Argentine legislature has played historically.

Smith's second study of the Argentine Congress between 1904 and 1955 had an even more general finding. There he found that legislative debates reflected political divides among regions and parties. Most interestingly, he found that heightened party-line voting foreshadowed coups.

In the postdictatorship era, the Argentine Congress has continued to have a larger policy role than often recognized. Despite the constant criticisms of Menem's heavy-handed political style, the legislature was not always an insignificant obstacle.[6] An important number of bills were initiated, modified, or blocked by the legislature. Table 1.1 provides an example of the legislature's assertiveness. It shows that both Alfonsín and Menem were pushed to use their veto powers relatively frequently. A dominated or inactive legislature would not have produced such controversial legislation. Furthermore, the legislature overrode one of Alfonsín's and at least eight of Menem's vetoes. It should be noted that these records are comparable to the "strong" U.S. Congress. Historically (1789–1984) the annual average of vetoes in the United States was 12.4, and Menem vetoed an average of 18.3 per year. More interesting is that the historical rate of U.S. overturns is 7 percent, while the Argentine legislature overturned 7.3 percent of Menem's vetoes (Molinelli, 1995).

These and other examples show that though the Latin American legislatures may be more reactive in comparison to the proactive U.S. Congress, they still retain significant influence over the policy process.[7] Their influence is frequently felt on specific policy issues, and battles in the legislature have precipitated democratic breakdown. Further, as democracy consolidates

---

[6] Both popular press and academic articles commonly pointed to Menem's decretismo. See, for example, Ferreira Rubio and Goretti (1998). But, Eaton (2002), for example, describes the legislature's important role in shaping tax policy.

[7] For more examples, see chapters in Morgenstern and Nacif (2002). In that volume I also discuss the origins of the legislatures' reactive status. See also Cox and Morgenstern (2001).

itself, the legislatures have become more professionalized and will potentially play larger roles in the future.[8] The legislatures' role in democratic
governability, therefore, is a highly significant issue.

Legislative Agents and a Critique of Party-Centric Theory

At least since Schattschneider's (1942) famous saying about the centrality of
parties to democracy, scholars have sought the characteristics of parties and
party systems necessary to sustain democracy. Sartori, for example, focused
on the importance of the number of parties, arguing that too many parties
fostered a dangerous level of polarization in the system. Following Linz's
damnation of presidentialism for generating executive-legislative conflict,
Mainwaring (1993; see also Jones, 1995) added that multipartism generally
created obstacles to policy making. Such conflict, in turn, invited intervention
by nondemocratic actors.

A second strain of this literature, founded by Mainwaring and Scully
(1995), focused on the "institutionalization" of parties. Their seminal work
highlighted the importance of consistent patterns of competition among parties, ties between society and the parties, the acceptance by parties of the rules
of the game, and stable party rules and organizations.

Sartori, Mainwaring and Scully, and other party scholars clearly recog-
nize the importance of intra- and interparty arrangements. Mainwaring and
Scully, for example, rank the strength of party organizations, but neither they
nor the other strands of literature carefully consider the effects of factionalism or interparty arrangements. As a result, the multitude of books and
articles on Latin American politics offer party-centric theories. Mainwaring
and Scully's volume, for example, is divided into sections indicating whether
the party systems are "institutionalized," "hegemonic . . . [and] transitional,"
or "inchoate." For another example, consider Pasquino's (1990, p. 52) pro-
nouncement that "[n]ot all the processes of transition [to democracy] have
been party dominated; but all processes of democratic consolidation have
indeed been party dominated." These strong proclamations ignore the determinant effect of sub- and supraparty actors on democratic breakdowns,
regime transitions, and policy decisions.

The importance of supraparty actors has been long recognized in studies of Western Europe, where coalition behavior has been a mainstay of
political science literature. But according to Foweraker (1998), work on
Latin American politics has focused too much on constitutional powers and
party unity and too little on coalition politics. Perhaps work on coalition
politics in presidential regimes is still in its infancy since news of successful

---

[8] Polsby (1968) argues that the U.S. legislature gained power as its legislators professionalized
around the turn of the century. Morgenstern and Manzetti (forthcoming) argue that Latin
American legislatures may be in a similar position today, though the degree of the legislators'
independence from their parties may prohibit such professionalization.

compromises is rather dull as compared with high-tension interparty (or faction) clashes. Furthermore, failure to reach an accord cannot generate the recall of a prime minister or the dissolution of congress as in parliamentary systems. In spite of these problems, the importance of coalition behavior in presidential democracies has begun to gain notice, yielding some recent advances in the study of Latin America. Deheza's already oft-cited dissertation portrays data on all coalitions for Latin America, dating to the 1950s. With this data she argued that presidents have had more support than is commonly recognized. With regards to Brazil and Uruguay, Amorim Neto (2002) and Altman (2000a), respectively, have taken up this issue as well. The former has focused on the importance of cabinet membership to legislative support of the president, and the latter has begun to theorize about coalition formation and survival in presidential regimes.

There has also been new work focusing on internal party dynamics, though little on factionalism per se. Studies of Brazil, for example, distinguish between the highly unified and ideologically focused Workers' Party (the PT) and the amorphous catch-all center or center-right parties. Since some parties are highly unified and coherent units, while others are so factionalized that the party loses its identity, discussions that focus on parties as if all were similar are nonsensical. Furthermore, factions vary too (Belloni and Beller, 1978; Morgenstern, 2001). Like parties, some factions are durable and highly unified with unique identities. Others are loose and ephemeral conglomerations of politicians that have joined together to serve a short-term goal. Not all parties "riven with factionalism," therefore, face similar problems, and political analyses that focus on parties without accounting for these differences are at best oversimplified and at worst misleading.

Consider, for example, the breakdown of the Chilean democracy in 1973, where both factionalization and cross-party alliances (or the lack thereof) were crucial. Central to this story is the *tres-tercios*, where the left, center, and right each held about one-third of the vote. In the election of 1964 the center and right joined together to defeat the leftists who had nearly won in 1958. Then, when the coalition attempts failed in 1970, the Socialist Party's Salvador Allende was able to win the presidency with only 36.6 percent of the vote. Allende's lack of an alliance partner, however, meant that almost two-thirds of the Congress (and society) opposed him, thus generating such high levels of interbranch conflict and societal polarization that the military eventually overthrew the government to restore their version of calm.

Behind this skeletal story of the failure of coalition politics is a less-well-known story of factional politics and of a crucial centrist party, the Radicals.[9] Divisions within the Radicals, a party formed in the 1880s, both made possible the Allende victory and contributed to his downfall. After a poor showing

---

[9] Divisions in the Christian Democratic Party also played a big role. For example, one splinter of the party (the MAPU; United Movement of Popular Action) even supported Allende in the 1970 election. Here, however, I will just focus on the less-well-known Radicals.

of their presidential candidate in the 1964 election and a history of supporting parties from both ends of the political spectrum, the Radicals split again
prior to the 1970 election. One wing supported the Allende coalition and the
others, after having been expelled from their party, supported the Christian
Democratic candidate, Jorge Alessandri (McDonald and Ruhl, 1989). The
supportive wing was important to Allende for both policy and political reasons. For policy, this centrist group lent support to Allende's initiatives;
for political reasons, the group validated Allende's claim of multisectoral
support. Thus when members of the Party of the Radical Left (Partido de
Izquierda Radical) walked out of Allende's cabinet in 1972, talks between
the government and the opposition broke down, and street demonstrations
ensued (see Valenzuela, 1978). Other Radicals, however, were still supportive. The Radical Party's Minister of Justice, for example, headed secret talks
that yielded significant concessions on both sides. These agreements, unfortunately, were abrogated by the conservative wing of the Christian Democrats
who, against the wishes of their more moderate party leadership, forced a
vote in the Senate before the resolution of final compromises (Valenzuela,
1978, p. 76).

A second example of the crucial importance of factionalism to the democratization process comes from Uruguay. Uruguay's factionalized parties are
consistent themes in discussions of that country, though many cross-country
analyses still count just two or three parties in that country. There is, in
fact, a debate about this issue. González (1991), for example, argues for the
centrality of parties due to their continuity and the stable competition, and
Mainwaring and Scully (1995) classify the Uruguayan parties as institutionalized for similar reasons. Others (including Lindahl, 1962; Solari, 1991;
Morgenstern, 2001) argue that factionalism is too central to the operation
of politics to focus on the parties as political actors.

Factionalism has been an issue for Uruguayan politics since the foundation of the parties in the 1820s. The parties grew out of the civil war disputes,
having earned their present labels in an 1837 battle of the Colorados (Reds)
versus the Blancos (Whites). Even at that time, however, factionalism was
a problem as the opposition was simply a "'rebel faction'" (Pivel Devoto,
1956, p. 229). Later (see Chapter 3) the Uruguayans designed a unique electoral system (in 1910) to accommodate the parties' factions, and factionalism
was key to the breakdowns in 1933 and 1973. Neither of those two ruptures
was party led; instead, both featured a coalition of leading factions from the
two principal parties working to subvert other factions in their parties (and,
in turn, democracy).

Historically Argentina's parties have been less institutionalized than those
in Chile and Uruguay, but Smith's (1974) study cited earlier shows that party
alignments were important to legislative activity in the first half of the twentieth century. Still, factionalism has played an important role there, too. Perón,
for example, won the support of a breakaway faction of the main opposition

party, the Unión Cívica Radical (UCR), and McGuire (1995) argues that Perón consistently used factional politics to undercut his opposition. In particular, by supporting weak factions in opposition groups, he successfully drove wedges into potential opposition movements. Later, claiming dissension within his support coalition, Perón sought to create a new more unified party (first named the Sole Party of the Revolution; Partido Único de la Revolución).

After the military removed Perón from power in 1955, a new type of electoral competition arose, which again featured the effects of factionalism. The main protagonist was again the UCR, but it now split into two wings, the Intrasigentes (UCRI) and the UCR of the People (UCRP). The former, under the leadership of Arturo Frondizi, courted Perón and his supporters, and in return won the 1958 presidential election. The latter, led by Ricardo Balbín, opposed Peronist policies. Not only did this split help Perón keep his hand in Argentine politics from his Spanish exile, but it also allowed the neo-Peronist parties to win a plurality in the 1962 and 1965 legislative elections (McGuire, 1995, p. 213).

Party ruptures did not end with those elections. After Frondizi was deposed by a coup, the UCRP gained the executive office, winning a mere 26 percent of the vote in 1963. Then Frondizi's UCRI split again. The Peronists were also split, with Augusto Vandor trying to wrestle the party from still-exiled Perón. Vandor, of course, was unsuccessful, as became evident when Perón's gubernatorial candidate – though losing to the Radical candidate – trounced Vandor's in Mendoza in 1966. According to McGuire, Vandor's failure to rebuild a labor party opened the way for the military coup.

Brazil's historically weak parties have not generated an abundance of party-centric political histories. Mainwaring's (1999) thoughtful volume on party systems focuses on the lack of institutionalization of parties in Brazil, and how this situation has affected the current democratization process. His main finding is that the country's party system has contributed to the presidents' reliance on patronage, which, in turn, has "had corrosive effects on public administration and policy implementation" (p. 5). In another recent and careful study, Barry Ames (2002) tests for and dismisses the parties' ability to structure legislative voting and then goes on to focus on the electoral incentives of individual legislators in a climate of weak party ties.

In sum, in none of these cases have parties been unified actors. Of course, the same is true for the United States where factionalism and the relatively weak organizational structure of parties have been the basis of studies of the current situation and historical periods. Therefore, at least in these cases, analyses of legislative behavior should not begin with an assumption of party unity. This does not imply that partisanship is irrelevant to understanding the behavior of legislators or voters. But, in many cases, factionship or coalitionship are more important to structuring behavior. As noted previously and as explained more fully in Chapter 2, this discomfort with a focus on parties leads me to apply the generic term "agent system" instead of the party system. I continue to use the terms "factions," "parties," and "coalitions" and to refer to specific groups that are commonly identified with these terms, but as a whole I will term them "agents" and an important focus will be the degree to which members of these diverse groups vote together on a consistent basis.

COMBINING THE ISSUES

In the preceding pages I have argued that the patterns of legislative politics can be described by considering the internal unity of legislative agents and the interactions among these agents. The first of these traits is a determinant of the identifiability of the agent, and the second I have here labeled flexibility. These traits not only help us to classify legislative types, but also redound to the quality of representation and governability, and hence the sustainability of democracy.

The legislative actors that I discuss in much greater detail in the ensuing chapters vary greatly in terms of their flexibility and identifiability. These two traits of political agents are independently important, but of course they also compete and interact. To some degree these are competing traits because highly identifiable agents must compromise their positions somewhat to become flexible. Further, the agents that lack identifiability on policy grounds are necessarily flexible, since an important number of their members consistently joins the opposition. The traits, however, are also interactive because unified legislative groups can either work with others or refuse to compromise. Responsible governance and the sustainability of democracy are a function of the manner in which legislative groups manage the interaction and competition of these traits.

The patterns of legislative politics are a function of the degree to which each agent maintains unity and is willing to compromise with other agents. If we compress the range on these traits to just high and low, their interaction can logically fill three of four quadrants in a two-by-two figure. Table 1.2 labels the interactions according to the resulting type of agent, with implications for democratic governance.

TABLE 1.2. *Agent Types*

		Identifiability	
		Low	High
Flexibility	Low		Exclusive governor or oppositionist
	High	Legislators for sale	Coalition partner

The agents in the bottom right corner are classic coalition-oriented agents. Members of the group are disciplined and/or cohesive, but as a whole, they are interested in negotiating with other legislative agents. Such agents may lose some identifiability in that voters may have difficulty in distinguishing among coalition members, but willingness to cooperate does not necessarily imply a lack of identifiability and such willingness may also be an identifiable (and desirable) trait. Unified European parties that consistently join coalitions, therefore, would occupy this box.

In the bottom left box, legislators are for sale to the highest bidder, rendering low levels of agent unity. If the bids take the form of logrolls or policy compromises, there would be forward progress of the policy process, but that type of system leaves voters without clear culprits if outcomes turn sour. Alternatively the bids can come in the form of pork or other targeted benefits, which at extreme levels would be detrimental to the coherence of policies, if not fiscal discipline and economic performance.

Though the southwest box implies a lack of responsible government and wasteful spending, it is important to recall that the high and low dichotomy is an artificial bifurcation of a wide range. Distribution of particularistic goods (pork) or logrolls can have wide benefits because they can help seal important compromises. To close the deal on the North American Free Trade Agreement, for example, U.S. legislators were clearly paid in pork, but the result included an important policy outcome with an important level of bipartisan support. This model also seems apropos to pre-Pinochet Chile, as described by Garretón (1989). Garretón explains that legislators' interest in local politics and the pork that fed these interests defused the potentially destabilizing polarization in Chile until the end of the 1960s. When the legislature lost its ability to provide targeted goods (due to constitutional changes that advantaged the president over the legislature), the fuse blew (see also Valenzuela, 1978; Shugart and Carey, 1992).

The northwest box is nonsensical, since a low score on identifiability implies a significant portion of a group's members frequently cross lines in voting, which implies high, not low, levels of flexibility.

Finally, the upper right box indicates highly disciplined or cohesive agents who are unwilling to compromise their ideals during policy debates. Agents that fit this description and are part of the majority could be labeled *exclusive*, and those in the minority would be *oppositionists*. Unless they see prospects for winning control in the future, majoritarian democracy offers little reward to those agents that are not considered as potential partners in legislative bargaining. Oppositionist groups such as the Chilean right of the 1970s, therefore, can become threats to democracy.

Different mixes of agent types yield different types of legislatures. As I argued in work with Gary Cox (2001), most Latin American legislatures fit into a reactive, instead of a proactive category, but within this category they can be, from the president's point of view, "recalcitrant," "venal or

parochial," "workable," or "subservient." In that paper, we argue that a
legislature's type is a function of the degree of support that the president
has in the legislature and the degree to which the legislators have parochial
interests. The typology of agents suggested here does not contradict that argument, but suggests that legislatures do not house legislators or legislative
agents of a homogeneous type. Instead, a single legislature might house different types of agents, and its type, then, reflects the predominant patterns
of interaction among a potentially heterogeneous set of legislative groups.
Legislatures replete with flexible and identifiable agents would tend to yield
what presidents would see as a workable assembly, or what the legislators
might view as a *coalitional* legislature. A legislature full of legislators willing
to make deals but agents that are unable to maintain unity in their membership would appear to fit the *venal* category, and those with important
inflexible groups would be recalcitrant if the majority opposed the president
or subservient if the president had majority support. From the legislative
minority's point of view (if not the majority's as well), these latter types
would look like an *exclusive* legislature. But, since the legislatures studied
here each house different types of agents, and since most agents' degree of
unity and their willingness to compromise varies at different times or on
different issues, the legislatures defy simple and stable classifications (which
is not unrelated to the oscillating types that Cox and I discuss). Still, roll-call
voting data provide information by which we can judge a legislature's type
on a particular vote, and the overall patterns of roll-call voting thus allow a
judgment about a legislature's typical posture. After reviewing the different
agents' positions throughout the rest of this book, Chapter 7 returns to the
classification issue. Based on the roll-call data, I show that, relative to one
another, the Chilean (and with caveats the Uruguayan) agents are the most
coalitional, the Brazilian and Argentine agents fit in the top right (exclusive/
oppositionist) box, and over time the U.S. parties have moved from the
bottom left (legislators for sale) box toward the position inhabited by the
Brazilians and Argentines.

A NOTE ON THE USE OF ROLL-CALL DATA

As noted, this book makes extensive use of roll-call data from the legislatures
in the United States and the four Southern Cone countries. Roll-call data provide concrete and systematic evidence of legislative behavior and patterns of
political competition. They can help show which groups form coalitions, resolve whether parties are unified or factionalized, and determine the issues on
which groups divide. Such questions have been at the heart of studies of the
U.S. Congress. There, the data have contributed to the debates about the role
of parties generally (Cooper, Brady, and Hurley, 1977; Cox and McCubbins,
1993; Aldrich, 1995), the parties' realignment and the changing position of
the Southern Democrats (Poole and Rosenthal, 1997), and other issues.

Recent studies of Latin America have also taken advantage of roll-call data to advance our understanding of those systems (Figueiredo and Limongi, 1995; Buquet, Chasquetti, and Moraes, 1998; Londregan, 2000, 2002; Weldon, 2000; Ames, 2001, 2002; Morgenstern, 2001; Desposato, 2002; Jones, 2002; Carey, 2002). The Brazilian data have received the most scrutiny; consequently, they have helped to spur a debate on the role of parties in Brazil, not unlike that among Americanists.

By and large, however, studies of the Latin American legislatures have been hampered by a lack of available roll-call data. Unlike the U.S. data, which are readily available in computerized form, the data on Latin America have to be compiled by hand through a laborious review of *Diarios de Sesiones* (Daily Legislative Records).[10] And this is only possible for the small subset of countries that take and record roll-call votes. This situation is beginning to change, as some countries have begun to employ electronic voting machines that facilitate the recording and, as such, will probably increase the use of roll-call votes.[11]

While quite useful, roll-call data are imperfect indicators of legislative politics. There are two primary concerns. First, because the data do not capture prevote pay-offs, logrolls, or other prevote bargains, the data miss the "real stuff" of politics. This challenge, however, neglects the fact that even if deals are cut and the voting outcomes are foregone conclusions, the roll-call data would still discriminate the Ins from the Outs. As such, the data on the final vote do yield valuable information about prevote agreements. Second, since the data only reflect votes that reached the legislative floor, the data are biased toward the less controversial legislation, or at least those bills for which proponents could overcome hindrances such as leaders in control of the legislative agenda. This is undoubtedly true to some extent, but for a variety of reasons some controversial legislation does reach the legislative floor, not all of it passes, and much yields acrimonious debate.[12]

Perhaps the sharpest critic of roll-call voting is Krehbiel (1991; 1993; 2000), who argues with those authors who use roll-call data to defend theses about changing levels of party discipline. He argues that while unity scores

---

[10] I have therefore been very fortunate that Barry Ames has shared his data on Brazil, Mark Jones has made his data on Argentina available, and John Carey has given me his data on the Chilean lower house. Though I have complemented this data with my own collections from Uruguay and both houses of the Chilean legislature, as well as data on the U.S. Congress available from the Inter-university Consortium for Political and Social Research (as well as Keith Poole's website), this project would have been impossible to complete without the generous apportions of these scholars.

[11] John Carey is currently heading a project to collect roll-call voting data from a number of countries. See Carey (2000; forthcoming).

[12] Budgets, for example, inevitably raise the ire of different groups, but legislative leaders cannot avoid dealing with them.

based on roll calls could represent changing abilities of leaders to force party members to vote in a particular direction, they may simply reflect changing levels of "preference heterogeneity" among the legislators. Since my goal is to consider the effects of both leadership powers and preference heterogeneity among legislators (which I discuss in terms of cohesion) on agent unity, Krehbiel's criticisms are not applicable.

In sum, despite their limitations, roll call data provide much more accurate and quantifiable information about the final move in the legislative process than any other concrete indicator. With these data, the following chapters will show that we can generate specific comparisons among parties and other legislative actors both within and among countries. The data leave little doubt that some legislative groups are much more unified than others, and they clearly indicate which groups cooperate with one another and which are more prone to join voting majorities.

Even though these comparisons are certainly valid within countries, there is still a concern about the intercountry comparisons. This concern is based on the different propensities of countries to employ roll-call voting. Table 1.3 details the database that I employ throughout this book.

These stark differences reflect different volumes of legislation, the interests of legislators in calling for a roll call, the employment of an electronic vote-

TABLE 1.3. *Number of Roll-Call Votes*

Argentina 1989–1991 (Lower House)	84
Argentina 1991–2001 (Lower House)[a]	331
Brazil 1991–1994 (Lower House)	211
Brazil 1995–1998 (Lower House)	421
Chile 1997–1999 (Lower House)	583
Chile 1992–1998 (Upper House)	94
Uruguay 1985–1989 (General Assembly)[b]	41
Uruguay 1990–1994 (General Assembly)	22
United States (Lower House; average number of votes/4 years) 1965–2001	1915

[a] Only summary statistics (not individual level data) were available for 1991–2001. These data are therefore only partially incorporated into the succeeding analysis.

[b] The Uruguayan data are based on votes of the General Assembly, which is a combination of the two legislative houses. The data here are based on General Assembly votes on veto overrides.

Sources: This table and all succeeding analyses use roll-call data from a variety of sources. Mark Jones collected and provided the Argentine data. John Carey and I culled the voting data for Chile Lower House from on-line legislative records, and my assistants and I extracted the Chilean Senate data from microfiche of the legislative records for all available years. Barry Ames graciously provided the Brazilian data. I also thank Argelina Figueiredo and Fernando Limongi for providing a similar data set, but unless otherwise noted the analysis uses Ames's data set. I collected the Uruguay data from daily legislative records. The U.S. data are available from Inter-University Consortium for Political and Social Research.

tallying machine,[13] and other factors. As a result, the sample of votes that we have to study may have substantive impacts on the data analysis. In the United States, the weight of the most politically relevant votes is more likely to be diluted by the sheer number of votes. At the same time, where roll calls are uncommon, the votes that are taken may not yield a fair (i.e., random) representation of common patterns.

Though more data are now becoming available, the data employed here was nearly exhaustive for the time period covered in this analysis, and it has therefore not been possible to add more observations for the Latin American cases.[14] But, we can deal with what is perhaps the greatest threat to questions about comparability, that the data overrepresent unimportant issues. In Chapter 3, I explain a technique (based on work by John Carey) for weighting the votes based on the level of controversy. With this system, we can be confident that the comparisons do deal with political decisions that raised serious debate. Further, there is enough data for even the country where I have the fewest number of roll-call votes (Uruguay) to place reasonably sized confidence intervals around estimates of the average unity of an agent. The indices, therefore, do provide a sufficient basis for a comparison of the average response of legislators to an average piece of divisive legislation.

While the weighted index assures us that the bills included in the analysis raised at least some level of controversy, the other important concern with cross-national comparability is that the rules under which the bills are chosen for roll calls could affect the cross-country comparability. That is, more or less restrictive rules could explain both the differences in the number of roll calls, as well as the type or the level of controversy of bills selected. This challenge fails, however, because it is not prohibitively difficult to petition for a roll-call vote in any of the countries.

The House rules in the United States state that any legislator can ask for a roll call, and that one-fifth of a quorum (forty-four legislators) must approve the request. Under this rule, hundreds of bills are submitted to roll-call votes each year. Argentine rules also require 20 percent of the legislature to approve a petition for a roll call, but they take this option very infrequently.[15]

---

[13] Among the four Southern Cone countries, only Uruguay still lacks such a machine. For most Latin American countries, however, the machines are recent acquisitions and are not always used.

[14] The data do represent all votes for Uruguay during the first two postdictatorship electoral periods. The Chilean data represent only a few years, because the website, which reports the legislative records, did not include earlier years. Since the Brazilian data set spans two full terms, I have not pursued other available years. Jones's data set for Argentina also represents all available data. For 1989–91 the few call votes that are not in the data set generated less than 10 percent dissent.

[15] In a few instances the constitution also requires nominal voting. Mark Jones reports that "on rare occasions nominal votes have been taken based on the discretion of the presiding president, a practice not mentioned in the Chamber rules. In none of these occasions however

Likewise, in spite of a relatively low hurdle in Uruguay (where the house rules require one-third of the legislature to approve a roll-call petition), my search of ten years of legislative records only uncovered sixty-three roll-call votes. Moreover, all of these votes were taken on issues where the constitution mandates a recording of the yeas and nays of individual legislators: veto override attempts. Because the presidents have used their veto power relatively frequently, and by definition these votes involved some degree of conflict, these data are still useful.

Roll calls are more frequent in the other two countries. This may be expected in Brazil which employs the least-restrictive rules. There, if only 6 percent of the legislature approves a petition for a quorum call, a roll call is taken.[16] The Chilean rules are perhaps the most restrictive, since they require that two committee chairs request a roll-call vote and that the floor vote to approve the request. The relatively large number of roll calls taken there, however, indicates that this is not a particularly high barrier.

These arguments may not erase all questions of intercountry comparisons, but they should increase our confidence about their validity. Further, notwithstanding their limitations, the voting data offers a unique view of legislative politics as they give concrete evidence about legislative divisions across a wide range of issues. Which actors opposed or supported the president? Which legislators concurred with the majority of their party, faction, or coalition? Which groups or individuals joined to pass a bill or prevent another from passing? These data can also reflect back-room deals, which would be reflected in cooperation on floor votes.

These types of questions have motivated many single country studies, and they are also central to the intracountry analysis in this book. The questions are also very pertinent for intercountry comparisons, and the roll-call data is particularly well suited to address them, in spite of its recognized limitations. In sum, while the data do not provide a complete picture, they are the best available objective source of information on legislative activity.

PLAN OF THE BOOK

While neither identifiability nor flexibility are sufficient for democratic survival, I take their importance to be relatively uncontroversial. My purpose, then, is not to test a theory about their role in sustaining democracy.

---

did any deputy object to the president's decision to hold a nominal vote" (Jones, 2002, p. 151, fn 13).

[16] There are also constitutional provisions that mandate roll calls on some important types of legislation, such as constitutional amendments. The rules actually limit the number of roll calls to one per hour. According to Amorim Neto et al. (1999), this rule was "designed to prevent the opposition from paralyzing floor decision-making by requesting roll calls all the time." Figueiredo and Limongi (2000) argue that party leaders only request roll calls on controversial votes due to this time limitation.

Instead, my primary goal is to identify the legislative agents, test their levels of identifiability and flexibility, and consider the origins of these traits.

As I have argued, the most relevant legislative actors are not necessarily parties as assumed in most studies. Instead, factions, coalitions, or state delegations are sometimes the most identifiable actors. Chapter 2 continues this argument, arguing for a move away from the idea of party-centric studies and toward an emphasis on identifiable voting blocs. In doing so, the chapter also offers further justification for my use of the term the "agent system" instead of the leading term "party system." The third chapter, then, describes the legislative agents in the five countries. The main hypothesis of the chapter is that the ballot structure determines whether factions, coalitions, or state party delegations will be more prominent than parties. While this hypothesis is substantiated, I find great variance in the voting unity of the agents. Chapter 4 explains that this variance is a function of two sets of variables. The electoral system can have a primary impact on agent discipline, determining whether leaders have control over prized candidate nominations. That variable, which has a similar impact on all agents within a given country, helps to explain cross-country variation. The electoral system, however, seldom grants leaders unambiguous nomination control, and that control can be supported or undercut by other factors. Further, since the electoral system applies equally to all parties, factions, and coalitions within a country, it cannot explain differences in unity rates among any single country's agents. That variation requires a second set of variables, most of which I group under the category of cohesion. That group includes ideology, polarization, the geographic concentration of legislators, the national orientation of the agent's vote, the ties between the agents and the executive, and electoral cycles. The fifth chapter operationalizes and statistically tests these hypotheses with regards to the voting patterns of legislators in Argentina, Brazil, Chile, Uruguay, and the United States. The sixth chapter then turns to the subject of flexibility. Its goal is to document and explain the degree to which the agents have formed voting coalitions with other agents. An important finding is that even the most ideologically pure agents are sometimes willing to bend and join with opponents on important votes. Thus, as opposed to the predictatorial period when some parties (agents) were considered pariahs, democracy appears much safer in these countries. The seventh and concluding chapter then summarizes the findings, provides a schematic comparative view of the legislative patterns in the five countries with regard to identifiability and flexibility, and discusses avenues for future research.

2

Representation and the Agent System

Representation requires that voters choose delegates and then hold them accountable for their actions. This relationship implies that the delegates act as agents of the voters. In some cases the voters will see their local representative as their agent; in others the voters can rationally aim their protests or praise toward factions, parties, coalitions, or local delegations. As I argued in Chapter 1, roll-call data show whether parties, factions, or coalitions can be held collectively responsible – or whether voters are more clearly represented by individual legislators.

Representation is not just a function of the relationship between voters and legislators. Interest groups, the executive, and coalition builders direct their time, money, and energy toward the individual or group whom they see as responsible for policy outcomes. Again, these principals do not necessarily see parties as their agents.

Since parties are not always the most relevant political or legislative actors in a system, the generic term "party system" can be misleading in terms of descriptions and explanations in comparative analysis. In this chapter, therefore, I propose to substitute a more neutral label, the "agent system," in its place.

Party-centric theories are unfounded where parties cannot make or enforce decisions. It is well recognized that not all parties have the requisite organization and strong leaders to act collectively. As Panebianco (1988) described, party leadership types range from "concentrated" to "diffuse." As a result, parties can have a defined hierarchy like those examined by Michels (1915), they can be loosely organized umbrellas for unorganized individuals or for smaller organizations (factions), or their organizational style can fall somewhere in-between. Parties can also be grouped into coalitions, which may put sizable constraints on their freedom of action.

Owing to this wide variance, it is erroneous to discuss all parties as if they come from a single class. Where parties are hierarchically organized, we can discuss them as relatively unitary decision makers.[1] In this case, the parties merit focus because we can identify a decision-making structure and consider the influences on the decisions makers – all with the presumption that all members of the party are bound by the decision. But, where parties are decentralized, it would be misleading to discuss, for example, the party's role in the policy-making process without asking about the role of individual legislators or factions.[2] In other words, where parties have difficulty in maintaining unity among their members (as in much of Latin America), they should not be used as independent actors, since there is not necessarily a unique party decision. Though not all factions can assure unity either, where they *are* strong, political bargaining operates at a different level than what would be assumed in a party-centered analysis. Likewise, some multiparty alliances have the tools necessary to generate cooperation among their members, and in these cases they may be more relevant to analyses than parties or factions.

Still, many comparative studies discuss the "party system" as if parties were the only (or at least the most prominent) organized political group in the legislature. With an overarching goal of attaining a more complete conceptualization of the relevant political actors, this chapter redefines the "party system" in terms of the relevant groups. Instead of presupposing that parties are unified and therefore reasonable objects to study, I argue for a prior consideration of whether parties are coherent enough to merit this focus or whether a faction- or alliance-based analysis would be more appropriate. That is, if a party is the largest group that can make and enforce decisions, then it should continue to be the focus of studies. But, if subsets of parties (as in Uruguay) are the primary organized group in the legislature, then this group, and not parties, should be the focus. Similarly, if alliances of parties (as in Chile) operate as a coherent unit, then studies should count alliances to determine fragmentation, consider the forces that act upon alliances to describe policy outcomes, and debate system changes by considering rising or falling support of particular alliances.

Because parties should not necessarily be central to the analysis, it seems appropriate to apply the term "agent system" where most studies use the phrase "party system." In this book, I use this new term to imply the collection of parties, factions, and coalitions operating in a given country. The term "legislative agent," in turn, can refer to any of the individual groups or may be construed to signify individual legislators if they are independent actors.

---

[1] This does not imply a lack of questions regarding the decision-making process, but it does imply that the party, as an organized unit, is able to enforce its decisions.

[2] This is a common scholarly trap. For example, in their chapter on Colombia, McDonald and Ruhl (1989) discuss both how the two main parties are "central actors in Colombian politics" (p. 77) and the complete lack of party unity.

My choice of terminology was motivated by two factors. First, an agent is the delegate of a principal with (limited) control. The literature on principal–agent relations makes clear that leaders (principals) constantly wrestle to control those to whom they delegate responsibility (the agents).[3] Managers worry that workers do not slack off, presidents concern themselves with appointees and lower-level bureaucrats who have to enforce and implement policies, and voters have to decide whether their elected representatives have acted to further their own, or the voters' interests. As it relates to legislative politics, the idea of an agent system, thus, implies a hierarchical relationship between voters and legislators, albeit one where the principals face important difficulties in controlling their subordinates.

Second, to have agency means the ability to take instrumental action. In some cases rank-and-file legislators have such power, but in others they are constrained by leaders. The idea of the agent system is meant to focus attention on independent decision making and actions. If individual legislators act independently, then they are acting with agency. But, where members of parties, factions, or coalitions all act in concert, then these groups appear as unitary actors with the ability to make decisions and move independently.

The term "agent system," in sum, is meant to capture both the idea of individuals or groups in the legislature with the ability (or propensity) to act independently, and the subordination (at least in theory) of these legislators or groups to voters. Most importantly, the new terminology expands the notion of the primary actors in a legislature from parties to encompass individual legislators and potentially coherent groups other than parties, such as factions, state delegations, and alliances. In some countries the parties do organize legislators and act with agency, but in other legislatures subsets or unions of parties, if not different groupings altogether, are the primary organizational units. In these alternative cases, voters and others who seek to hold their delegates responsible will focus less on the parties than other agents. Describing the agent system for a particular case thus implies a description of the unity with which different groups act, as principals will seek to hold responsible those individuals or groups that make the decisions that affect policy.

This new term aids studies of comparative politics, which requires definitions that are widely applicable in order to identify common patterns and causes. In addition, rational choice accounts require assumptions that groups are coherent enough to act as a unit in pursuit of some goal. In recognition of the range of party and faction types, a comparative and rational account of legislative politics, therefore, requires a change from a focus on the vaguely defined parties to the specifically identified legislative agents and their conjunction in the agent system. These more specific definitions, in turn, will improve tests and comparisons among agents.

---

[3] See, for example, Kiewiet and McCubbins (1991).

As it encompasses both representation and legislative decision making, the agent system is inseparable from discussions of legislative politics. The lobbying system, for example, looks very different where individual legislators are not seen as agents. Similarly, the U.S. president would waste little time on rank-and-file legislators if it were not for their independence. Further, the shape and stability of policy coalitions are very much a function of whether individuals independently decide to join, or whether party or faction leaders can line up their ducks and keep them in a row.

In order to more fully justify the utility of the agent system concept, the next section of this chapter will highlight some inconsistencies in the standard definitions of parties and party systems. There I show that factions and alliances cannot be distinguished from parties using well-known definitions. The subsequent section turns to the analytical consequences of poor definitions. In particular, I describe how the unsubstantiated use of unitary actor assumptions yields incomplete and misleading analyses. The basic point of these sections is that factions and coalitions, if not individual legislators, should be a part of any analysis of what we have hitherto called the party system – especially in Latin America but elsewhere in the world as well. Following this critique, the third section asks how to identify agents, and the fourth section concludes.

PARTIES, FACTIONS, AND ALLIANCES: A CONGRUENCE OF DEFINITIONS

New terms and definitions must improve upon the weaknesses in those they are replacing. To justify the shift from parties to agents, this section explains how the literature on parties and party systems fails in a basic task: differentiating parties from other political actors. This is the case for the two basic classes of party definitions – those based on party goals and those based on labels.

Can Goals Define Parties?

Epstein's (1967) classic study exemplifies the general conception in political science of parties as goal-oriented organizations. Specifically, Epstein states that parties, unlike other political organizations, seek "to elect governmental office-holders under a given label" (p. 9; see also Schlesinger, 1991).[4] Other studies operate under similar assumptions, differentiating parties from

---

[4] In updating and expanding this definition in a new work on political parties in Latin America, Mainwaring and Scully (1995) concur that parties are organizations that seek a particular goal; they conceive a party more broadly as including a "political group that would present candidates for public office, but is unable to do so either because it is proscribed or because elections are not being held" (p. 2).

factions based on particular types of goals. Sartori (1976), for example, states that "parties are instrumental to collective benefits. . . . In short, parties are *functional* agencies – they serve purposes and fulfill roles – while factions are not" (p. 25; emphasis in original). Instead of a vehicle for pursuing collective benefits, Sartori sees factions as "nothing but the expression of personal conflicts" (p. 25).[5] Similarly, Aronoff (1993) states that "all political groups, including parties as well as factions, are by definition self-interested in the sense that they are competing for political power" (p. 17), the difference being that factions pursue more particular interests while the parties are larger and thus pursue broader interests. In general, then, authors assume parties are goal-oriented and differentiate parties from factions, interest groups, or other political organizations based on different types of goals.

This definition is insufficient for two reasons. First, many parties are too amorphous to be considered "goal-oriented." While individual members of a party may all possess political goals, without effective organization and leadership, it may be impossible to identify a unique partisan goal. In systems such as Brazil and Colombia, for example, many legislators promote their individual policy agendas and campaigns to a much greater extent than they promote those of the party. Second, other legislative actors can desire the same goals that analysts often attribute to parties. The party goals of winning elections, enacting policy, gaining an appointed office, or attaining some mix of the these goals[6] are also primary ambitions for organized factions, legislative and electoral coalitions, unassociated maverick legislators, and even some interest groups. For example, the Chilean Concertación, an alliance of parties, has had a much clearer platform than the Liberal Party in Colombia or the Colorados in Uruguay. Moreover, the relationship between goals and size cannot differentiate between factions and parties generally, because some factions are clearly more relevant contestants for executive power than some parties. In short, neither the possession of goals nor the types of goals sufficiently differentiates parties from other political actors, and thus neither serves as a means to define parties.

Can Labels Define Parties?

The inability of electoral goals to distinguish among parties and interest groups was not lost on Epstein; thus he continues: "Having a label (which may or may not be on the ballot) rather than an organization is the crucial defining element [of parties]" (1967, p. 9). Since interest groups generally refrain from lending their own label to candidates, Epstein's full definition does distinguish parties from interest groups (Beck and Sorauf, 1992).

---

[5] Sartori later substitutes the word "fraction" for "faction" to avoid etymological problems.
[6] See Strom (1990).

Neither goals nor electoral labels, nor their conjunction, however, is sufficient to separate parties from some factions and alliances. In particular, defining parties by their ability to confer a label upon candidates is dubious for two reasons. First, voters can identify (or label) some factions and alliances as easily as parties, especially where multiple candidates or lists from the same party are in direct competition. Epstein's definition points out that not all systems allow the parties to put their names on the ballot. In pre-1993 Japan, for example, though multiple candidates from the same party competed against one another in the same district, voters were forced to remember their preferred candidate's name, as the ballots did not provide these, the names of the parties, nor the names of the factions. The opposite system also exists; in Uruguay and Chile multiple candidates also compete against one another in a single district, but in these countries the faction names, the party names, and the individual candidates' names all appear on the ballots.[7] Moreover, even where faction names are not specified on the ballots, as in Colombia and Japan, the factions are identified in the media and various publications.[8] Finally, factions that are not labeled for the general elections may be readily identified in primaries.[9]

The second reason that labels fail to differentiate parties, factions, and alliances is that some factions and alliances have as much or more control over the use of the party's label as do the parties themselves. As explained in more detail in Chapter 4, while nomination control is sometimes held by national party leaders, it may be held by the candidates themselves, as well as regional parties, faction heads, or alliance leaders.

In systems where primaries determine candidates (such as the United States) or where multiple candidates compete together and candidates cannot be denied the use of a label (as in Colombia and Brazil[10]), the candidates have effective control over the labels. Local or regional party leaders often have an important voice in systems where candidates are named to closed lists in different electoral districts, as in Argentina.[11] In some closed list systems, candidates are determined by national party leaders, but in others,

---

[7] See sample ballots in Appendix 3.1.

[8] In the past, faction names were specified in Colombia. When they were taken off the ballot in 1994, labeling was so important to one faction of the Liberals that it ran under a separate party name, the New Liberals.

[9] On Argentina, see Jones (2002); on Norway, see Valen (1988); on Israel, see Aronoff (1993).

[10] A Brazilian law (*candidato nato*) guarantees all current legislators the right to retain a spot on the party list (see Mainwaring, 1991). This law was overturned by the high court in 2002.

[11] Open and closed list systems are described in the next chapter. Briefly, in closed list systems voters choose among lists of candidates and seats are distributed according to the list in proportion with the number of votes it receives. The rank order of the candidates on the list – which voters cannot alter – determines which candidates will take the seats won by the list. In open list systems, alternatively, voters determine the order by which candidates on the list will enter the legislature.

candidacies may be determined through debates and votes among competing local groups in a caucus-like setting as in Norway (Valen, 1988), or, as in some Argentine districts, through primaries (cf. Chapter 4).

Nonregional factions are important to the labeling process in other countries. In pre-1993 Japan, multiple candidates competed with one another, but use of the party's label was restricted, and factions played a key role in dispensing the Liberal Democratic Party (LDP) endorsement (Cox and Rosenbluth, 1993).[12] Likewise as will be explained in more detail in Chapter 4, in Uruguay the factions – not the parties – bestow labels upon the candidates.[13] The presidential winner is solely an electoral by-product of whom the factions promote because the factions, not the parties, control the nomination process. The Chilean alliances offer one further example. There, though candidates run as alliance members, the parties that make up the alliances bargain amongst themselves to place candidates in propitious districts (Molina Armas, 1993). These alliances, therefore, are analytically equivalent to a factionalized party with the Chilean parties acting as the factions. Finally, though Israel employs a single nationwide district, factions of the Labor Party maintain a role by competing for propitious places on the national lists.[14] In short, since control of naming candidates for competition in legislative elections can be held by the individual candidates, or leaders of the factions, parties, or alliances, nomination control is not a distinguishing feature of any of these organizations.

Can Organizational Types Define Parties?

Like goals and labels (as noted in Epstein's definition cited earlier), the level of organization is insufficient to differentiate parties from factions or alliances. This results from the great differences among party, subparty, and supraparty organizational models.

Panebianco (1988) explains how the "power" of party organizations varies, based on whether the leadership is "monarchical," "oligarchical," or divided as in a "polyarchy" (p. 172). Further, the author measures party

[12] Japan changed its system to a German-style mix of single member districts and closed list proportional representation in 1994. Henceforth I will generally refer to pre-1994 Japan to avoid the confusion. Prior to the change, some would-be LDP candidates who were not bestowed with the party label ran as independents. These candidates, however, were not always fully independent. Because the factions had to divvy up a limited number of potential seats in a district, not all factions were represented in every district. Therefore, they sponsored independent candidates who, if successful in their campaigns, quickly joined the LDP, often with the membership retroactive to the start of the campaign.
[13] See Morgenstern (2001).
[14] Israel's Labor Party was formed as the union of several smaller labor parties, which now comprise the Labor Party's factions (Luebbert, 1986; Aronoff, 1993). Though there are not formal primaries (as found in some Argentine districts), the factions bargain intensely about which (and in what order) candidates will appear on the party's list.

institutionalization by the degree to which (1) the party develops intraparliamentary organizations, (2) the party's organizations at similar levels in the hierarchy (e.g., all local organizations) have a similar form, (3) finance is routinized, (4) the party dominates external organizations, and (5) there is correspondence between a party's written rules and the actual power structure. Mainwaring and Scully's definition of institutionalized parties is similar:

> The [institutionalized] party...[is] autonomous vis-à-vis movements or organizations that initially may have created it for instrumental purposes. It is a sign of greater institutionalization if party structures are firmly established, if they are territorially comprehensive, if parties are well organized, and if they have resources of their own. (1995, p. 5)

These indicators, however, fail to separate parties from factions or alliances because they, like parties, fall along a continuum according to these variables (Morgenstern, 2001). As a result, in some cases the factions or alliances have more highly developed organizations than do the parties with which they are associated. For example, Thayer (1969) describes the Japanese factions as "formal political entities, with a headquarters, regular meetings, known membership, an established structure, and firm discipline" (p. 15). Similarly the pre-1994 Italian factions were well organized, as are some of the Uruguayan factions. Moreover, some countries' factions compete for votes throughout the country. In sum, like parties, factions or coalitions may have inchoate organizations that form around emerging candidates to machine-like organizations with defined hierarchies, meeting houses, and campaign organizations.

WEAKNESSES IN PARTY-CENTRIC DEMOCRATIC THEORY

The inconsistent and incomplete definitions do not fully justify my peddling a neologism to replace the "party system." The larger reason is that such problems yield oversimplified and potentially misleading comparative analyses. To explain, the following subsections criticize some well-known works where parties are taken as collective actors without proper care to that assumption. I have drawn examples from the literature regarding coalition theory and theories of system fragmentation as well as those works considering the organization and institutionalization of parties and the party system.

Coalition Theory, Representation, and System Fragmentation

First, theories of coalition formation and cabinet durability have failed to deal with the rational actor assumption satisfactorily. Such theories have moved from a focus on minimum winning coalitions (Von Neumann and Morgenstern, 1944; Riker, 1962) to more recent strategic or game-theoretic approaches (Axelrod, 1984; Laver and Shepsle, 1990; Strom, 1990), but most theories have continued to rely on a discussion of (unitary) party interests and strategies. A first example would be Riker's (1962) theory of "minimal winning coalitions," and the subsequent tests of that theory which count how many parties are included in cabinets.[15] Likewise, game-theoretic approaches are based on the parties weighing the costs and benefits of accepting (or later renouncing) portfolios. Strom (1990), for example, makes a similar assumption in his comprehensive analysis of how parties strive for some mix of policy influence, vote maximization, and elected or appointed office. But while the assumption of party unity may be right for parties in much of Western Europe (as asserted by Laver and Schofield, 1990), it is incorrect for many Latin American parties. Moreover, even in the Western European cases that Luebbert (1986) studies, "Most negotiation in cases of protracted government formation takes place between leaders and their followers and among rival factions within parties" (p. 52). Thus, to characterize legislative coalitions correctly, especially in Latin America, we must assess subparty actors and the unity of the parties.[16]

Second, the lack of care to the rational actor assumption is evident in analyses that rely on the number of parties in a system. Counting parties is illogical without an accompanying description of party unity, and this opens to scrutiny conclusions based on the number of assumed-to-be-rational parties.

One primary issue in these studies is the translation of voters' preferences into legislative representatives, as in studies that seek to explain which party and electoral systems are biased for or against minority representation. The general assumption is that multiparty systems are more representative than two-party systems because voters have a broader range of choices (Sartori, 1976; Lijphart, 1984). But, although the multiparty systems always permit voters multiple choices, some systems with just a few parties do as well. In countries such as Colombia, pre-1994 Japan, or Uruguay, voters have had much more choice than suggested by figures that solely enumerate the number of parties, since they must choose among factions or candidates within the two or three main parties. Moreover, in Israel the two main parties are really coalitions of small parties that give representation to many small groups (see Aronoff, 1993). Even in the United States one could argue that geographically concentrated groups gain representation. Thus, because parties are not all unified, it is often misleading to suggest that small groups lack legislative representation in two-party systems.

---

[15] Riker's theory predicts that coalitions will form with only the bare minimum of parties to guarantee a majority, in order that the resources controlled by the governing group be divided into as few pieces as possible.

[16] See Druckman (1996) who challenges the assumption for European parties. He finds that factionalized parties impede cabinet durability.

It is equally problematic to count only parties in characterizing political fragmentation or polarization. Sartori (1976) asserts that the number of parties indicates "the extent to which political power is fragmented or non-fragmented, dispersed or concentrated . . . [and] we are alerted to the number of possible 'interaction streams' that are involved. . . . [T]he greater the number of parties (that have a say), the greater the complexity and probably the intricacy of the system" (p. 120). If factions and not parties account for the primary "interaction streams," is it not misleading to count only parties? Sartori does spend a chapter discussing factions but does not integrate this analysis into his well-known conclusions about party systems. He demarcates, for example, the transition to extreme multipartism at "five to six parties" (p. 131), without counting factions as among the "relevant" actors. Many factions would meet his criteria of relevance, which he defines as "coalition" or "blackmail potential" (pp. 122–3), and thus too much is lost by confining the discussion of fragmentation to parties.

Japan and Norway provide clear examples of subparty actors that meet Sartori's definition. First, Cox and Rosenbluth (1995) explain that the fall of the LDP government in 1993 was due to an internal party schism. Though factions have generally held together in Japan out of the common desire to control the prime minister's office, in 1993 several factions found other interests more pertinent and voted against their copartisan prime minister. Second, Strom (1994) describes how in Norway a majority opposition was unable to bring down a minority government as a result of differences among the coalition members. Though each of the opposition members desired the ouster of the socialist government, they differed on the vehicle for the no-confidence vote. Additionally, Strom describes how internal party politics reduced the latitude of the leaders of the member parties sufficiently that they were unable to negotiate a satisfactory method for reaching the ultimate goal of defeating the socialists. As a result, though two motions of no-confidence were presented, neither generated the necessary support, and not only did the socialist government survive, but the party also trounced the opposition in the next elections as a result of the nonsocialists' embarrassment and divisiveness. In sum, in each of these cases, "coalition and blackmail potential" was determined by subparty actors, and thus Sartori's definition is insufficient.

In Latin America, similar problems arise when discussing Chilean or Uruguayan politics under standard definitions of parties. In Uruguay, the lack of a clear definition has led to a largely semantic debate about whether their factionalized parties are really only facades for multiple smaller parties (Solari, 1991; González, 1991, 1993, 1995; see also McDonald, 1978; Dix, 1984; McDonald and Ruhl, 1989). González argues that the parties are relevant in that they are identified by the electorate, have long histories, and act as catch-all parties found in other parts of the world. On the other hand, Solari argues that factions are the more relevant political unit because parties are little more than an electoral grouping of very diverse factions that do not necessarily work together. In fact, he states "party discipline is practically non-existent" (p. 121). What end does this debate serve? For studies of policy, fragmentation, or legislative politics, the important analytical distinction between factions and parties is the extent to which each influences policy decisions. This is a function of their ability to make and enforce decisions among their ranks – that is, sustain collective action. Thus, it again seems appropriate to apply a generic term to the collective actors.

A similar argument can be made about definitions of alliances of parties as found in Chile. In Chile two coalitions – the center-left Concertación and a rightist coalition (that has used several names) – compete electorally, are ideologically differentiable, and are frequently unified in their voting. Given that these two coalitions act as two distinct voting blocs, is it correct to consider them as simple alliances? Should they be taken as factionalized parties? Again, these labels are much less important than an understanding of the extent to which these groups structure legislative behavior.

Party Organization and System Institutionalization

The second type of party study that has disregarded unitary actor assumptions and alternative legislative agents are those concerned with the organization and institutionalization of parties and party systems. Party and legislative organization have received much attention in both the American (Mayhew, 1974; Weingast and Marshall, 1988; Rohde, 1991; Cox and McCubbins, 1993) and comparative literature (Michels, 1915; Duverger, 1954; Panebianco, 1988) because, as Michels stated, "democracy is inconceivable without organization" (p. 21). In spite of the attention, the unitary actor assumption has escaped serious scrutiny.[17] The oligarchical leaderships that Michels found, or Duverger's inner circle, for example, could be a group of close-knit leaders controlling a unified party or loosely banded leaders heading unified factions. Panebianco's discussion of the degree of leadership "concentration" is a first step toward rectifying the problem, but all of these studies neglect looking at the factional (or alliance) organizations, which in some cases may fit Weberian models better than the parties.

Likewise, the literature on party system organization in Latin America treats factions inadequately, thereby limiting broad application of the conclusions. This literature is best evidenced in Mainwaring and Scully's (1995)

---

[17] Laver and Schofield (1990) are an exception (see their Chapter 2). Also, I do not mean to imply that these other authors ignore the issue of factions. In fact, Duverger explains that within the inner circle, "cliques," "wings," "tendencies," or "teams" can and do form as "personal oligarchies" (pp. 153–4). The point is simply that factions can be organized just like parties – hierarchical or not, disciplined or not. Moreover, some coalitions among parties also organize themselves hierarchically, and this is not accounted for in the literature on party organization.

introduction to their book about the role of party systems in building democratic institutions (see also Huntington, 1968; Dix, 1992). Among other consequences, Mainwaring and Scully state that the degree to which a party system is institutionalized "implies stability in inter-party competition . . . and is important to the process of democratic consolidation" (p. 1). They define an institutionalized party system as "stability in the rules and nature of inter-party competition. . . . A venue in which major parties regularly appear and then just as quickly evaporate is not characteristic of an institutionalized party system" (p. 5). This definition, however, fits poorly for systems with factionalized parties because an appearance of party stability may mask great internal changes. Similarly, the definition ignores issues related to the stability of alliances. Discussions of the longstanding control of the legislature by the U.S. Democrats, the Chilean Concertación, or Japan's LDP, for example, hide the change from Southern domination in the United States, the changing weights of the Concertación's member parties, and the intense rivalries and shifting fortunes among Japan's powerful factions. Similarly, the Uruguayan parties, which Mainwaring and Scully code as institutionalized, have undergone tremendous internal changes. The Communists who until 1994 dominated the Frente Amplio's legislative contingent, for example, are now a small minority – a fact that has scholarly implications for categorizing the party and the party system, as well as practical consequences for both the party and the country.

In sum, coding a party as institutionalized for its stable electoral results, or a party system as such due to stable competition among parties, may hide fluid competition within the parties. Such coding may also neglect the level of stability at the alliance level, which may be unrelated to the consistency of support for the member parties. The concept of institutionalization, then, is applicable to legislative groups other than parties, and a coding scheme for an institutionalized system should account for the stability of competition of the groups that pertain to the party's label and a consideration of the alliance structure in which the party is embedded.

Weaknesses: Justifications and Ramifications

The preceding characterization of the extant party and party system literature simplifies some complex and detailed analyses in an effort to highlight the neglect of factions and alliances. It should therefore be noted that the importance of factions or alliances is not always lost to party theorists; these other agents are just ignored for simplicity. Lijphart (1994), for example, cites the need for simplicity in excluding factions from his analysis, though he does note that "the definitions [for parties] one chooses are by no means inconsequential" (p. 74). Similarly, Shugart and Carey (1992) note that factionalized systems can confuse the calculation for the number of parties, but they shrug off the issue stating that their indicator of party leadership strength "is justified, because it is the closest that we can come to expressing, with a simple number, both electoral efficiency and representativeness" (p. 179). The ramifications of this simplification, however, are evident in a later passage: "If the number of parties varies, so perhaps do such outcomes as the extent and quality of representation and the stability and effectiveness of the system" (p. 226).[18]

DEFINING THE AGENTS

If parties, factions, and alliances are difficult to distinguish based on traditional definitions, a different strategy is required. Recall that the search for analytical distinctions was based on a need for a definition of which individuals or groups take independent or unified action in the legislature. This suggests the need to downplay the traditional labels and focus on identifying groups that vote together on a consistent basis. In a pure form, a legislative agent would be a group of legislators who consistently act in concert, thus rendering them collectively responsible to the voters. Roll-call data would thus reveal which groups could be considered agents. This does not paint a complete picture, since it will not distinguish, for example, unified British parties from factionalized Japanese parties, since both unite their members for floor votes. But even in this extreme case, the definition does serve to highlight important similarities among legislative agents. Although Japan maintains consistent factions, and Britain only grows "tendencies" during leadership contests, legislation passes through the Diet and House of Commons on party-line votes. The factionalism in Japan implies more internal bargaining than in Britain (see Thies, 1994), but if we are concerned with the coalitions that support policy decisions, taking parties as unified in these countries is not problematic.

The similarities between Britain and Japan result from a strong sense of a collective fate that is due to single party majorities within parliamentary systems. The Latin American systems, which are my primary concern, are presidential instead of parliamentary, and few have single-party majorities. This decreases the costs of dissension from an executive proposal and should therefore expose factions during legislative voting. Unfortunately, the empirical exercise of identifying agents is complicated because roll calls are taken irregularly, if at all, in many countries. In a few countries, this is not problematic because dissension from the majority party is so rare that it is well publicized.[19] But, in the countries where dissension is the rule (such as Colombia, Ecuador, and Brazil) or those that fit in the middle (such as

---

[18] See also Tsebelis (1995).

[19] In Venezuela, for example, Carey (1996), citing discussions with Michael Coppedge, reports only two dissensions between the mid 1940s and 1993 (p. 138). Mexico is another case where, at least until the late 1990s, dissension was extremely rare.

Argentina, Chile, or Uruguay), we have lacked the voting data necessary for identification of patterns.

For this book, however, I detail a significant sample of such data for the four Southern Cone countries. These data are still more limited than those for the United States because roll calls are infrequent in two of the countries, and the available time series is rather short. Still, the data open a new window on Latin American legislative politics, which the subsequent chapter begins to explore.

IMPLICATIONS AND CONCLUSION

It is difficult to analytically distinguish parties from either factions or alliances in terms of their goals, their level of organization, or their ability to control labels. Further, is clear that both sub- and supraparty actors are often central to the political process. Still, academicians continually assign a prominent role to the "party system" in their models. At least in comparative work, this yields misleading interpretations and oversimplified analyses.

A prime example of this is Sartori (1976) who spends a chapter discussing factions but then fails to incorporate them into his well-known theory correlating the number of parties with political stability or polarization. Studies of representation that leave out factions or alliances cannot hope to explain how a group's votes are translated into legislative seats or the ideological compatibility between voters and representatives because they would be missing distinctions among a party's factions or an alliance's parties. Without defining the unity of and relations among legislative groups, a model of executive-legislative relations would miss the mark. These differences are central to understanding, for example, why some presidents facing a multiparty legislature (e.g., in Chile) may have fewer problems getting legislation through the Congress than other presidents (e.g., in the United States) who "enjoy" a single-party majority.

These aspects of the agent system also account for the differing focus of presidential, lobbyist, and voter attention. Voters' focus on factions, parties, or coalitions rather than individuals, for example, has implications for how legislators run their campaigns, deal with constituents, or build the legislative institution. U.S. presidents and lobbyists do deal with party leaders to try to generate support, but since U.S. legislators are relatively independent of their leaders, such meetings are insufficient. As a result, the president and lobbyists are forced to meet with, cajole, and occasionally buy off individual legislators. This second step would be unnecessary were the parties consistently unified. It is therefore no surprise that in countries where legislators are less independent from their parties (e.g., Britain or Canada) pressure groups focus much more attention on the bureaucracy and the executive, seldom resorting to pressures on individual legislators. The agent system thus distorts the electoral and legislative process, and as a result it has a marked effect on policy outcomes.

By simply recognizing the possibility that groups other than parties may be reasonably coherent and thus influential, substituting the term "agent" for "party" resolves a number of definitional and methodological traps. Further, the new term conjures images of independent action by groups of legislators, and a delegation game in which the legislators are playing. Therefore, in the ensuing chapters I apply the terms "agent" to general cases of relatively unified groups of legislators and "agent system" to refer to the conjunction of those groups. For specific agents, however, I will use the names that they themselves or others generally apply – factions, parties, delegations, and coalitions or alliances.

Other studies of legislative politics are also moving away from party-centric analysis. Underpinning the works of LaPalombara (1987), Laver and Shepsle (1990; 1996), Panebianco (1988), Cox and Rosenbluth (1993), Cox and McCubbins (1993), and others is the importance of breaking legislatures into their component parts in order to understand the legislative process as a conjunction of rational actors. Roll-call data can aid in the task of identifying coherent or unified groups of legislators, and the following chapter therefore describes the voting unity of different legislative groups. It also argues about the importance of the balloting system in determining which groups are likely candidates for agency.

3

Identifying Agents

Having replaced the term "party system" with "agent system," this chapter identifies whether parties, factions, or coalitions will be the focus of analysis, based on two factors. The first is the voters' ability to hold the collective group of legislators responsible for their actions given the country's voting system. The second is the degree of unity the group maintains when voting on legislation, though I also take into account the historical trajectory of the agents.

The balloting systems are so significant because they determine whether voters are directed to choose only among parties (or candidates of those parties) or whether the ballot specifies the choice among factions or coalitions as well. The ballot structure thus determines whether voters can hold parties responsible, or whether they can direct their retrospective or prospective votes to the factions or coalitions. I also argue that the electoral systems are important determinants of factionalism.

In Argentina, Brazil, and the United States, ballots only note the partisanship of a candidate or group. In Chile, however, the ballot allows voters to indicate their party and coalitional preference, while Uruguayan voters can choose among factions and parties. Parties are thus vulnerable to voters in all countries, but the coalitions and factions are also open to voter retribution in Chile and Uruguay, respectively. In Argentina and Brazil, as explained more fully in what follows, voters choose a slate of party candidates in each state or province to represent them, and thus the voters may react to the actions of these delegations or those of the national party.[1]

Consistent with these balloting systems, parties in the United States, parties and perhaps state or provincial party delegations in Argentina and Brazil, parties and coalitions in Chile, and factions and parties in Uruguay are

---

[1] The Uruguayans also elect a slate of candidates, but because most of the districts send only a few members to Congress, and the others are divided into factions, the regional slates are less viable. Chileans only elect two members per district.

the durable elements of the agent systems in their respective countries. This does not imply that other agents do not at times play important roles in these countries, or that these agents are always unified in the legislature and stable in terms of electoral competition. It does imply, however, that these are the consistently central elements of the agent system in each country. I substantiate this claim later through short historical descriptions of the agent systems.

In addition to an electoral system that allows voters to target their anger or praise, accountability requires, as I argued in the introductory chapter, that groups of legislators demonstrate a reasonable level of unity in their actions. Thus, the chapter offers a first look at the agents' unity on roll-call votes. Using the U.S. parties as examples, I show that while not all of these agents have equally high unity rates, each has shown their ability to achieve unity on at least a limited set of issues. Thus while these agents may not be equally identifiable in terms of all policies, voters do have a basis on which to judge these agents as collective bodies.

In sum, this chapter identifies the countries' agents – which then become the focus of analysis for the rest of this book – based on which legislative groups the ballot targets. The chapter also provides historical overviews of the agent systems to show the consistency with which parties, factions, or coalitions have shaped the agent system in the respective countries. Finally, it explores the agents' unity on roll-call votes in order to address the relationship between voters' ability to direct their votes at a particular agent and that agent's collective behavior in the legislature.

THE BALLOTING SYSTEMS

Voters in these five countries deal with very different ballots when they go to the polls (see Appendix 3.1 for schematic examples). In the United States, voters choose among a list of candidates, each one identified with a particular party. In Argentina, voters choose from among preprinted lists of candidates for each party. Seats are distributed to the parties in accord with the proportion of votes the party receives, and thus the voters' selection is only influential in determining the number of representatives elected from a particular party, not the actual identity of the new legislators. This "closed-list proportional representation system" is contrasted with Brazil, which uses "open lists." In Brazil, the ballot only lists party labels, but voters can and do write in the name or code number of a candidate from their preferred party.[2] Thus, while candidates are prominent in Brazil and the United States, these cases plus Argentina focus attention on partisanship.

The Chilean and Uruguayan ballots are quite different. In Chile voters elect two lower house members in each of their sixty districts and another two senators from each of the nineteen senatorial districts, but voters can

---

[2] Some states now use electronic machines, but the system is the same.

only indicate their first preference.[3] The ballots are organized into alliances, and under each alliance there are one or usually two candidates listed, each identified by their party affiliation. When choosing their preferred candidate, the voters are thus identifying a coalition preference and a party preference within that coalition.[4] This voting system is consistent with an agent system that revolves around parties within recognizable and durable coalitions. Prior to Pinochet, the Chileans used a system similar to the current Brazilian system, and like Brazil, their earlier system did not revolve around durable coalitions.

As in Argentina and Brazil, Uruguayans select a slate of candidates for their district. It is a misnomer, however, to talk about the Uruguayan ballot, for instead of marking a single ballot, Uruguayans choose among dozens or even hundreds of different (and nonseparable) ballots and deposit their favorite in an urn. The large number of ballots results from the parties presenting multiple combinations of factions instead of a single party slate. Until a 1996 reform (which took effect for the 1999 election), each of a party's many unique ballots named one of that party's presidential and vice-presidential tickets, one of the party's lists of senators, and one of the party's lists of lower house representatives with that group's factional name. Prior to the reform, the number of lists was quite large since the Blanco and Colorado parties generally ran more than a single presidential candidate, and each of these executive tickets, as well as the Frente Amplio's tickets, was tied to different sets of senatorial and house factions. The reform forced the parties to designate a single presidential candidate, but voters still must choose among the factions when voting for the legislature.

Around the world, factions come in many shapes and sizes. They can be geographically or nongeographically based, single- or multidimensional, and can also vary in terms of their level of institutionalization and unity. This variety is, of course, not explained solely by the ballot structure. But, the Uruguayan ballot structure is consistent with the persistence of the highly organized and visible factions as central parts of the country's agent system (see Morgenstern, 2001). No other Latin American country specifies factional affiliation on the ballots for the national legislature,[5] and in no other country are the factions consistently a prominent part of the agent system.

In important ways the Chilean and Uruguayan systems are parallel. As noted in the previous chapter, if we consider the Chilean alliances as parties and the small parties that make up the alliance as factions, the results are not too dissimilar from the Uruguayan combinations of relatively institutionalized factions housed within a system of parties. These two systems are also

---

[3] The senatorial districts that hold elections are staggered, such that only the odd-numbered or even-numbered senatorial districts are in play at one time.

[4] In a few cases the two candidates from a coalition belong to the same party.

[5] Similar systems, however, have been used to elect regional legislatures in some cases.

similar in providing incentives for the smaller groups to remain within the larger umbrella. In Chile, the individual plurality winner of the election wins the first of the district's two seats. But unlike most electoral laws that are biased to favor the largest agents, this law favors the second largest list. It does so by awarding the district's second seat not to the second-place candidate, but to the candidate on the second-place list with the most votes. The list that won the most total votes is only awarded both seats if its vote total doubles the two-candidate total of the other list. Thus if the second place coalition wins just one-third of the votes, it is guaranteed one of the two seats. As a result, the two coalitions split the two available seats in most districts. But, if the parties in one of the coalitions were to split, they would run the risk of throwing both seats to the opposition (see Jones, 1995). Similarly, factions stay within their parties in Uruguay, in order to improve the chances of victory at the presidential level. As explained in Chapter 4, the factions' votes are pooled to determine which party will be awarded the presidency, and the prize is then given to the largest faction in that party. There is little reason for factions to run independently because they are not limited in presenting candidates and independents cannot take advantage of the votes won by other factions in their party.

In sum, the electoral systems put the focus of voters' attention on parties in Argentina, Brazil, and the United States, while they must consider their role in choosing coalitions in Chile and factions in Uruguay. With the exception of the Chilean system which is a radical departure from the pre-Pinochet days, the main elements of the other systems have been in place for many years. It is no coincidence that only the general shape of the Chilean agent systems has undergone significant change.

ANALYSIS AND INTERPRETATION OF ROLL-CALL DATA

While the electoral systems justify the focus on different agents in the different countries, the consistency with which parties, factions, or coalitions have played central political roles and have operated as relatively unified actors substantiates this focus. The following section therefore highlights the role of these different agents in recent history and uses the legislative voting data to explore the agents' unity. Before proceeding with that discussion, it is necessary to explain the measurement of voting unity and discuss the interpretation of the statistics.

The measure of agent unity that I apply is a weighted version of the Rice index (Rice 1925; see also Özbudun, 1970). The Rice index for agent i for a single vote j is simply the difference between an agent's yea and its nay votes divided by the total number of votes. In symbols, it is calculated as

$$\text{Rice}_{ij} = \frac{|\text{yea}_{ij} - \text{nay}_{ij}|}{\text{total}_{ij}} * 100$$

This yields a score ranging from 0 to 100, where 0 indicates a 50–50 split in the agent and 100 indicates unanimity.

Because many votes are uncontroversial, the Rice index can easily overstate an agent's degree of unity. Therefore it has been typical for authors to throw out all votes in which at least 10 or 25 percent of the legislature is not in opposition to a particular bill. This, however, is an arbitrary cut-off. Carey (2000; 2002), following Riker (1959), therefore developed a weighted Rice index that discounts the score by the inverse of the total number of voters and the difference between the number of yeas and nays for the whole legislature. The first piece of the weight assumes that more important votes are heavily attended. The second piece adds more weight to a vote depending on the level of controversy among the legislators. A unanimous vote receives a weight of 0: $1 - (100 - 0)/100$, while a perfect split would receive a weight of 1: $1 - (50 - 50)/100$.

In the analysis that follows, I have applied the weight based on the closeness of the vote but have not used the abstention calculation. This is the result of the sometimes strategic use of abstentions, which negates the suggested positive relation between high levels of turnout and the importance of a vote.[6] Throughout this book, I therefore use average weighted unity (AWU) scores defined as

$$\mathrm{AWU}_i = \frac{\sum\limits_{j=1}^{n} \mathrm{Rice}_{ij} * \mathrm{weight}_j}{\sum\limits_{j=1}^{n} \mathrm{weight}_j}$$

where n is the number of votes, and Rice is as defined previously. The weight on any single vote (which is the same for all agents) is simply

$$\mathrm{weight}_j = 1 - \left| \frac{\mathrm{total\ yeas}_j - \mathrm{total\ nays}_j}{\mathrm{total\ votes}_j} \right|$$

Of course, there are alternatives to this weighting system. Londregan (2000) has recently developed a sophisticated system that yields much more information about bills (based on the bills' valence properties instead of simple weights) and allows a scaling of the legislators on an ideological scale. In order to generate his scale, his system puts more weight on bills that originate from the most-polarized legislators. Because my interest is simply in revealing general voting patterns, I prefer the simpler system that weights votes according to the level of controversy, without regard to the ideological

---

[6] On votes where all members of an agent abstain, I code them as having received a unity score of 100.0.

content of the bill. Further, running Londregan's model requires information about who initiated each bill – information that is not available for most of my data set.

Interpretation of Data and Identifiability in the United States

Interpretation of these scores is, of course, not unambiguous. Unity in the U.S. legislature has been extensively studied, and two interpretative camps have formed. On one side, Krehbiel (1993; 2000) claims that parties are not unified and that politics are legislator-centered. On the other side, Cox and McCubbins (1993), Aldrich and Rohde (1997), and Berger (2000) argue that parties play key roles in organizing national legislative politics. In terms of the weighted Rice scores, the U.S. parties score considerably lower, on average, than the agents from the Latin American countries that I will discuss in this book (Table 3.1), though recently the scores of the U.S. parties have risen considerably.

Two competing spheres of discourse define discussions of U.S. legislative politics. First, almost since the inception of the country, two parties have dominated the political system. At the same time, however, "all politics are local," and legislators are relatively free from the dictates of party leaders.

TABLE 3.1. *Average Agent Weighted Unity Scores*

	Average AWU[a]
Argentina	
House parties 1989–1990	86.0
House parties 1990–1991	89.9
Brazil	
House parties 1991–1994	78.2
House parties 1995–1998	74.5
Chile	
House parties 1997–1999	84.3
Senate parties, 1992–1998	89.3
House coalitions 1997–1999	75.4
Senate coalitions 1992–1998	76.9
Uruguay	
Gen. Assembly parties 1985–1989	95.7
Gen. Assembly parties 1990–1994	68.7
Gen. Assembly factions 1990–1994	82.2
United States	
House parties 1965–1985	52.3
House parties 1985–2001	68.6

[a] Simple averages of AWU scores for major agents.

TABLE 3.2. *Are U.S. Parties Agents?*

Sessions	Year	No. of contentious votes[a]	Democrats		Republicans	
			AWU	% Contentious votes where party near unanimous[b]	AWU	% Contentious votes where party near unanimous[b]
89–90	1965–69	574	53.7	8.6	58.8	17.5
91–92	1969–73	705	42.1	4.3	50.4	8.5
93–94	1973–77	1,668	47.9	5.9	50.8	9.4
95–96	1977–81	1,865	47.4	5.0	56.5	12.1
97–98	1981–85	1,174	57.9	14.6	57.4	13.2
99–100	1985–89	1,395	69.8	37.8	58.2	15.6
101–2	1989–93	1,383	67.7	36.6	60.1	19.3
103–4	1993–97	2,001	69.1	29.4	77.1	45.6
105–6	1997–01	1,642	70.5	30.6	76.3	43.8

[a] "Contentious" defined as votes with at least 10% dissent (weight > 0.2).
[b] "Near unanimous" defined as Rice scores of at least 90.

This competition of ideas has led to a debate about the role of parties in the U.S. Congress.

While Krehbiel and others argue that parties are little more than amorphous bodies that are unable to structure their members' actions, Cox and McCubbins and Aldrich and Rohde make a convincing case in favor of parties' ability to structure the legislature. They argue that where the leadership is united, the rank-and-file fall into line. Further, they provide evidence that the rank-and-file willingly delegate powers to their leaders and that the leaders use this power to further partisan goals.

The debate between those who find an important role of U.S. parties and those who do not is particularly rich, since both sets of authors analyze similar data. Table 3.2 presents both sides of the argument, showing the AWU scores for the two parties, alongside the number of contentious votes on which the parties do achieve very high unity. The antiparty authors contend that the remarkably low AWU scores are evidence that legislators are independent operators. The other side, however, contends that the important subset of contentious votes on which the parties do unify supports their hypothesis that parties matter, at least on procedural votes or important national issues. Appendix 3.2 lists a subset of these near-unanimous votes and shows that many, though not all, of these votes were important issues on which the parties could define themselves. Further, the remarkable change in these figures since the mid-1980s implies that parties have become much more salient. In sum, the data do support the contention that the parties are identifiable to voters on some issues – even though they project an amorphous image on the great bulk of legislation.

These well-founded competing theses imply that we must treat low unity scores with care. While high scores certainly identify cohesive and/or disciplined agents, low averages do not necessarily imply that agents lack discipline or cohesion on all issues. As Rohde (1991), Cox and McCubins (1993), and Aldrich and Rohde (1998, 2001) discuss in terms of "conditional party government," an agent that is not unified on all issues can still work as an effective organization, structuring procedural and other votes.[7] In these cases the agent could maintain a highly identifiable policy agenda. These cases, however, clearly belong in a different category than those where agents maintain high unity on almost every vote. Thus in the data analysis that follows, I consider the frequency that agents are unified to capture the "conditional" agents, but use average unity rates to separate the conditionals from the unconditionals. As explained earlier, the data are complemented with a discussion of each country's political histories that highlights the role of parties, factions, or durable coalitions.

POLITICAL HISTORIES AND AGENT UNITY

Argentina

Consonant with the focus on parties in the elections, Argentine politics have been focused on parties, though the parties have suffered important splits, and coalitions have been central to several elections, including those of the late 1990s. Unlike the cases of Chile and Uruguay that I discuss subsequently, however, the Argentine factions and coalitions have been neither institutionalized nor durable. The parties, in turn, have both maintained their identities and achieved rather high levels of voting unity.

The two main Argentine parties, the UCR and the Justicialista or Peronist Party (PJ), have competed against one another since the 1940s. For much of their history, the Peronists have been considered more of a personalist movement than an institutionalized party, and the democratic credentials of the parties have, at times, been questionable. More recently, however, the PJ and UCR have transformed themselves from movements trying to dominate the political system (and willing to turn to the military when their opponents win) to democratically oriented and nationally competitive political parties (McGuire, 1995). Further, McGuire argues that voters have come to judge the incumbent party as responsible for the economic situation.[8]

The Radicals trace their roots to their victory over the Conservatives in 1916. They retained power until 1930, but between 1930 and 1943 an

---

[7] Citing Rohde (1991), Cox and McCubins (1993) explain that "Conditional party government refers to a system in which the majority party leadership is active on an issue only when the party rank-and-file is substantially in agreement on what should be done" (p. 137).

[8] McGuire (1995) cites the strong showing of the Radicals in 1985, when the economy was still doing well, as evidence (pp. 223–4).

important UCR faction was restricted from electoral competition. During that time, however, the other primary UCR faction (known as the anti-Personalists) competed in coalitions under the banners of Demócrata Nacional in 1931 and Concordancia Demócrata Nacional in 1937, placing their leaders (Agustin Justo and Roberto Ortíz) into the presidential palace (McGuire, 1995).

In 1943 the elected government (Ortíz had resigned his office due to illness) was overthrown by the military. Juan Perón, a member of the group responsible for the coup, was named labor secretary.

Perón set out to organize the underpoliticized labor movement in support of his 1946 presidential campaign. With their support, he founded the Laborist Party, under which he won the election with 53.7 percent of the vote. He soon dissolved the Laborist Party and founded in its place the prescriptively named Partido Único (the Only Party), which was the forerunner to the Peronist Party (renamed in 1947).

As the party's final name implied, the organization was more of a movement than an organized party. Perón dominated the party with strong-arm tactics, restricting the advance of alternative leaders and mass participation. The party's identity, therefore, was almost inseparable from that of its leader.

Under Perón the party dominated the political scene, taking 90 percent of the lower house in 1951 and 1954 (Nohlen, 1993), and winning the presidency in 1951 with 63.5 percent of the vote. The Peronist image was hardly diluted when Perón was removed from office by the military in 1955. The military quickly restored electoral politics but disallowed the Peronists to participate. From his exile home in Spain, however, Perón continued to control his highly influential movement, and his followers cast millions of blank ballots in protest to the electoral restrictions. An alternative strategy was to make deals with parties that were allowed to compete, and an important split in the UCR allowed a neo-Peronist party to campaign to win legislative pluralities in 1962 and 1965 (McGuire, 1995). The deals that parties made to win Peronists' support (such as Frondizi's secret promise to relegalize the Peronists in return for Perón's support in the presidential election) quickly brought military intervention. This "impossible game" of the military's proscription of the party with the largest mass base but the elected government's necessity of support from those masses lasted until 1966 (O'Donnell, 1973). In that year the military again stepped in to resolve the political disputes, but this time they did not quickly restore elections and instead imposed a harsh regime that lasted for six years. Then in 1972, in an attempt to quell new instability, the military legalized the Peronists, now under the label of the Justicialist Party, but (again) Perón himself was not able to compete in the elections.[9] In response, the Peronist candidate, Héctor Cámpora, competed

[9] Perón refused to return to Argentina from Spain by the date set by the military for inscription of candidacies.

on a platform of "Cámpora to the Presidency, Perón to power!" Shortly after his overwhelming victory,[10] Cámpora called for a new election in which Perón was allowed to run. In October 1973 Perón returned to Argentina's presidential residence. For a short time he was reasonably successful in righting the economy and calming the social pressures. But he died after only nine months in office, and his wife, Isabela, took over as president.[11] Isabela was unprepared for the tremendous challenges and quickly proved to be incompetent.[12] The military, to the relief of most, dethroned Isabela in 1976.

The cure, however, had terrible side effects. The military regime was much harsher than its predecessors, prosecuting the "dirty war" (which had inaugurated under Isabela) in which thousands of suspected communists, Peronists, and others were killed. The military regime also failed to resolve the economic instability, and by the early 1980s the situation was again in crisis. Maybe to divert attention from their domestic problems, the military fought and lost a hapless war with Britain over a small island, the Malvinas/Falklands. The humiliation led to a relatively quick retreat of the military from power and the return to democratic rule.

In the elections of 1983, the two old rivals – the Justicialists and the Radicals – competed again. This was, however, the first election in which the parties would compete since the death of Perón. The PJ's appeal had always focused on just one person, and without that identifiable leader, voters gave a surprising victory to the UCR candidate, Raúl Alfonsín.

The Peronists were not the only group that faced an identity crisis in 1983. The Radicals had been split since the 1950s into several parties, and the surviving groups remained competitive (the Partido Intrasigente and the Movimiento de Integración y Desarrollo) (McGuire, 1995). Alfonsín, however, had been instrumental in negotiating the retreat of the military and thus was able to capitalize on his public opposition to the human rights abuses. Still, there was not united party support for his candidacy, and he was forced to win a primary to gain the nomination.

Alfonsín quickly implemented an economic stabilization program, which helped contain the crisis for a while. But as his term ended, the economy got out of hand, with unemployment and wages running in the wrong directions and hyperinflation taking off. This new crisis helped the little-known Peronist candidate, Carlos Menem, to win the 1989 election with 47 percent of the vote. Soon after the election, Alfonsín agreed to step out of office early so that Menem could implement his new stabilization plan as early as possible. Menem's plan ran directly contrary to the Peronist legacy, but by tying the peso to the dollar and implementing large-scale privatization, hyperinflation

---

[10] Cámpora won just under 50 percent of the vote, but the Radical candidate won only about 20 percent.

[11] Evita, his well-known and popular wife, had died many years earlier.

[12] There were widespread reports that she used a fortune teller to help make decisions.

disappeared and the economy began to grow. This success led to Menem's successful reelection bid (after negotiating to change the constitution to allow reelection) in 1995.

During the postdictatorship period, the Argentine Congress has also been dominated by the PJ and the UCR, though the UCR has passed through some very hard times and the upheaval of 2001–2 may yield significant changes (Table 3.3). When Alfonsín was elected in 1983, his coattails were sufficient to bring a bare majority of his party into the lower house, and he retained that majority in the first interim elections of 1985. In the Senate, Alfonsín's party was unable to muster a majority during his tenure, as the Radicals held only about 40 percent of the Senate seats during that time. In the lower house, his majority disappeared after the 1987 elections, and the party's vote continued to shrink through the 1990s. During Menem's two terms, the UCR never earned more than 37 percent of the legislative seats, leaving them little option but to join an alliance with the Frepaso for the 1997 congressional election. This alliance was maintained for the 1999 presidential contest, which Fernando de la Rúa of the UCR won, and the alliance captured a near majority of the lower house. The alliance, however, quickly ran into serious problems, and then the economic crisis and resulting riots forced de la Rúa into early retirement in December 2001. After several caretaker presidents who lasted just a few days a piece, Eduardo Duhalde, the Peronist who lost to de la Rúa in the 1999 campaign, was chosen by the Congress to deal with the political and economic storm.

The Peronist legislative support was relatively stable between 1985 and 1999, with the number of seats held by the party oscillating from a low of 41 percent at the beginning of Alfonsín's term to a high of 52 percent toward the end of Menem's second term (1995–7). With de la Rúa's election in 1999, the PJ won under 40 percent of the lower house seats, but during Menem's term, his party held a small majority in the House during eight of his ten years in office. The PJ also held a solid majority in the Senate during Menem's whole tenure. These numbers, however, are a bit misleading due to the rise of several alternative parties and the breakaway of several factions from the Peronists. In particular, a leftist party, the FREPASO (National Solidarity Front), used its Buenos Aires base to score a sizable number of seats in the 1995 and 1997 elections. The UceDé (Unión del centro Democrático) also rose on the strength of capital city voters, and won 10 percent of the vote in 1989. It then fell back, however, as the PJ usurped its main policy positions (a focus on free-market economics). In addition, a group of eight PJ legislators started voicing opposition from within the PJ and broke away at the end of 1990. This was an important blow to Menem, since these eight legislators broke his majority control.

This history suggests that both parties should have been highly percep-tible to voters, at least until quite recently. The image of the UCR was severely tarnished by the hyperinflation that initiated while its leader, Raúl

TABLE 3.3. *Percentage of Seats Held in the Argentine Chamber of Deputies: 1983–2001*

	1983–85	1985–87	1987–89	1989–91	1991–93	1993–95	1995–97	1997–99	1999–01
Partido Justicialista	43.7	40.6	42.9	50.0	50.2	50.2	52.1	46.7	38.9
Unión Cívica Radical	50.8	51.2	46.1	37.0	33.1	32.7	26.9	26.5	33.1
Center-right	3.2	4.3	5.9	7.1	9.3	9.3	8.2	10.5	9.3
Provincial parties									
Left & center-left parties	1.6	2.8	2.4	1.2	2.0				
FREPASO						3.1	9.7	16.0	14.0
Other	0.8	1.2	2.8	4.7	5.5	4.7	3.1	0.4	4.7
TOTAL SEATS (No.)	254	254	254	254	257	257	257	257	257

Source: Data provided by Mark Jones.

TABLE 3.4. *Argentine Party Unity*

	AWU and Rice Scores[a]						
	1989–90	1990–91	1991–93	1993–95	1995–97	1997–99	1999–01
PJ	79.7	91.4	93.1	95.4	95.7	92.2	91.4
UCR	92.2	96.5	100.0	100.0	100.0	100.0	100.0
UceDé		81.9					
AVERAGE	86.0	89.9	96.6	97.7	97.9	96.1	95.7

[a] AWU scores for 1989–90 and 1990–1, Rice scores for other years.

Alfonsín, sat in the *Casa Rosada* in the late 1980s, and the economic collapse of 2001–2, which occurred under the watch of President Fernando de la Rúa, will certainly affect its support for years to come. Throughout, however, the party has maintained its position as the alternative to Peronism. The Peronists, meanwhile, are still central to the political dialogue and strong electorally, in spite of important internal fissures.

The complete roll call data for Argentina is quite limited, covering just the first two years of Menem's term (1989–91), but I also have summary statistics for the years 1991–2001 (Table 3.4). The very high AWU scores for the 1989–91 period and the Rice scores for the 1990s all suggest that the parties have structured legislative behavior. The Peronists achieved quite high AWU scores, earning a weighted score of 80 for the first year of Menem's term and 91 in the second. They then earned (unweighted) Rice scores in the 90s during the next decade. The UCR scored even higher, with AWU scores over 90 in the 1989–91 period and perfect unity during the rest of the 1990s.

While these numbers imply that on average at least 90 percent of PJ and UCR legislators vote with their copartisans, Jones argues that these types of unity scores overrepresent party unity, since legislators who oppose their parties often post their objection by abstaining or absenting themselves from the vote. This strategy can be costly, and in Chapter 6 I note a number of cases where abstentions or divisions among the PJ resulted in the party losing votes, in spite of their majority position. Still, the very high level of unity among the voting members suggests an important role of partisanship in structuring legislative behavior.

The Electoral System and Provincial Factions. While the electoral system puts an emphasis on parties in determining slates of candidates for each party in a province, there is also a possibility that the provincial delegations of the parties could develop as organized factions. Only a few of the provinces, however, are large enough to generate a sizeable provincial faction, as only Buenos Aires, the Federal District, Cordoba, and Santa Fe send more than ten delegates to Congress, and these are divided among parties. With its seventy representatives, however, the Buenos Aires delegation represents more than one-quarter of the legislature, and the other three large provinces elect between eighteen and twenty-five deputies.[13] Though divided by parties, these numbers are certainly large enough to swing votes, thus making provincial-based factions viable.

In addition to the electoral possibilities, Argentina has long had meaningful federal divisions on both political and economic indicators. McGuire (1995) highlights their importance to elections in his discussion of Yrigoyen working to gain control of four provinces after an electoral loss (p. 207). In addition to their economic clout, the provinces have maintained their political clout by electing senators through the provincial legislature (the case until 1994), and keeping significant control over the composition of lower house electoral lists (see Chapter 4). Further, the provinces have maintained some independence from the federal parties, as shown by the relatively high representation of provincial parties (around 10 percent of the federal legislature).

At least during the 1989–91 period, these provincial divisions manifested themselves on only one roll-call vote for each of the parties.[14] There were other divisions, but these cannot be attributed to provincial boundaries. Between 1989 and 1990, PJ voting unity was quite high, though on thirty-five of the forty-three votes the party had at least one dissenter. Eight legislators were much more likely to defect than others, having dissented on between nine and twenty-eight of the votes, while no other legislator defected more than five times (and most never defected). All but one of these dissenters were elected from Buenos Aires or the Capital district (the lone exception was a legislator from Tierra del Fuego), thus suggesting a regional affinity among the defectors. This, however, does not imply that the legislators were able to organize an identifiable provincial faction, since not all (or even most) PJ legislators in these provinces were counted among the defectors. In order to measure (and hopefully increase) their support, these eight formed the Movimiento Peronista, better known as the Group of 8. They then separated from the Peronists for subsequent elections.[15]

Brazil

Brazil's ballot system, which as already noted only lists party affiliations for lists of candidates (and a space to write in candidate names or codes), again

---

[13] The terms are staggered such that half of each provincial delegation is elected every two years.

[14] On the one vote that aligned the PJ members in this manner, those from Buenos Aires voted yes, all those from the Federal District voted no, and all the others abstained. The vote that divided the Radicals along regional lines saw twenty-one of the twenty-four provinces unifying in one way or the other, yielding a total party vote of 33 to 12.

[15] The other prominent dissenter also formed a new group, along with two other legislators. Information about the Group of Eight (and the smaller dissenting group) comes from correspondence with Mark Jones.

puts the focus on parties and state-party delegations. As also explained earlier, this does not imply that the parties are well organized or highly unified. Indeed, the emphasis of the Brazilian electoral system on candidates to the detriment of parties has been a constant issue in the literature (Mainwaring, 1999; Figueiredo and Limongi, 2000; Ames, 2001, 2002). The argument is that voters' ability to choose among candidates within each party generates intraparty competition in the elections. The candidates' independence from their parties in the elections is carried forth into the legislature. While there is ample evidence that legislators do maintain independence from their parties, there is also evidence that at the collective level the parties serve to organize Brazilian legislative politics. Further, in recent years the support of the main parties has stabilized, and most show a reasonable level of unity in roll-call votes.

Prior to Brazil's twenty-one-year dictatorship (1964–85), parties were not solid organizations (Mainwaring, 1999). From 1937 to 1945 their populist dictator, Getúlio Vargas, ruled mostly without the need for parties. In the waning months of the dictatorship, however, he allowed parties to form and then compete in the democratic elections of 1945. The democracy, with Vargas winning the 1950 election, endured until the coup d'état of 1964.

During the 1945–64 period, the parties were unable to institutionalize. In Mainwaring's terms: "The precoup parties in Brazil had moderately weak identities and roots in society, and political elites' attachments to them were sometimes shallow" (1999, p. 93). The states, alternatively, have always played critical roles in Brazilian national politics. Ames (2001) dates the power of the states and municipalities to colonial times, and after 1889 (the end of a monarchical period) states "could write their own civil codes, negotiate foreign loans, and sell bonds outside the country. The states also maintained their own military forces. Vargas imposed a plan of governmental centralization, but states retained their vitality" (p. 20).[16]

During the dictatorship, unlike other Latin American dictatorships, the Brazilian military government allowed some restricted partisan competition, though it was mostly limited to federal and state legislatures. Executive posts at all levels were filled by central directives until 1982, when elections were held to choose state governors (Mainwaring, 1999). For these competitions, the dictators set up an official party, the Alliance for National Renewal (ARENA), and an official opposition, the Brazilian Democratic Movement (MDB). These parties had important restrictions, and the legislature had been emasculated. Their temporary status was highlighted when the military dissolved them in 1979 to make way for new electoral rules and a new system of dividing the opposition. But, by 1982 the opposition reorganized and did surprisingly well in statewide elections, taking numerous governorships and

---

[16] Ames (2001) also notes that state taxes as a percentage of federal taxes were about 55 percent during the Vargas years.

TABLE 3.5. *Brazilian Party Unity: 1991–1998*

Brazil	Given legislators' party at time of vote		Using legislators' party affiliation for election	
	1991–94 (AWU scores)	1995–98 (AWU scores)	1991–94 (AWU scores)	1995–98 (AWU scores)
PDT	79.6	79.4	73.9	46.2
PFL	74.2	82.9	72.9	85.8
PMDB	71.9	56.2	68.1	57.0
PPB	71.7	52.2	69.4	52.6
PSDB	76.9	78.3	72.5	72.0
PT	96.8	97.7	94.5	97.7
PTB	72.3	74.5	67.2	74.4
AVERAGE	77.6	74.5	74.1	69.4

winning a small majority in the lower house of Congress. The opposition then took an important role in the democratic transition, and voters began to identify with the MDB and other parties (Mainwaring, 1995, pp. 363–9). But, the parties' identifiability soon faded.

In the foundational democratic election of 1985, the MDB, now renamed the Party of the Brazilian Democratic Movement (PMDB), ran as its presidential candidate Tancredo Neves, who was well known for his association with ex-presidents Vargas and Goulart (as well as his experience in public office). He won handily, and his party won 53.6 percent of the legislature. Neves, however, died before taking office, and his vice president, José Sarney, who had been a leader of rightist parties that grew out of ARENA, became president.

Though the 1986 legislative election produced a majority party, the PMDB, no government-opposition cleavage developed. The PMDB majority quickly crumbled, unity in the legislature failed quickly, and the party's left wing broke off to form the Party of the Brazilian Social Democracy (PSDB) during the constituent assembly that convened in 1987 (Ames, 2001). Further, the rest of the opposition was highly splintered. The legislature's fragmentation was heightened after the 1990 election when the biggest party in the chamber held barely 20 percent of the legislature's 503 seats, the next largest party held 17 percent, and no other party held even 10 percent.

Turning to unity rates, Table 3.5 shows that only the leftist Workers' Party (PT) scored very highly, though a few other parties scored around 80.[17] At least in one case, part of this success is attributable to the sport of "party jumping." Since legislators frequently change parties, dissidents may

[17] Figueiredo and Limongi (2000) report relatively similar numbers for these parties throughout the democratic period. Different weighting schemes account for the small differences.

leave the party instead of driving their initial party's Rice scores down.[18] The data in the first two columns reflect legislators' parties at the time of a particular vote. The second two columns take this problem into account, assigning legislators to the party under which they first voted. The change was not dramatic for most parties, but for the Democratic Labor party (PDT) between 1995 and 1998, the statistics change from indicating a relatively united party (on average 90-to-10 splits) to a deeply divided party (on average 73-to-27 splits). Other parties also exhibited important differences, though not nearly as large as the PDT.

The fact that the unity scores do not improve for most parties confirms Mainwaring's (1999) statement that legislators do not switch for ideological reasons. They switch, he explains, to position themselves with a powerful state governor, to win more access to executive resources, to receive better legislative assignments, or even to search for direct payments from legislative leaders (pp. 142–7). Apparently even these pay-offs were insufficient to secure members' voting loyalty on a consistent basis.

As in the United States, the relatively low levels of unity have led Ames (2002), Mainwaring (1997), Figueiredo and Limongi (1995; 2000) and others into a debate about the role of political parties in structuring legislative voting. Figueiredo and Limongi (2000) argue that the low scores underestimate the party leaders' abilities to cajole their followers on important votes. They find that when the party leaders take a stand on an issue, party unity is quite high. Further, they argue that the unity level of the president's coalition is over 85 percent (implying a Rice score of about 70).

Ames and Mainwaring contest these claims by pointing toward the difficulty Brazilian presidents have had in passing important legislation. Ames tests for discipline, running a regression that shows that leader pre-announced positions do not influence the votes of other party members. Mainwaring and Pérez Liñan (1997) also counter that the Brazilian unity levels are not high relative to Argentina or Venezuela.

Still, it may be that the two sets of authors are not fully contradicting one another, since Figueiredo and Limongi may be pointing to cohesion, while Ames, Mainwaring, and Pérez Liñan are pointing to the absence of discipline. This is evident in the relatively large number of votes in which the Brazilian parties did vote unanimously (or close thereto). Table 3.6 shows that while parties are not consistently unified, all parties did gather most of their members together on a significant number of controversial votes. Using a cut-off of a Rice score of 90 to determine unity, all parties in the first period were unified on at least one-quarter of the votes, and in the second period four of the seven parties collected at least 95 percent of their members on at least 38 percent of the votes. If the cut-off is a Rice score of 80, then all the

---

[18] Legislators may move to gain ideological reasons, but it is more likely that they move to win new benefits. Either way, the result is higher party unity.

TABLE 3.6. *Contentious Votes in Brazil Yielding High Party Unity, 1991–1998*

	Rice > 90		Rice > 80	
	1991–94 (%)	1995–98 (%)	1991–94 (%)	1995–98 (%)
PMDB	34.5	7.0	56.3	19.1
PTB	26.8	38.1	47.2	58.5
PDT	47.2	18.5	63.4	60.5
PFL	36.6	48.2	59.9	76.2
PPB	34.5	0.8	54.2	11.5
PSDB	39.4	39.2	57.0	65.6
PT	78.2	93.0	95.1	97.5

Note: $n = 142$ for 1991–95, 357 for 1995–98. "Contentious" defined as votes with at least 10% dissent (weight > 0.2).

parties except the Brazilian Progressive Party (PPB) and PMDB were unified on well over half of the votes in both periods, and even those two parties reached that level for the first period.

Especially if we put these figures into the context of the United States where, until the mid-1980s, the Democrats and Republicans reached high levels of unity on a much smaller subset of votes (usually around 10 percent), these tables suggest that voters could detect an identity for the Brazilian parties. Unfortunately we lack the data to evaluate the issues on which this identity is based, but it is clear that most parties could campaign on platforms based on their unified voting positions.

State and State-Party Delegations. As in Argentina, the use of party slates forces a consideration of the agency of Brazilian state-party delegations. Even more than in Argentina, discussions of Brazilian politics frequently cite the strong role of the states, often assuming that the full legislative delegation operates in concert (e.g., Samuels, 2002). In part, this is related to the great influence of state governors in national politics and, in turn, their hold on national legislators (Mainwaring, 1999; Samuels, 2000). The legislative voting data suggest that few of the states have shown an ability to maintain their full contingent of legislators unified, but that the party delegations in many states do function as unified agents.

Overall, the average unity of states' party delegations was just above 60 for 1991–4 and a bit under 60 for the 1995–8 period. There was, however, a great deal of diversity among the states. Using data from the latter period, Table 3.7 shows that the wealthier, industrialized states (Mato Grosso, São Paolo, Rio de Janiero) are all on the low unity side, likely because these

TABLE 3.7. *State Delegation Unity in Brazil: 1995–1998*

High (>70)			Low (<70)		
State	AWU	PT/Total legislators	State	AWU	PT/Total legislators
Amazonas	86.3	0/7	Acre	58.0	0/10
Amapá	71.6	0/5	Alagoas	59.5	0/7
Mato Grosso do Sol	72.9	0/6	Bahia	67.9	2/28
			Ceará	58.0	1/16
Mato Grosso	81.5	1/2	Distrito Federal	47.5	2/3
Piaui	84.0	0/10	Espírito Santo	44.3	1/6
Rio Grande do Norte	83.9	0/9	Goiás	55.4	1/12
			Maranhão	60.5	2/16
Roraima	82.6	0/5	Minas Gerais	52.6	5/44
Tocantins	82.6	0/5	Paraná	37.3	2/16
			Paraibá	63.5	0/10
			Pernambuco	38.2	2/10
			Pará	44.3	3/22
			Rio de Janeiro	25.1	3/35
			Rondonia	56.7	0/6
			Rio Grande do Sul	25.6	6/31
			Santa Catarina	45.2	0/15
			São Paulo	31.0	11/47

Note: Database identifies party and state for 390 legislators.

are the states where the PT has a significant representation. Other states without PT representation, however, failed to unify. On the other hand, several states had unity indices of at least 80. These states all have relatively small delegations (except for Piauí, which had ten Lower House legislators) and only one of them, Mato Grosso (MT), had any PT representatives (one of its two legislators; the other belonging to the PSDB).[19]

The ideological divisions in some state delegations suggests that parties within states may be better candidates for identifiable agents. In some of the least unified states, the party delegations were unified. In Rio de Janeiro, for example, while the state delegation was badly split, each individual party for that state had weighted Rice scores between 87 and 99. This pattern generally held in other states, though the average unity rates of the state-party delegations was often a bit less than in Rio. In São Paulo, for example, several parties had AWU scores in the mid 70s. Table 3.8 illustrates this

[19] The data base identifies the party and state of 390 legislators. The Rice scores are based on these legislators, as are these statistics about the number of party representatives from each state.

TABLE 3.8. *PMDB AWU Scores, by State,*
1995–1998

	No. of PMDB legislators[a]	AWU
Acre	3	91.7
Bahia	7	83.0
Ceará	3	85.4
Espírito Santo	4	69.3
Goiás	8	78.4
Minas Gerais	12	74.5
Paraíba	6	87.4
Pará	4	82.7
Pernambuco	3	90.4
Paraná	5	87.7
Rio de Janeiro	2	88.4
Rio Grande do Norte	3	93.9
Rio Grande do Sul	8	81.9
Santa Catarina	5	84.8
São Paulo	9	81.1

[a] States where the PMDB had at least three members identified in the database. Rio de Janeiro included because it is discussed in the text.

pattern with a look at the PMDB, the large party that scored the lowest on overall unity scores. While the party did not exhibit unanimity in any state, neither did it portray the disunity evident when these delegations came together. Since most delegations are small, the AWU scores of around 80 indicate that, on average, only one person dissented from the rest of the group on every second or third vote. In the state with the largest PMDB delegation, Minas Gerais, the relatively low score of 74.5 implies that on average, one or two members dissented from each vote.

Aside from its importance in defining identifiability, this finding has important repercussions for the explanation of the weak party organizations and high level of personalism in the Brazilian parties. As noted above, that explanation is largely based on the intra-party competition in the general election. But, if that explanation were correct, then we should see very significant divisions at the state level. These data suggest, alternatively, that the greatest source of intra-party conflict is among state delegations or among legislators who do not compete against one another.

This survey of the Brazilian data suggests two principal findings. First, it is well known that PT's members vote together on almost all issues; however, the PTB, PFL, and PSDB reach high levels of unity on about one-half of salient votes. With a slightly lower threshold of unity, the PDT would also be counted with these parties and even the PMDB gathers 90 percent of its members together on 20 percent of the controversial votes. In sum, it is reasonable to study the parties as collective agents.

Second, even though there is anecdotal evidence of state influence, few state delegations achieved high AWU scores. The groups that do appear identifiable – and that voters can single out – are the party delegations from within the states. In the analysis of agency it would therefore be valid to focus on state-party delegations. The number of these different agents, however, would makes this analysis unwieldy, and with few exceptions a focus on parties' national delegations as agents remains valid.

Chile

Chile's long-standing parties were central to the downfall of democracy in 1973. Pinochet's dictatorship, however, destroyed the extant parties by arresting or exiling the left and proscribing the right. Seventeen years later, maybe owing to their long traditions, the parties were able to regenerate themselves for the fight to end the dictatorship. This fight, plus the odd electoral system that Pinochet created, forced the parties into two identifiable coalitions, though the parties still retain their separate identities within the coalitions.

Previous to the coup, there were five principal parties in Chile, divided into three groups. On the left, the Socialists and Communists accounted for 34.9 percent of the vote in 1973. The Socialists, then headed by Salvador Allende, had been serious contenders for the presidency in the elections since the 1950s. They nearly won the 1958 election with 28.5 percent of the vote, lost again with 38.6 percent in 1964, and then in 1970 Allende claimed the presidency in spite of a slight dip in his support to 36.6 percent of the vote. Under Allende, politics and economics were transformed; factories were taken over by the workers, the poor were politically empowered, and the wealthy were fighting for their property.

The radical changes polarized the Chilean political landscape. In the Congress, Allende began his term with the support of about 38 percent of the legislature, but this number increased to 46 percent after the midterm elections of 1973 (Valenzuela, 1978, Table 5). These midterm elections were clearly a referendum on Allende's policies, and his supporters and opponents mobilized for that election.

After the election, the polarization that had yielded not only plant takeovers by the workers but also economically crippling counterstrikes by business owners reached crisis levels. In the Congress, though the opposition was divided among several groups with distinct perspectives on the Allende regime, these groups united to successfully censure and remove several of Allende's ministers and block *every* initiative (Valenzuela, 1978; Maira, 1979). At this time, therefore, the left and right were clearly identifiable agents.

While the pre-coup Socialist agenda was clear, the shifting center left the meanings of center and right murky. The rightist parties have traditionally been identifiable by their strong class and rural bases, but the Christian Democrats (DC) have taken much of the rural base away. Further, the strength and ideological position of the DC and the other centrist party, the Radicals, has shifted over time. Just prior to the dictatorship, however, the Radical Party, that had been electorally strong for most of the century, fell to hopeless division. Thus, when they won just 4 percent of the vote in 1973, they were unable to play the mediator/king-maker role of a centrist party.

The Christian Democratic Party had won the presidency in 1958 under Jorge Alessandri (with just 31.2 percent of the vote), and in 1964 the rightist National Party had supported the DC candidate, Eduardo Frei Montalva, to prevent a possible victory by Allende. But in 1970, the DC and the National Party could not agree on a common candidate, and both thought they had a chance to win. This division opened the way for Allende's victory.

The DC's role in favoring the coup was a defining time for the party. The party had moved from the center toward the right, as evidenced by their dealings with the National Party. Further, they had been working hard to solidify and expand their electoral base, which grew very fast from 1957, when they won less than 10 percent of the vote, to 1964 when they jumped to 42 percent (Scully, 1995). Most of this new support came at the expense of the right, but the DC proved unable to hold onto their new position, dropping to support levels of under 30 percent for the next two elections.

By 1969 the National Party supplanted the old parties of the right, the Conservatives and Liberals. The older parties had attracted large portions of the Chilean electorate (ranging from 25 to 44 percent) until their pact with the Christian Democrats in 1964. In 1965 the combined share of the congressional vote for the Conservatives and Liberals fell to just 12.5 percent. In response to this electoral disaster, the parties merged into the National Party, and recuperated much of their traditional vote share in 1969, rising to 20 percent. In 1973, after intense campaigning in opposition to Allende, they improved by just one percentage point. Leaders of the National Party then led the call for Allende's removal from office by whatever means necessary, constitutional or not.

After the coup Pinochet consolidated his power and eliminated party politics. Allende died during the siege on the presidential palace (most likely by his own hand), and leftist party members and supporters were rigorously pursued, exiled, and worse by the armed rulers. The rightist parties were also proscribed during Pinochet's rule.

The parties on both sides, however, reemerged in 1987 to participate in the national debate and the 1988 plebiscite that would have allowed Pinochet to continue in power for eight more years. Among others, the Socialists, Communists, and now, importantly, the Christian Democrats united to form the

"Concertation of Parties for the No" (Scully, 1995, p. 124). In the campaign, the Christian Democrats and their leader, Patricio Aylwin, took the lead. The campaign was severely handicapped by Pinochet's continued control of the media, but the "No" campaign emerged victorious, winning 54.7 percent of the vote.

On the right, Pinochet relied on a conglomeration of his supporters plus the traditional rightist parties. Their electoral effort failed, but they did succeed in reawakening rightist party politics. Two parties formed in this process. The National Renovation (RN), which had some centrist leanings, was an outgrowth of the old National Party. The RN is quite different than its predecessor, however, having developed into a more institutionalized party with technical and political expertise. It also has come to "elaborat[e] its own strategies, plans, and platforms, rather than simply reacting negatively to its opponents' programs of transformation" (Siavelis, 2000, p. 117).

At the extreme right is the highly ideological Independent Democratic Union (UDI). Their founder, Jaime Guzmán, had been an important advisor to Pinochet and was a particularly charismatic and ideologically motivated leader. He took special care in choosing candidates and took them through a thorough indoctrination process. After his assassination in 1991, his followers remained highly motivated in pursuit of Guzmán's goals. One current diputado (deputy) explained how a primary focus was in winning over districts traditionally held by the left.[20] In this effort, the party had sought to focus on local issues and case work, as well as to sell the voters on ideological positions. He further explained how angry citizens often chastised him when we was making his rounds. When asked why he continued in spite of the very unpleasant process (he said that he could hardly sleep the night before he had planned to go to public markets in anticipation of the rude reception), he answered that it was to promote the ideals of Guzmán and the party, and that he would not give up the job until he was confident that a copartisan could take his place.

In terms of policy, the UDI's ideological colors have shone brightly on issues relating to Pinochet and the military. When Pinochet was arrested in Britain, the UDI helped stage a few protests and earlier they had fought against constitutional revisions that would have ended military advantages and the provision for the "designated" senators (discussed later). That said, along with the RN, the UDI has moderated its extremist position considerably, and has now come to show a commitment to democracy (Siavelis, 2000, p. 118).

The new and reconstituted parties have had to compete under electoral laws that Pinochet's team devised with the intention of breaking the old party model, which included multiple parties divided into three teetering blocs. His two most important innovations were requiring the president to

---

[20] Interview, Santiago, 1998.

win a majority of votes instead of just a plurality (he devised a runoff in the event that no candidate won 50 percent in the first round) and replacing the multimember electoral districts that had been used to elect representatives with the unique two-member district system.

The majority rule (with a run-off) for presidential elections has two conflicting effects. First, it forces leaders to try to cobble together coalitions to meet the high electoral standard. It certainly has this effect in the second round, but Duverger (1954) and others have argued that it has the opposite effect in the first round. Since an agent need only be "second-best" to make the second round, they can carve out small niches and hope that other agents' niches are even smaller. Duverger shows that "almost all countries with a second ballot are also countries with a multi-party [i.e., agent] system" (p. 240).

The rule change for the legislative elections has had two important effects in regard to these issues. First, it identifies the coalitions to the voters on the ballot. Second, as explained earlier, by awarding one of the two available seats to a coalition that wins only half what the largest coalition wins, the system gives the parties an important incentive to stay within the coalition. This system has thus helped to reinforce the compression of Chile's parties into two electoral blocs, each of which has composed single slates of legislative candidates since the foundational democratic election of 1989 (Scully, 1995, p. 125). Further, in pushing the parties into coalitions for the legislative elections, the congressional electoral system congress has reinforced (if not driven) the bi-coalitional nature of the presidential elections.

The campaign for the "No" certainly helped divide the electorate and parties along a clear cleavage, yet, it was no small achievement for the parties to unite and maintain themselves within two blocs. Thirteen parties had participated in the "No" campaign, and all had leaders to support and demanding followers, in addition to a wide array of ideologies. Further, similar campaigns did not result in bipolar politics in other countries. The electoral system must therefore be credited with forcing the parties to enter into stable coalitions.

The multipartism housed within two stable coalitions is clear in a review of the electoral returns since 1989 (Tables 3.9a and 3.9b). As noted earlier,

TABLE 3.9a. *Chilean Presidential Elections, 1989–1999*

	Concertación		Right[a]	
	Candidate (party)	%	Candidate (party)	%
1989	Aylwin (DC)	55.2	Buchi (UDI)	29.4
1993	Frei (DC)	58.0	Alessandri (Indep)	24.4
1999	Lagos[b] (PPD)	48.0	Lavin (UDI)	47.5

[a] The rightist alliance has used different names in each election.
[b] Results for the first round. Lagos won in the second round with 51.3%.

TABLE 3.9b. *Partisan and Coalition Representation of Elected Legislators in Chile (Number of Seats), 1989–2001*[a]

	1989 House	1989 Senate	1993 House	1993 Senate	1997 House	1997 Senate	2001 House	2001 Senate
Agent								
Concertación	**72**	**22**	**70**	**21**	**70**	**20**	**63**	**20**
Christian Democrats (DC)	39	13	37	13	39	14	24	12
Party for Democracy (PPD)	7	1	15	2	16	2	21	3
Socialists (PS)	18	4	15	5	11	4	12	5
Radical Social Democrats (PRSD)[b]	6	4	2	1	4	0	6	0
Independent (I-Conc)	0	0	1	0	0	0	0	0
Alternative Dem Left Mvmt (MIDA)	2	0	0	0	0	0	0	0
Right	**48**	**15**	**50**	**17**	**49**	**18**	**57**	**18**
National Renovation (RN)	32	13	29	11	23	7	22	7
Democratic Independent Unión (UDI)	14	2	15	3	17	5	35	11
Center-Center Unión (UCC)[c]	0	0	2	0	0	0	0	0
Independent and other	2	1	4	3	9	6	0	0
Independent and Other	0	0	0	0	1	0	0	0

[a] Excludes designated senators. Also note that senators' terms are staggered so the figures refer to the total number of seats held by each agent, not the number won in the election.

[b] The Radicals and Social Democrats merged before the 1997 election to form the PRSD.

[c] The Center-Center Unión Party was part of the rightist coalition in 1993 but independent in 1997.

Sources: Carey (2002), Siavelis (2002).

the rightist coalition has had two prominent parties, the RN and the UDI. The coalition has coalesced behind singular presidential candidates, though there has been tension in the selection process. In 1989, the parties settled on Hernán Buchi, who had served as Treasury Minister under Pinochet. The RN wanted to impose one of its members for the 1993 campaign, but owing to its own internal division and the UDI's strenuous opposition, the coalition settled on Arturo Alessandri, formally an independent but a grandson and nephew of former presidents. In 1998 the coalition almost won the election behind Joaquín Lavín, the popular UDI mayor from a wealthy Santiago suburb.

At both the presidential and the legislative levels, the Concertación has had three prominent parties, the Christian Democrats, the Party for Democracy (PPD), and the Socialists (PS). The PPD was formed to represent the left in the democratization movement and originally allowed dual membership with the PS (Siavelis, 2000). The two parties then formally split, and though there are some disagreements, they are considered ideological brethren.[21] Some of the leaders of both parties were tied to the Allende regime (the current Chilean president, Ricardo Lagos of the PPD, was slated to become ambassador to the Soviet Union), and the parties have ties to Socialist International. In the post-Pinochet and Berlin Wall era, however, the parties' platforms signal concerns with economic distribution and market regulation without embracing radical versions of socialism. The PPD platform specifically disavows an ideology (saying it is a party of pragmatism and ideas) and states concerns for social democracy, equal opportunity, and access to health, education, housing.[22] This movement toward the center has surely aided their coalition with the DC, which has aligned with the PS and PPD in supporting democratization, though the DC membership has frequently disagreed with its PPD and PS partners on many economic and social issues.

Like the rightist coalition, the Concertación has been successful in holding the parties together, in spite of some important conflicts over candidacies at both the legislative and presidential levels. For the 1989 elections, the Concertación chose Patricio Aylwin, leader of the DC and, importantly, the democratization movement, as its candidate. Over some opposition from the Socialists who thought it their turn to put up the presidential candidate, the coalition chose another DC leader, Eduardo Frei Ruiz-Tagle (whose father had been president from 1964 to 1970) in 1993. Finally, in 1998 the Concertación held a primary and anointed Ricardo Lagos, a long-time Socialist Party member and founder of the PPD. While there was considerable

---

[21] Siavelis (2000, p. 113 n. 12) states that the PPD "is now seen as more pragmatic and 'modern,'" and Drake and Jaksic (1991) note that the more moderate PS members joined the PPD.

[22] The declaration of principles is available at http://www.ppd.cl/declaracion.htm. The declaration does note that the party is associated with Socialist International.

discussion about the DC's continued participation in the alliance given Lagos's victory, the alliance survived through the election and now the first several years of Lagos's term.

Table 3.9b shows how the two coalitions, with the same embedded parties, have competed in the congressional elections. In the first three congressional elections, the Concertación won a solid majority, holding about 60 percent of the seats, of which the DC held slightly more than half. On the right, the RN started with about two-thirds of the coalition's seats, but they lost some of that support to the UDI and rightist independents over time. While the 1989, 1993, and 1997 elections showed tremendous stability in the returns at the coalition and to a lesser the degree the party level, the 2001 election proved to be a watershed. At the coalition level, the right nearly caught the Concertación, cutting the margin to just six lower house legislators and two elected senators. Within the coalitions, there was more change; the UDI surged ahead of the RN, the DC lost more than one-third of its seats, and the PPD gained significant ground.

Elections, however, do not tell the full tale of the Chilean legislature. Under the Chilean Constitution bequeathed by Pinochet, ex-presidents who served at least six years gain Senate seats for life, and the president names an additional nine senators who serve for eight years.[23] As a result, though the Concertación has held a slight majority among the elected senators, the "institutional" or designated senators have held the swing votes. Since Pinochet named the institutionals who served from 1990 to 1998, the rightists could block any Concertación proposal. This constitutional provision, thus, has helped to reinforce the left–right division. That perceptible division has not diminished since 1998, since the choice of the new senators has been so critical to the Senate balance.[24]

The sum of these factors points to voters' ability to identify both the coalitions and the embedded parties as potential agents. The coalitions' identity is aided by the ballot that directs the voters to choose among coalitions in the congressional elections, the bimodal nature of the presidential contest, and the provision for institutional senators that advantages the right in the Senate. It is also reinforced by the societal cleavage with regard to Pinochet and other military issues, which is mirrored by the coalition lines. Finally, the remarkably stable electoral returns at the alliance level in the elections of 1993 through 1997 (which were followed by an advance of the right in 2001) have reaffirmed the coalitional lines.

---

[23] Eduardo Frei thus took up his Senate seat in 2000, and for a short time the Senate housed Augusto Pinochet until his 1998 arrest in Britain. Pinochet had only taken up his seat in the same year of his arrest, and he officially resigned in 2002 after the Chilean Court declared that he was unfit to stand trial for human rights abuses.

[24] See Chapter 6 for more details about the "institutional" senators. I explain there that though President Frei was able to choose some moderates, the Constitution still gives an advantage to the right, as presidents are severely limited in whom they are able to appoint.

The clear coalitional lines have not, however, subsumed the parties' identities. Candidates' partisanship is displayed alongside their names on the ballot, and the voters have shown shifting support among the parties. Whether Chilean politics surrounds parties or coalitions has therefore become a debate among students of Chilean politics. Siavelis (2002) argues that the parties are still primary, given that they have important continuities from the pre-dictatorship years. Londregan's (2002) study of the Senate shows important ideological differences among members of the coalitions, and thus he too sides with the party-centered hypothesis. Carey (2002), however, shows that legislators are much more likely to side with others who are part of the same rather than the other coalition, regardless of the ideological space between the parties. He therefore concludes that the coalitions have a primary role in organizing legislative politics.

The voting data offers some support to both views, though it more strongly supports the idea of parties as agents. In support of the coalitions as agents, Table 3.10 shows that while neither coalition is as highly unified as the Argentine parties, their AWU scores of about 75 still imply a relatively structured vote. Further, the Concertación's score in the Senate was high enough to suggest that the coalitions – or at least the Concertación – does consistently structure politics.

While high enough to suggest that the votes are generally structured along coalitional lines, the evidence is not particularly strong that core issues help them generate higher levels of unity. Table 3.11 shows that only on foreign policy issues and bills affecting organic or constitutional laws did the Concertacón achieve AWU scores over 80, and the right never scored higher than 76. Further, most of the bills across the issue areas were approved with a high degree of consensus in the legislature. Seven of the ten bills relating

TABLE 3.10. *Chilean Agent Unity*

	Lower House 1997–99 (AWU scores)	Senate 1992–98 (AWU scores)
Concertación	75.9	90.0
DC	79.4	90.6
PPD	87.3	97.4
PS	82.9	96.4
PRSD	89.6	100.0
Right	74.9	63.7
RN	81.4	69.3
UDI	90.4	92.9
Institutionals		64.5

Note: For House, $n = 583$ votes, 251 contentious (defined as at least 10% dissent); for Senate, $n = 94$ votes, 83 contentious.

TABLE 3.11. *Chilean Unity and Issues*

Issue	Economic (AWU scores)	Social/ military (AWU scores)	Foreign (AWU scores)	Government (AWU scores)	Constit. & org. laws[a] (AWU scores)	Miscellaneous (AWU scores)
Left						
DC	65.4	80.0	93.9	70.8	97.3	51.1
PPD	74.2	81.7	88.8	92.2	95.6	62.1
PS	74.8	85.8	100.0	82.5	100.0	100.0
PRSD	85.9	91.5	96.5	66.1	100.0	83.1
	86.5	99.9	100.0	87.8	100.0	62.4
Right						
RN	70.3	70.3	51.4	76.0	41.0	73.7
UDI	84.5	73.1	44.2	81.5	100.0	50.3
	94.7	92.5	79.5	95.9	1.0	94.6
TOTAL NO. BILLS	96	64	16	30	10	10
% Contentious[b]	36.4	43.8	25.0	26.7	30.0	30.0

[a] Constitutional and organic laws included here are not used in other chapters, since quorum rules are different.

[b] "Contentious" defined as votes with at least 10% dissent (weight > 0.2).

Note: Data covers only legislative sessions 335 and 336, 5/97 through 1/98, or 216 of the 491 votes.

Source: Issue codings provided by John Carey.

to organic and constitutional issues, for example, did not yield even 10 percent of the legislature in the minority. Further, the last three votes united the Concertación and the RN against the UDI.[25] These issues, then, could not be the basis for coalition identity. The social-military issues were the most contentious group of votes, where twenty-eight of sixty-four (43.8 percent) votes reached the plateau of at least 10 percent voting on the minority side. But, on these contentious issues, the coalitions were not unified; the AWU scores imply that both suffered a significant number of defections. Finally, the economic issues produced a surprising degree of unity across the coalitions, such that forty-five of ninety-six votes were unanimously approved, and only thirty-five (36.4 percent) generated at least 10 percent dissent. The unity scores for both coalitions are low in this issue area as well. In sum, there is no issue area that clearly and consistently divides the two coalitions.

Both on average and with relation to the issue areas, the parties exhibit unity rates that are at least moderately higher than the coalitions, suggesting that the parties sometimes vote in unison against their coalition partners. The PPD on the left and the UDI on the right stand out, with AWU scores more than 15 percent higher than their respective coalitions. This pattern is also evident in Table 3.11. For the right, while the UDI was very highly unified on the economic and social-military issues, many from the RN (and independents) crossed to the other side. Similarly, the PS showed great unity on the economic issues, but others from the Concertación frequently split away.

In sum, when Chilean voters cast their ballots, they can choose between two coalitions that are much more highly unified than U.S. parties. Still, those coalitions do not display particularly high rates of unity on some of the most contentious issues. As such, at least some of the parties have issue-based identities that are much clearer than the coalitions to which they belong.

Uruguay

Like Chile, Uruguay enjoyed a long democratic history in which the military played a secondary role to political agents until 1973. Its democracy was founded in 1918, when the electoral playing field gained legitimacy (González, 1995, p. 141). The democracy was disrupted twice thereafter, in 1933 when a semiauthoritarian regime took and held power for eight years and between 1973 and 1985 when a repressive dictatorship installed itself.

---

[25] On two of the votes the UDI was joined by one independent from the rightist coalition and one DC legislator.

As noted previously, Uruguay's electoral system forces voters to indicate both their preference among parties and among their preferred party's factions. As a result, both parties and factions play roles in the voters' calculus. The historical record and the voting unity data suggest that both these levels are candidates for identifiability, but that the factions are more consistently collective actors.

The two "traditional parties," the Colorados and Blancos (the latter is also known as the Partido Nacional), were formed as organizations prior to the civil war that inaugurated in 1836. This and later wars, which continued until 1904, helped seal loyalties to the parties (González, 1991, p. 140), but ever since their origination, the parties have failed to overcome serious factionalization. As noted in Chapter 2, the factions have been so prominent that Sartori (1976, p. 107), as well as Uruguayan specialists such as Lindahl (1962), Solari (1991), and González (1991), have entered into a debate about whether Uruguay has had a multiparty system, masked by umbrella party labels. This entrenched factionalism makes Uruguay a particularly useful case for this analysis.

The case for the parties as identifiable agents begins with the long dominance of the Blanco and Colorado Parties, which were virtually unchallenged by third parties until the 1970s. The Colorados held the upper hand electorally for most of the first forty years of democracy, the Blancos from 1959 to 1966, and then the Colorados again until the coup in 1973. These parties, however, were rife with highly organized factions, which consistently opposed other copartisan factions. Even presidents with a partisan majority in the legislature (which they did not always have), therefore, were often derailed by factions of their own party.

While factionalized, the two parties have been built on traditions of highly recognized leaders. At the turn of the twentieth century, José Batlle-Ordóñez, leader of the Colorados, was elected president twice (1903–7 and 1911–15) and his legacy still affects Uruguayan politics and society. As president, he promptly won the civil war against the Blancos but instead of harsh terms, he gave control of some departments to the losers.[26] Additionally, he is still revered today by Colorados (and probably Blancos) for increasing suffrage and setting up one of the world's most liberal social welfare states. He also was a political engineer, campaigning for an end to the presidential system that he saw as leading to antagonism between the two parties. After he left office, a plan for a collegial executive was implemented for the years 1918–33, and Uruguay has experimented with such systems at various times in their history (Gillespie, 1991). The initial plan called for a sharing of executive power between a nine-member collegiate plus a president. The

---

[26] Uruguayan "departments" are roughly equivalent to provinces or states, though Uruguay is not considered a federal system.

collegiate councilors were elected in threes every two years, with the plurality winner in the election given two seats and the second place finisher the remaining seat.[27] There was also a president whose powers were limited, except in areas of foreign policy and law and order. The system was seen to boost the Blancos from opposition to coparticipation (Taylor, 1985). It may also have helped the Blancos develop a party identity, but it ended up highlighting the important factional divides among the Colorados. While Batlle had championed the idea of a collective executive, he opposed the particular plan that was put forward. Other Colorado factions, however, did support this new plan; therefore, it was approved by a coalition of Blancos plus Batlle's opponents within the Colorado Party.

The Blancos' predictatorial history was largely formed by Luis Alberto de Herrera. Herrera had inherited the party's leadership in the aftermath of the civil war against Batlle's Colorados. The party had its base in the countryside, claiming to represent "the gentlemanly, pure-blooded and patrician tradition of Uruguay" (cited in Taylor, 1985, p. 322). The strong urban immigrant wave that Batlle had mobilized, however, was too much for the Blancos, and they were rendered to an opposition mode for the first half of the twentieth century. Like the Colorados, the Blancos' storied history is also replete with factionalism. Herrera was a firm leader, but faced strenuous opposition from Blanco moderates.

Factionalism was an important contributor, if not a primary cause, of Uruguay's two democratic breakdowns. Frustrated by a lack of power owing to Uruguay's use of the collegial president and a lack of legislative support from within his own party, President Gabriel Terra concocted a self-coup in 1933. To bring about the coup, Terra pacted not with other members of his own Colorado Party, but with the largest Blanco faction (headed by Herrera). Terra took on the problem of a lack of legislative support by installing a new constitution that restored a singular executive and guaranteed extra legislative seats not for the largest party, but for the largest factions of each of the two parties. In particular, he divided the Senate in two equal pieces, one for the Colorados' largest faction (namely Terra's) and the other for his coup-partner, Herrera's Blanco faction. This deal lasted through 1936, and the *dictablanda* through 1942, until another coup restored democracy.[28]

Factionalism, and the concomitant lack of legislative support for the president, also played a role in Uruguay's coup of 1973. After a successful economic period through the 1940s, Uruguay began a long economic decline. Various factions of the Colorados had held power since the redemocratization in 1942, but the Blancos finally broke through in 1958, largely as a

[27] In a later reincarnation of the collegial executive (1952–66), there was a single election for the councilors, in which the largest party was given six seats and the second largest party the remaining three.
[28] For more details, see González (1991).

result (again) of fights amongst the Colorado factions over economic policy (Taylor, 1963). The Blancos came to power under Herrera's leadership, but within a renewed collegial executive. Herrera died after a few short weeks in power, and the Blanco plan for economic revitalization was (again) blocked by factional squabbles. Another Blanco faction of the party took control after the next election, but it too failed to resolve internal disputes and the economic decline. The Colorados gained back the (again) singular presidency in 1966, under a popular president who seemed to promise a change. Oscar Gestido, however, died shortly after taking office. In his place stepped a relatively unknown politician who had been Gestido's third choice for a running mate. Since he was not already an important political leader, Jorge Pacheco lacked partisan or even factional support. Further, he entered at a time when Uruguay was in the midst of an economic slide and much of the world was experiencing growing political polarization. In Uruguay, this polarization was characterized by growing social unrest, labor mobility, and a new urban guerrilla movement. Though the level of threat was limited, Pacheco used it to increase his own power. He decreed a state of emergency and invited the military to assist him in attacking the security threats. Then, as his term ended, he succeeded in installing a political weakling, Juan María Bordaberry, as his successor. Even more than Pacheco, Bordaberry lacked legislative support. In his case this was the result of an eleventh hour change of partisan identification, from the Blancos to the Colorados. Because of the switch, Bordaberry did not command a following in either party and thus followed Pacheco's lead of using the military and a state-of-siege to bolster his position. He was not, however, able to control the military, and its leaders continued to encroach on the democratic space. Eventually the legislature resisted, but Bordaberry sided with the military. This was democracy's denouement.

In addition to the two traditional parties, leftist parties have been relevant since the mid-1960s, when the Communists and others formed an alliance named FIDEL (Leftist Liberation Front; Frente Izquierda de Liberación) (González, 1995, p. 149). In 1966, they (plus the Socialists and other small parties) won only 10.1 percent, but the leftist coalition, renamed the Frente Amplio (Broad Front), zoomed to win 18.3 percent of the vote in 1971.

Much of the leftist success must be owed to the polarizing effect of a growing, but small, guerrilla group, the Tupamaros. The "Tupas" were initially an urban protest movement, largely supported by the educated middle class (González, 1995, p. 151). Their movement, however, turned from "sporadic mischief and Robin Hood acts" (Taylor, 1985, p. 336) into violent attacks after government provocation. By 1968 the government felt it could no longer handle the guerrilla tactics, and, as noted earlier, imposed a sort of state of siege, which resulted in significant repression (González, 1995, p. 152). These actions precipitated the formal coup of 1973.

For our purposes, the importance of the leftist movement is that they generated a strong identity for the Frente Amplio. In the 1960s the parties carefully kept an arm's distance from the Tupas, but the Communists avowed that they supported the Tupas' aims, if not their means (González, 1995, p. 151). During the dictatorship, those tied to the Communists and other leftist parties were targeted especially by the military, but others, such as Blanco leader Wilson Ferreira Aldunate, were not immune to exile or torture.

After twelve long years of military repression, democracy began to sprout, and the parties were at the center of the debate. Though limited in their freedom, leaders of all parties campaigned against the military in the 1980 plebiscite. Others in the traditional parties, however, continued to support the regime, and some Colorados even held jobs in the military government (González, 1995, p. 153). This division certainly worked against future party unity.

Though they forbade the Blancos' most outspoken leader from participating in the 1984 transitional election, the outgoing Uruguayan military did not try to alter the electoral rules or attempt to alter party competition as the Chilean dictator had done. Therefore parties reorganized in ways very similar to their pre-coup days, and their electoral strength was virtually unchanged after the twelve-year democratic hiatus. The Colorados won the presidency in 1984 with 41 percent of the vote, followed by the Blancos with 35 percent and the Frente Amplio with 21 percent. In 1971, the numbers were 41 percent, 40 percent, and 18 percent, respectively. The highly proportional electoral system converted these votes almost perfectly into the same percentage of seats in both houses of the legislature.

The party totals, of course, hide the factional divisions. The Colorados were split into three main factions. The right was led by Jorge Pacheco, the ex-president who had conspired with the military in the 1970s and continued to support the military through the transition process. The center and center left were led by other leaders who had also been central to their parties since the 1960s. Jorge Batlle Ibáñez, son and grand-nephew of past presidents, headed one faction, and Julio Maria Sanguinetti, a leader of the prodemocracy movement, headed the other. Batlle and Sanguinetti agreed on a singular candidacy for the election, though Pacheco headed his own list. By virtue of his being the most-voted candidate within the party that had won the most votes, Sanguinetti (with 31 percent overall) was declared president.

The Blancos faced a very different situation. Their unchallenged leader, Wilson Ferreira Aldunate, had been in exile during much of the dictatorship. He returned just prior to the election and was immediately imprisoned by the dictators and banned from taking part in the 1984 elections. Without the charismatic Ferreira in the race, the Blancos were unable to challenge the Colorados effectively. The party's leading presidential candidate, Alberto Zumarán won almost as many votes as Sanguinetti, but the party as a whole fell far short. Ferreira died soon after the election and with him went hopes for a relatively united party.

TABLE 3.12. *Uruguayan Party Unity, 1985–1989*

Party	AWU scores
Partido Colorado	93.6
Frente Amplio	96.6
Partido Nacional	96.8
AVERAGE	95.7

Note: Based on 41 veto overrides.

The Frente Amplio, unlike the traditional parties, ran a single presidential candidate for the election. Their primary leader, Liber Seregni, an ex-military officer and presidential candidate in 1971, had been imprisoned during the miltiary regime. Like the Blancos' Ferreira, Seregni was banned from participation in the 1984 election. The Frente Amplio, using the banner of the Christian Democrats, thus chose Juan Crottogini to run in his stead.[29] This singular candidate surely made the party appear more identifiable than the other parties, yet the Frente Amplio still had some important internal divisions. The party included both extremists, such as members of the Tupamaros who had been imprisoned during the dictatorship, as well as some moderates, such as the Christian Democrats. Part of the moderate wing eventually broke from the Frente (forming the Nuevo Espacio in 1989), and another group has floated between the Frente, the Colorados, and independence.

During the first post-dictatorship term, consolidating democracy was the principal challenge for the Sanguinetti government. The major issue during the period was the Colorado plan for an amnesty for the military conspirators, which was eventually approved in a national plebiscite. The economy was not healthy, but it did not reach crisis levels either. During that period the three parties also showed extremely high unity, at least when voting to overturn the vetoes (Table 3.12).[30] Identifiability at the party level was short lived, however. The economy turned sour toward the end of Sanguinetti's five years (inflation reached 100 percent). The high unity of the Colorados aided voters in casting blame on the party and throwing them out. But, the 1989 election, which awarded the presidency to the Blancos' Luis Alberto Lacalle, also showed that voters were oriented toward the factions, as Sanguinetti's faction lost more support than others. Some of this decline is attributable to the economic situation, but some is also attributable to the loss of Sanguinetti

[29] The electoral law forced the Frente to use an existing party label for the election. The Christian Democrats proved to be a convenient choice, in spite of the fact that their presidential candidate was not a member of that party.

[30] As noted in Chapter 1, with very few exceptions, the roll calls taken in Uruguay have been for the legislature's attempts to override presidential full and partial vetoes.

TABLE 3.13. *Uruguayan Party Unity, 1990–1994*

Party	AWU scores
Partido Colorado	61.6
Frente Amplio	99.4
Partido Nacional	45.1
AVERAGE	68.7

Note: n = 24.

as a candidate.[31] Either way, the shifting factional support was quite evident in the primary that the Colorados held prior to the 1989 election in which Sanguinetti's faction (led by Sanguinetti's vice president, Enrique Tarigo) was defeated by the group led by Jorge Batlle.

Unlike the 1985–9 term, the parties showed deep internal divisions in the next *quinquenio*. President Lacalle was opposed on many issues by other factions in his party and on only thirteen of the twenty-two vetoes did a majority of his own party vote to sustain the veto. The Colorados, meanwhile, did not mount a united opposition, earning a Rice score of only 62. Only the Frente Amplio maintained tight voting unity (Table 3.13).

In spite of this lack of party-level unity in the traditional parties, voters were not left without identifiable collective political actors, as most of the factions were highly unified in both the Blanco and Colorado camps (Table 3.14). The Colorados were divided into four important factions, the Foro Batllista, Cruzada 94 (C94), the Batllists (B15), and the Unión Colorada y Batllista (UCB). The FORO and the C94 were led, respectively, by Sanguinetti (and Tarigo) and a rising center-right leader, Pablo Millor. These two factions showed great success in unifying their followers. In contrast, the long-standing Batllista faction, known by its number 15 on the ballots, and the rightist UCB showed more internal divisions. The first of these was headed by Jorge Batlle, who had defeated the FORO in the primary. His loss in the general election, however, damaged his stature (though he recouped it for the 1999 election). These two groups' poor showing in 1994 may help confirm the importance of presenting the voters with an identifiable legislative contingent.[32] Likewise, the UCB was a faction in decline, still led by its aging leader, Jorge Pacheco.

The Blanco factions also earned relatively high Rice scores. On average, just under 90 percent of the president's Herrerista faction voted together, as

---

[31] The constitution prohibits immediate reelection of the president. Ex-presidents can, however, run again after sitting out for one term.

[32] Batlle won his party's primary in 1999 and the ensuing general election (though he won only 31 percent of the vote in the first round).

TABLE 3.14. *Uruguayan Factional Unity, 1990–1994*

	AWU scores
Colorado factions	
C94	95.9
B-15	65.8
Foro Batllistas	90.4
UCB	61.3
Factional average	78.4
Party average[a]	61.6
Blanco factions[b]	
Herreristas	87.1
MNR	86.6
RyV	88.5
Factional average	87.4
Party average[a]	45.1

[a] AWU for the party as a whole. If cohesive factions oppose one another, the party unity score would be lower than that of the factions.

[b] There were also two small factions that often voted 2 to 1.

did 95 percent of the MNR (the small RyV faction was only slightly worse).[33] The Herreristas score was even higher until the faction collapsed in the last year of Lacalle's term when legislators started jockeying for position among new potential leaders.

In sum, though most Colorado and Blanco factions were unified, the factions within the parties did not always align. Party unity, therefore, has only been achieved by the contingent consent of the factions. The high party unity during Sanguinetti's first term was likely an anomaly explained by the special circumstances surrounding the reinstallation of a democratic regime.

González takes the opposite position, arguing that in spite of the lack of party unity, the parties are more than facades hiding a multiparty system. He supports this argument in several ways, most importantly by noting that partisanship binds the factions. This point is evidenced in Altman's (2000a) study, which shows that presidents have offered principal cabinet posts to members of their own parties. As argued in Chapter 4, there is also a crucial electoral link among a party's factions. But, Uruguay's history, including the

---

[33] The RyV had only six members and voted together perfectly until the end of 1992. Starting in 1993, some of their members commonly failed to vote and the faction frequently split 2 to 1, yielding their low score.

experience of the Lacalle government, has shown that cooperation among copartisan factions is often problematic. Factions cooperate only when their own leaders find such cooperation in their interests. Thus, while the parties have long recognizable labels, the factions are more identifiable in terms of their legislative behavior.

WHO ARE THE IDENTIFIABLE AGENTS?

The ballot structure in each of our five countries reflects the political histories of the countries: parties are active everywhere, but state or provincial delegations appear where slates are elected for the region (particularly in Brazil, though also in Argentina), durable coalitions are evident (in Chile) where voters see coalition labels on the ballot, and institutionalized factionalism appears (in Uruguay) where voters choose among factions.

This broad analysis, however, fails to capture the diversity of the voting unity of the agents both within and among countries. Externally, though the Argentine and to a somewhat lesser extent the Chilean parties divide much less frequently than parties in the other countries, even these parties divide on some salient issues. Further, the agent systems in these countries differ in that the ballot system and voting records provide bases for the identifiability of the Chilean coalitions as well as the parties. Internally, the rightist coalition in Chile, at least in the Senate, divides more frequently than the Concertación, and the RN's Senate delegation is less unified than its coalition partner.

In Brazil, the parties also exhibit diversity, with the PT showing much more unity than other parties. Still, many of the others unified on a significant percentage of the roll-call votes, and even the least unified party (the PMDB) has shown a greater ability to gather its membership than have the U.S. parties, at least during much of the period reviewed in this book. Thus, even though several state delegations also exhibit traits of identifiability, and some parties only act collectively on a limited number of issues, the parties are still a reasonable focus of inquiry.

In Uruguay, finally, the electoral system directs voters to identify their factional preference, and the result is that the parties only act collectively as a result of factional assent. Again, however, one party, the Frente Amplio, stands out as an exception.

While the prominence of agents is explicable by the ballot structure, that lone variable is insufficient to explain the different levels of voting unity. Even if the electoral system could explain the differences among countries, it would, of course, be unable to explain differences among agents in a single country that all face the same system. The next two chapters argue that in addition to the electoral system, ideology, common electoral interests among legislators, and the electoral cycle all add to a fuller explanation of these patterns.

APPENDIX 3.1. SCHEMATIC VIEWS OF BALLOTS

PARTY A		
Presidential Candidate	Senate Candidate 1	Deputy Candidate 1
	Senate Candidate 2	Deputy Candidate 2
	Senate Candidate Substitute 1	Deputy Candidate 3
	Senate Candidate Substitute 2	Deputy Candidate 4
		Deputy Candidate 5
		Deputy Candidate 6
		Deputy Candidate 7
		Deputy Candidate 8
		Deputy Candidate 9
		Deputy Candidate Substitute 1
		Deputy Candidate Substitute 2
		Deputy Candidate Substitute 3
		Deputy Candidate Substitute 4
		Deputy Candidate Substitute 5
		Deputy Candidate Substitute 6
		Deputy Candidate Substitute 7
		Deputy Candidate Substitute 8
		Deputy Candidate Substitute 9

FIGURE A3.1. Schematic view of Argentine Lower House ballot (for a Lower House district of magnitude 9). On this ballot the voters can either deposit the whole ballot or tear it at the "dotted" lines if they prefer to choose delegates for the different offices from different parties. They cannot, however, alter the order of the candidates.

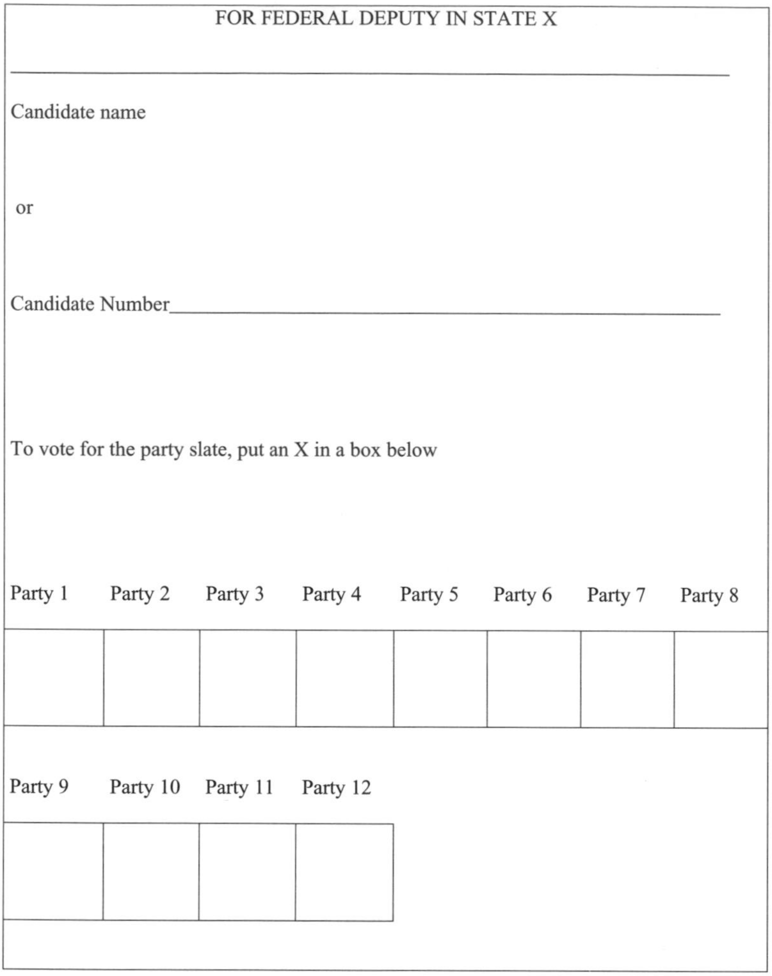

FOR FEDERAL DEPUTY IN STATE X
_____

Candidate name

or

Candidate Number_____

To vote for the party slate, put an X in a box below

Party 1	Party 2	Party 3	Party 4	Party 5	Party 6	Party 7	Party 8

Party 9	Party 10	Party 11	Party 12

FIGURE A3.2. Schematic view of Brazilian Lower House ballot. Voters indicate their party preferences and may write the name or number of their preferred candidate. (The ballot also has a section, which can be torn off, for governor and senate races. In some states the paper ballot has been replaced with an electronic system.)

```
┌─────────────────────────────────────────────────────────────────┐
│                 LOWER HOUSE  ELECTION, DISTRICT X                 │
│                                                                   │
│                                                                   │
│   Coalition A                      Coalition C                    │
│                                                                   │
│   Party I Candidate 1              Party V Candidate 1            │
│                                                                   │
│   Party II Candidate 2             Party VI Candidate 2          │
│                                                                   │
│                                                                   │
│   Coalition B                                                     │
│                                                                   │
│   Party III Candidate 1                                           │
│                                                                   │
│   Party IV Candidate 2                                            │
│                                                                   │
└─────────────────────────────────────────────────────────────────┘
```

FIGURE A3.3. Schematic view of Chilean Lower House ballot. Voters indicate their choice of candidate.

```
┌─────────────────────────────────────────────────────────────────┐
│                             PARTY A                               │
│                                                                   │
│                                                                   │
│   President and Vice Presidential Candidate                       │
│                                                                   │
│                                                                   │
│   Senators, Faction I                                             │
│                                                                   │
│   Senator 1                        Senator substitute 1          │
│                                                                   │
│   Senator 2                        Senator substitute 2          │
│                                                                   │
│   Senator 3                        Senator substitute 3          │
│                                                                   │
│   ...                              ...                            │
│                                                                   │
│   Senator 30                       Senator substitute 30         │
│                                                                   │
│                                                                   │
│   Representatives, Faction Ia                                     │
│                                                                   │
│   Deputy 1                         Deputy substitute 1           │
│                                                                   │
│   Deputy 2                         Deputy substitute 2           │
│                                                                   │
│   Deputy 3                         Deputy substitute 3           │
│                                                                   │
└─────────────────────────────────────────────────────────────────┘
```

FIGURE A3.4. Schematic view of Uruguayan ballot (for a Lower House district of magnitude 3). Voters choose among different ballots, each indicating a presidential candidate, a list of senators, and a list of house representatives. The candidates are all listed, but voters cannot alter the order of the lists. Starting in 1999, the president was elected separately.

APPENDIX 3.2. SAMPLE OF CONTENTIOUS ISSUES ON WHICH ONE
OR BOTH U.S. PARTIES UNIFIED (CONGRESSIONAL SESSIONS 91
AND 97)

Descriptions are paraphrased from ICPSR summaries. "Unified" is defined as Rice scores > 90. "Contentious" is defined as votes with at least 10 percent dissent in the legislature (weight > 0.2).

Unified Democrats, Session 91 (1969–1971) (14 votes)

1. To elect a speaker of the House for the 91st Congress.
2. To recommit the conference report on S. 2917 regarding improvement of the health and safety conditions of persons working in the coal mining industry.
3. To recommit HR 15091 to Committee on Banking and Currency with instructions.
4. To strike various parts of an omnibus private claims bill HR 15062 (four votes taken).
5. To recommit HR 15931 to the Committee on Appropriations with instructions to report it back forthwith containing an amendment that would limit expenditures to 97 percent of the total funds available in the bill.
6. To override the president's veto and pass HR 11102, which would amend the Public Health Service Act, relative to hospital construction.
7. To order an open rule providing for the consideration HR 1182 relating to pay rates for government employees.
8. To pass HR 17795 amending the Housing and Urban Development Act of 1965.
9. To recommit HR 9306 providing for the reestablishment of the Apostle Islands National Lakeshore in the state of Wisconsin, with instructions to amend the bill by excluding certain mainland areas from the lakeshore.
10. To adopt the conference report on HR 17809 relating to pay rates for government employees.
11. To adopt HR 1238 relating to the speaker of the House of Representatives in the 91st Congress.

Unified Republicans, Session 91 (1969–1971) (30 total votes)

1. To elect a speaker of the House for the 91st Congress.
2. To extend the period within which the president may transmit to Congress plans for reorganization of agencies of the executive branch of the government.
3. To adopt HR 270 authorizing the expenditure of certain funds for the expenses of the Committee on Internal Security. (2 votes)

4. To adopt a substitute to HR 514, which extends programs of assistance for elementary and secondary education.
5. To pass HR 5554, which provides a special milk program for children.
6. To adopt HR 414 waiving points of order against the section of a bill that places a ceiling upon the amount of expenditures that the president can make within fiscal year 1970.
7. To pass HR 247 relating to the administration of the national park system.
8. To pass HR 14000 related to military procurement authorization for fiscal 1970.

Unified Democrats, Session 97 (1981–1983) (44 total votes)

1. To elect the speaker of the House of Representatives and approve house rules (three votes).
2. To commit HR 44 to a special committee designating minority membership on certain standing committees of the House, with instructions to report it back containing an amendment to provide for two additional minority members on the Committee on Ways and Means.
3. To agree to HR 115, which authorizes for calendar year 1981 a total of $39,605,373 for investigations and studies to be conducted by House committees other than the Budget and Appropriations Committees for all of the entities funded under the resolution (two votes).
4. To suspend the rules and pass HR 3423, which provides vocational education and training opportunities for certain Vietnam-era veterans and establishes a small business loan program for Vietnam-era veterans.
5. To agree to HR 148 to amend the Legal Services Corporation Act to provide authorization of appropriations for additional years.
6. To suspend the rules and pass HR 287, to support the implementation of the World Health Organization voluntary code on infant formula.
7. To pass HR 3238, fiscal year 1982 authorizations for Corporation of Public Broadcasting.
8. To resolve into the committee of the whole for consideration of HR 4560, the 1982 fiscal appropriations for the departments of Labor, Health and Human Services, and Education, and for related agencies.

Unified Republicans, Session 97 (1981–1983) (76 total votes)

1. To elect the speaker of the House of Representatives and approve rules (three votes).
2. To commit to a special committee HR 44, designating minority membership on certain standing committees of the House.

3. To recommit HR 115, which authorizes 1981 funding for House committees to the Committee on House Administration.
4. To authorize $35.3 million for all of the entities funded under the resolution.
5. To suspend the rules and pass HR 3132, which amends the Truth in Lending Act to encourage cash discounts.
6. To agree to a substitute to HR 115, which sets fiscal year 1982 levels at $777.9 billion in budget authority, $709.8 billion in outlays, and $717.7 billion in revenues, with a surplus of $7.8 billion.
7. To agree to a substitute to HR 115, which sets fiscal year 1982 levels at $793.7 billion in budget authority, $716.5 billion in outlays, and $717 billion in revenues, with a surplus of $500 million.
8. To agree to an amendment of HR 115 to set fiscal year 1982 levels at $764.5 billion in budget authority, $688.8 billion in outlays, and $657.8 billion in revenues, with a deficit of $31 billion.

4

Influences on Agent Unity

Discipline and Cohesion

The previous chapters have challenged the notion of parties as necessarily unitary and rational actors and turned our attention to other legislative agents. Chapter 3 argued that the ballot structure provides a succinct explanation for whether parties, factions, or coalitions will gain prominence in the political dialogue of a country. It also showed, however, that the level of voting unity of these agents varies greatly. This chapter seeks a theoretical understanding of this variation.

Following Özbudun (1970), agent unity can result from two broad factors: cohesion and discipline. A group of legislators are *cohesive* when they vote together as a result of shared goals or common beliefs; *discipline* yields voting unity as the result of influential leaders (see also Ranney and Kendall, 1956). Thus, two interrelated and complementary – not competing – sets of variables contribute to an agent's unity. The first set, pertaining to cohesion, includes those that measure the extent to which an agent's legislators share ideological or electoral affinities. When groups lack ideological fervor or common interests, voting unity requires strong leaders who can impose discipline.

As unity levels vary both across and within countries, the variables that determine the phenomenon can be analytically subdivided according to whether their primary effect is on inter- or on intracountry variation. By and large, the factors determining the level of cohesion among a group's members are particular to the group and thus explain the different unity rates of agents within a country. As this chapter describes, these factors include the level of ideological agreement among members, the degree to which the agent is polarized from others in the system, the extent to which legislators have common geographic ties, and the importance of the national campaign to local electoral outcomes. By contrast, a primary source of leaders' powers to discipline legislators stems from their control of candidate nominations (and associated powers). Since, as I argue in this chapter, nomination control is a function of the electoral system, it applies to all agents in a country equally and thus helps to explain differences among countries.

In developing these hypotheses, this chapter continues the focus on Argentina, Brazil, Chile, Uruguay, and the United States, but it also discusses other cases to fill out the comparisons. The chapter is broken into three primary sections. The first describes the different factors affecting cohesion, and the second focuses on discipline. While I argue in the second section that certain electoral laws can endow leaders with significant disciplinary powers by giving them control over the nomination of candidates, the laws of most countries ensure that national leaders must share nomination control with the candidates, voters, or regional leaders. Moreover, factors such as low reelection rates or weak ties of voters to agent labels can loosen the nominators' control. A primary conclusion, therefore, is that for most cases voting unity requires an important degree of cohesion. I also argue that both discipline and cohesion should vary across the electoral calendar, and that the forces determining unity differ depending on whether an agent is associated with the president or is in the opposition. Finally, prior to concluding, there is a note about the effects of electoral systems on the formation of factions.

COHESION

To an important degree legislators join parties or other legislative groups due to their affinities with that group. As a result, legislators often vote with other members of their party, faction, or coalition on ideologically charged issues. Ideological affinities, thus, drive voting unity. Ideology, however, is not the only source of common thinking among legislators. Legislators of a particular region may also band together for a particular vote when the issue affects their common constituencies. Similarly, ethnicity, race, and religion conjoin different legislators. Further, considerations of the party's, faction's, or coalition's electoral needs may help bind legislators together. Cohesion, in short, encompasses, but is not limited to, ideology. I will define "cohesion" here as agreements among legislators that are driven by ideological affinities, common interests in electoral goals, or common geographic ties.[1]

Ideology

Ideology is the most common source of cohesion that enters into questions of legislative voting studies. Ideology in these studies refers to a common belief system among the members of a group that leads them to react similarly to

---

[1] Shared religious, ethnic, racial, gender, or other traits can also yield cohesive groups, but here I will take these influences as subsumed under geography and ideology.

a variety of specific issues. In their analysis of legislative voting, Jackson and Kingdon (1992) define ideology as "a set of core beliefs that organize perceptions of political issues and that underlie individual preferences" (p. 814). Londregan (2000) explains the concept through the example of the "visceral" reactions of different groups to a policy under which workers would have to "punch out" for their coffee breaks. While the liberals yell, "That's not fair!" the conservatives react to the high pay of workers and might yell back something about the "outrage" of paying the overpaid workers to "loaf openly."[2]

While there are some shades of difference in definitions of ideology and as I discuss in Chapter 5 much controversy about the concept's measurement, it is unsurprising that numerous studies have found an important role for ideology in determining legislative patterns. Poole and Rosenthal (1991, 1997) and Londregan (2000, 2002) offer ideologically based explanations for the structure of legislative voting in the legislatures of the United States and Chile, respectively. Scully and Patterson (2001) find that even accounting for partisanship, ideology has a separate and measurable impact on legislative voting in the Ohio State Legislature. Aldrich and Rohde (1997, 2001) address specific questions about the changing force of party leaders and the changing levels of unity within parties, which rose substantially in the 1990s. Their studies focus on the conditions under which rank-and-file legislators will delegate more power to the their leaders and, in turn, generally follow the leader's voting recommendations. Their explanation for this change centers on changes in the House rules, internal party rules (in the Democratic Party), and most importantly, increasingly homogeneous policy preferences (2001).[3]

While a high level of ideological agreement facilitates unity, its effect is magnified when an agent stands firmly in opposition to other agents. In other words, more polarized agents should be more unified than centrists.[4] By definition, centrists have pulls in multiple directions and, as such, have a less–well-defined platform. Ideological fervor rises as agents move toward extreme positions. Where this fervor is high, it will be much tougher for coalition builders to buy off legislators with the promise of future pork or policy concessions. Further, since ideologically extremist agents build their reputations on coherent policy platforms, policy compromise is more costly to their members than to groups oriented close to the political center.

The importance of polarization to unity is clear in both the United States and Latin America. Conditional party government, for example, requires

---

[2] For other definitions, especially as applied to voters, see Downs (1957) and Hinich and Munger, (1994, 1997).

[3] In addition to preference homogeneity, the second condition Scully and Patterson add is conflict between the parties.

[4] Following this logic, Poole and Rosenthal (1991) find that most prediction errors occur for legislators close to the ideological center.

separation of the parties (Aldrich and Rohde, 2001). When the parties are in
general agreement, there is little reason for rank-and-file legislators to wage
partisan battles that require delegation of significant powers to their leaders.
More poignantly, the fall of Allende is largely attributed to the polarization
of the agent system, which precluded compromises among centrist members
of all agents. Smith (1969, 1974) argues that Argentina's conflict-ridden history is also a product of polarized politics. Tracing roll-call voting from the
early 1900s through the Perón period, he finds that policy alliances transformed from temporary groups based on individual issues into solid pacts
that divided on multiple issues. In moving toward a unidimensional pattern
of conflict, the heat of battles rose. This, in turn, melted the prospects for
democratic development.

In sum, where preferences among a group of legislators converge across
a range of issues, as with regionally or ideologically tied groups, agent unity
should result. Further, since the intensity of feelings is particularly strong
where agents are polarized from one another, ideologically extreme agents
of the left and right should also be the most highly unified agents.

Geography

Multiple studies of diverse countries have grouped legislators according to
geographic categories to explain different aspects of legislative behavior.[5]
Geography affects cohesion in two primary ways. First, geography may be
related to ideology, as it presupposes link to a common ethnic, religious, or
cultural heritage. Second, geography can link legislators who are trying to
appeal to a common constituency. This could yield unity for agents whose
members pertain to a single region, but it could create dissent if members
represent different types of voters. There are many countries where agricultural policy, for example, has created tensions between an agent's rural and
urban legislators.

Electoral Affinities

The electoral component of cohesion is built around the idea that agent
members' electoral fates rise and fall with the group's collective popularity.
Common electoral fates are routinely invoked to explain partisan (agent)
unity in parliamentary systems. In a parliament, a defeat of an executive proposal may imply new elections. On top of this, studies of Britain (e.g., Cain,
Ferejohn, and Fiorina, 1987) show that the fates of all members who support
a given executive are closely tied together, since voters choose their member

[5] On the role of federalism and geography on legislative behavior in Brazil, see Samuels (2000);
in the United States, see Poole and Rosenthal (1997); in Argentina, see Smith (1969, 1974);
and in Japan, see Scheiner (1999) and Thies (1998).

of parliament expressly for whom that member will support in the executive. Thus, for both the individual and the group, the costs of defection are generally higher than in a presidential system. Division may hurt the group by bringing down the government, and since all fates are tied, internal group conflict may unseat the individual dissenters.

In presidential systems, where defeats of executive proposals do not imply new elections, conflicts among group members do not have such direct consequences. As a result, common fates cannot work as well in holding legislative groups together. Yet, since Stokes's (1965, 1967) work, it has been clear that copartisan legislators share a common fate even in U.S. congressional elections. The work on incumbency advantage has implicitly acknowledged this tie, since the value of the advantage is to shield incumbents from falling party tides. In their study of parties in the U.S. Congress, Cox and McCubbins (1993) argue that legislators have a strong interest in supporting partisan agendas to ensure their party's success. If the party falls, the legislators must reason, then they too are at risk. These authors therefore conclude that the common electoral fate drives the legislators to delegate power to their leaders who, in turn, work to enforce a high level of unity on important votes.[6]

The Uruguayan experience helps substantiate the converse. As noted in Chapter 3, Batlle and Pacheco, the leaders of the Colorado UCB and B15 factions, were aging and appeared to be declining in stature after the 1990 election. The rank-and-file in these factions should therefore have seen dissipating prospects of electoral benefits by continuing to follow these leaders. Without these benefits the expectation would be that the faction members would put less weight on the faction's collective interests when considering which way to vote. This expectation is consistent with the much lower unity rates that these two factions upheld.

DISCIPLINE

Studies of U.S. congressional roll-call voting show that ideological positions or the cohesion of legislators are strong predictors of voting patterns in the United States. Poole and Rosenthal (1991), for example, report that their models generate correct classification percentages of between 80 percent and 85 percent. Still, these models make no assumptions about the role of discipline or other factors in driving legislators' voting decisions. Their results, therefore, would be nonsensical for a case like Britain, for example, where the parties house a wide variety of opinions yet vote as a unified bloc. In short, the application of models built solely on cohesion may have validity for studies of some single cases, but for comparative studies (or perhaps time series) the leaders' ability to enforce voting discipline cannot be excluded in the analysis.

[6] They focus on leadership votes, those votes where party leaders agree on the party's direction.

Leaders of factions, parties, and coalitions are able to enforce discipline when they control resources that the rank-and-file desire. Leaders may control the paths to cabinet posts, the votes necessary for the approval of policy, campaign funds, the distribution of budgetary resources, and the placement of pork projects, staff resources, or even access to graft opportunities. Further, many legislators owe their current (and future) posts to the leaders who helped them win nominations and/or supported their fund-raising and campaigning efforts.

While all these tools can be effective, since all legislators must win nominations to attain a spot in the legislature, control over those nominations is perhaps the key power that some agent leaders enjoy. Further, even though probably all leaders control some resources (at least rhetorical), a bit later I will use the example of campaign funds to argue that the control over nominations is strongly correlated with control of other important resources.

The assumption here is simply that nomination control is a key determinant of an agent's unity because leaders who possess this power should be able to discipline their followers. Where an alliance leader nominates candidates, all members in the alliance will owe allegiance to that leader for their current posts, and must at least consider whether dissenting on a given vote will bring retribution from that leader in the form of withholding a future nomination (or other resources). Nomination control at this level, thus, should bring about a disciplined alliance. If there are alliances but nomination control is one level down, at the party level, disciplined parties should form amidst undisciplined alliances (which may or may not be cohesive). This relation is parallel to that for factions within parties. If, however, there are no leaders at any level with nomination control, unity will require cohesive forces or pressure from the president or other external sources.

The Electoral System and the Strength of the Nominator

Electoral laws assign formal powers over nomination to agent leaders by declaring how candidates gain ballot access. The candidates' desire for access creates a power relationship; whomever controls the sought-after labels will then have important controls over the candidates they choose to nominate (Schattschneider, 1942; Duverger, 1954; Gallagher, 1988). In Schattschneider's (1942, p. 64) words: "The nature of the nominating procedure determines the nature of the party; he who can make the nominations is the owner of the party." Not all systems, however, require candidates to have a leader inscribe them on a ballot. Those systems that do make this requirement give agent leaders an important power advantage over leaders in systems where candidates gain access by collecting signatures or winning primaries. In addition to determining whether candidates require a nominator's seal of approval, the electoral system has a part in determining to what degree control of this seal is an effective tool for leaders. For example, in some systems, the leaders must nominate multiple candidates for a given district, and the voters, not the leaders, determine which among these people gain office. Though crucially important, the electoral laws are not the only factor in determining a leader's control over nominations. Internal agent rules, laws concerning campaign finances, the value that candidates put on ballot access, federalism, and the electoral cycle can dilute the nominating power. This section categorizes electoral systems by whether or not there is an official nominator and explains how electoral laws and other factors affect the degree of influence a nominator is likely to have. An important conclusion is that even though the power over nominations varies greatly across countries, few systems afford their leaders full control over nominations, and even where leaders do have control, a number of factors can reduce their potency.

Electoral Systems and Formal Nomination Control

While many systems require that agent leaders officially sanction candidacies, two types of systems negate nomination control by allowing candidates to participate in elections without official leader approval: those that call for intraagent primaries to determine general election candidates and those that put no restrictions on the labels used by candidates in the general election.[7] Primaries weaken leaders, since the privilege to compete is not bestowed upon a candidate but must be won from the other candidates who compete for the agent label in the primaries. Primaries are not just a U.S.-style single-member-district phenomenon. In Argentina, a country that employs multimember districts and closed lists, the Radicals (and to a lesser extent the Justicialistas) allow factional slates to compete in primaries for propitious slots on the party's general election ballot.[8]

The other type of system that does not provide a role for nominators (at least above the faction level) is actually a specialized primary system. In Colombia and Uruguay, primaries are, in a sense, held concurrently with the general election (cf. Chapter 3). In these countries multiple closed lists of candidates for each agent compete against one another and against lists of other agents. Party leaders in these two countries have virtually no say over

---

[7] Note that rules for choosing candidates are not generally determined by statute. That is, though the United States is an exception, most parties can choose whether to hold primaries or use another method for choosing candidates.

[8] Jones (2002) offers an interesting account of the relation among local and national party leaders and the use of regional primaries for the case of Argentina. He argues that though the national leaders have the power to impose their choices on the list, they often let local leaders make these decisions to shore up local support. If the local leaders are divided, he argues, then they employ primaries.

the composition of the lists, and thus would-be leaders cannot rely on the nomination gate as the basis for their power.[9]

This is not the case for leaders operating under other electoral rules. In contrast to the preceding cases are (a) the British system in which the party[10] chooses a unique candidate to represent it for each district and (b) the ideal-typical closed list systems in which agent leaders create an unchangeable list of candidates and no more than one list per agent can participate in a given district. In these cases, as typified by pre-1993 Venezuela, Costa Rica, and Argentina, the party leadership is quite powerful, since their pre-rogative in determining the rank order in which candidates appear on the ballot means that the leaders very much determine which candidates will be elected.[11]

The Extent of Nomination Control

The preceding paragraphs presume that leaders either have control over nominations or lack such powers. Clearly, however, there is a large gray area between these poles. This section explains that the extent of nomina-tion control is strongly influenced by intraparty competition and the district magnitude, and it should also vary in accord with federalism, the strength of partisan identification among the electorate, the value candidates put on reelection, and other factors. Nominators' effectiveness should also depend on the agent's association with the executive and the electoral clock.

Intraagent Competition and District Magnitude. Some systems that per-mit leaders to choose candidates dilute that power by permitting intraparty competition in the general election (Katz, 1986). In these systems, the lead-ers may have a hand in choosing multiple candidates for each district, but voters choose among those nominated. Effectively, then, the leaders must share their nominating power with the voters.

---

[9] An important difference between the Colombian and Uruguayan system is that seats in Colombia are distributed to the lists based on proportional representation, disregarding party affiliation (see note 17). As explained in detail later, in Uruguay the votes are pooled at the party (and factional) levels before distributing the seats. In both systems, few lower house lists elect more than a single candidate, and thus most lists are essentially candidacies of the top person on the list. Thus, even though the leaders of the individual lists could be considered as nominators, they control too few legislators to form viable factions.

[10] Gallagher (1988) emphasizes that the local party officials, not national leaders, make the choices.

[11] As is explained later, the Argentine and Venezuelan cases differ in that the provincial leaders in Argentina maintain significant control over nominations, while the Venezuelan power resides with national party leaders. I also used Argentina as an example of a country with primaries. The primaries, however, are an internal matter to the Radical Party and not regulated by law. The law only stipulates that the parties cannot present more than one list in the general election.

There are two systems that allow voters intraagent choices in the general elections: open list systems (as employed in Chile, Brazil, and Peru and for some seats in Ecuador) and ones that combine primaries with general elections (as used in Colombia and Uruguay). The district magnitude (M; the number of legislators elected from a district) interacts with these systems to either attenuate or strengthen the nominators' powers (Carey and Shugart, 1995). When ballots are closed, M determines the number of legislators over whom a leader has influence. But where ballots are open, the district magnitude has a negative relation with nominator influence. When voters are represented by just a few legislators, then winning a nomination is more consequential than where many coagent legislators appear on the same ballot.

Consider the Chilean open list where nominators must present just two candidates for each seat. Leaders who choose these candidates must whittle their choice from many potential candidates, and their final choice has a large bearing on who eventually wins. Though the low number of candidacies affords the leaders an important power, the leaders are handicapped by the assurance that most districts will elect only a single candidate from each coalition (cf. Chapter 3). This motivates intraalliance competition that can be at least as keen as the between-alliance fight, thus diluting the role of the nominators in determining the eventual winner.

The system helps to maintain nominators at two levels, each with somewhat limited powers. As explained in Chapter 3, the electoral system gives the parties a strong incentive to work within the alliance structure. Thus, plus the limit of just two candidacies per alliance in each district, leads the parties to bargain amongst themselves to determine how many candidacies each will have for an election and in which districts they will run. Interview subjects explained that, to create the district lists, party leaders in each of the country's thirteen regions send a priority list to the national leaders who then create a master list for the party. This list takes into account the party's strength (based on recent local elections and success in past national elections) in a given district and the characteristics of the candidates (including their experience, electability, and importance in the party). Some parties also use primaries to help create these lists. Thus, at one level, the party leaders, both regional and national, are quite important for the nominations.

The party leaders' nomination powers, however, must be shared with the coalition leadership since the parties must compromise in creating the two member lists. Armed with their priority lists, the members of each coalition come together to bargain for the right to place their candidates in the most propitious electoral districts. The parties must also take care in determining which candidates they pair for a particular district, since in only a few cases can both candidates be elected. Since there are no residence restrictions, however, it is relatively easy for the parties to place their highly valued candidates into winnable districts where they are not paired with titans from other coalition parties.

This shared nomination control, however important, is limited by the intraagent competition. Since two coalition partners compete in each district, the electoral outcome has an important personal and/or partisan component. For many districts, this might imply that the party nominator has more power than the coalition nominator since in most districts there is only intracoalition competition, not intraparty.[12]

Lastly, it should be noted that numerous interview subjects protested the idea that party leaders use the threat of withholding a nomination to an incumbent who failed to maintain discipline in the legislature. One DC senator explained that the party has tried to "capture, not isolate" one of their members who is known to dissent frequently. A RN lower house member, who described frustration with the party leadership and called himself an "independent," explained that the party was mostly concerned about winning the seat. Thus, though he did not win a nomination to the Senate as he would have liked, the party would not deny him his lower house nomination, since he is a "proven winner." One lower house DC member did, however, insist on the importance of the party's nomination power. His first reaction to the question about party leaders' ability to influence legislative nominations was: "Thank God we have primaries!" This reaction stemmed from his belief that the party leaders (including the president) saw him as a "loud obnoxious brat" for his role in pushing a controversial debate about reforming the constitution to end some military prerogatives. He did concede, however, that in spite of his overwhelming primary victory (he claimed to have won 80 percent of the vote) the party could "sacrifice" people during the interparty negotiations.

In contrast to Chile, party leaders in Brazil name between eight and seventy members to their lists, and as a result, their nominating power is seriously diluted. Since voters can choose among so many lower house candidates in Brazil, the candidates' winning of office has more to do with the their own campaigns than with the leaders' power over nominations. As explained in Chapter 3, the Brazilian lower house ballots allow voters to choose from among the many parties, and if they so desire (and about 90 percent do), the voters can indicate their preference for individuals from within their favored party.[13] Thus although a party leader officially has power to compile

---

[12] In a few districts both candidates pertain to a single party, thus reducing the party nominator's influence. The Concertación parties have grouped themselves into two subpacts, each of which has rights to one candidate on the list. After the 2000 election, the pacts were rearranged, with the DC on one side and the other parties in the other pact. This means that the DC will have rights to a candidate in all sixty districts. The other parties, thus, will have to bargain amongst themselves to fill the other slot in each district.

[13] The figure of 90 percent comes from Ames (2001, p. 42).

the list,[14] this and other open list systems with high district magnitudes limit the nominators' influence in the election. Further, the Brazilian *candidato nato* law allows all incumbents to participate under their party's banner in subsequent elections, further limiting the power of nominators over current legislators.[15] In sum, for open list systems, the district magnitude determines whether the nominator's role is very important, as in Chile, or minimal as in Brazil.[16]

I argued previously that party leaders in Uruguay and Colombia lack nomination control because they cannot limit the number of lists participating in the general election. In Uruguay, however, the electoral system does vest faction leaders with an important level of control over candidate nominations. This results from Uruguay's unique double (or triple) simultaneous voting (DSV) system, which was briefly discussed in the previous chapter. Under the system in place until 1999, voters chose among many unchangeable ballots that linked their vote for president, the thirty senators (who competed in a single nationwide district), and the ninety-nine House members (who competed in multimember districts). The new system is similar for the House and the Senate elections, but the vote for the president is now separate. Both the old and new systems challenge the voters by allowing multiple party candidates to compete against one another for the same posts, creating a multitude of intraparty competitors for seats in both houses of Congress and, until 1999, for the president. In 1994, for example, the Colorados postulated three presidential candidates. Like his copartisan (and his cross-party) competitors, the winner, Sanguinetti, was supported by several lists of senators, each of which was linked to dozens of lists of diputados (only the latter of which differed across the provinces). Sanguinetti was proclaimed the victor since the sum of the vote for the Colorado presidential candidates was greater than the sum for the other parties, and among the Colorado candidates, the sum of the senatorial lists (which is the sum of the diputado lists) that were linked to Sanguinetti was greater than the sum for other Colorado candidates (Table 4.1).

The key reason why factional rather than party leaders wield nomination control is that the law, although very lenient in terms of using the party label, explicitly states that all candidates on a ballot must assent to their inclusion. This provision created, for the system in place until 1999, nomination control for presidential candidates over senators and of both presidential and

---

[14] Mainwaring (1999, p. 157) notes that the 1995 Law of Political Parties freed the parties to nominate their candidates as they wished, but he states that most parties continue to use the mechanisms set up in the 1971 law.

[15] See Chapter 2, footnote 10, about the *candidato nato* law.

[16] As is explained later, this relationship also depends on an important degree of partisan identification. In Brazil, where many argue that voters are not swayed by party labels, nomination control would be unimportant, even if the district magnitude were small.

TABLE 4.1. *Uruguayan Presidential Voting, 1994[a]*

Party and presidential candidates	Votes
Colorados	**656,428**
Sanguinetti	500,760
Batlle	102,551
Pacheco	51,935
Other and undistributed[b]	1,192
Blancos	**633,384**
Ramirez	264,255
Volante	301,665
Pereyra	65,660
Undistributed[b]	1,804
Frente Amplio	**621,226**
Vazquez	621,226

[a] Excludes Nuevo Espacio (104,773 votes) and minor parties (13,470 votes).
[b] Votes counted for the party but undistributed among candidates.

senatorial candidates over representatives on a given list. The reform maintains the control of the Senate candidates over the Lower House aspirants. Of course in some cases the presidential candidates court popular politicians at the lower levels, but, in general, aspirants to posts in the Uruguayan Congress need the backing of presidential candidates. Since 1999, diputados have not needed presidential support to earn a place on a ballot, but they still require the backing of senatorial aspirants. It should also be noted that prior to 1999 presidential candidates also ran for the Senate, and future losers in the presidential primaries may continue to do the same. Thus while some senators have built factions, the presidential candidates have generally been the factional leaders.

The district magnitude has an ambiguous effect on the nomination control for Uruguayan faction leaders. In Montevideo about forty-five seats are at play, and the nominators can thus name many candidates on their closed lists. But, since the nominators cannot prevent alternative lists under a party label, the high district magnitude invites extra intraparty competition; as a result, few lists elect more than a very few legislators. Other Uruguayan districts elect as few as two members, thus limiting the number of factions competing but also giving the leaders few legislators to control. More important than the magnitudes of the districts for diputados is the single nationwide constituency in which the senators compete. Because the same sets of senators compete in all the provincial districts, the leaders of the Senate lists have influence over diputado lists in every district. Thus while each senator's level of influence in a given district may vary according to the district magnitudes, at least a reasonably sized percentage of the full (ninety-nine member) lower house will necessarily be tied to each elected senator.

Both the multiple list and more typical open list systems also decrease nominator powers because there is an adverse electoral interest in not exercising nomination control. In open list systems, votes for all candidates on the list are summed (pooled) in order to determine the number of seats to which the list is entitled. After determining the number of seats pertaining to the list, then the seats are distributed among the individuals with the highest vote totals. This means that every candidate who attracted voters helped the entire list and thus if there were no limit, a purely vote-seeking leader should offer nominations to anyone who would not drive voters away. Likewise, in Uruguay, the votes for all lists are pooled to determine the party's quota of seats. The actual seats are then distributed to the lists in accord with how many votes each contributed to their parties' total. There again, if party leaders were pure vote maximizers, they might encourage the formation of any list that could attract even a few new votes because votes for even very weak lists help others in the party. This seems to explain why the Uruguayan parties, which have the legal power to limit candidacies, allow hundreds of lists across a vast political spectrum.

An important difference between the open list systems and that of Uruguay or Colombia are the limits most place on the number of candidates per party. Under most open list rules, leaders must restrict the number of entrants into the campaign, thus helping them to retain some powers. Most countries set the limit on the number of candidates a group can present equal to the district magnitude, though in Brazil the limit is 1.5 times the district magnitude. In Uruguay, however, there is no effective limit. Each list can present "only" as many candidates as there are seats available, but because there is no limit on the number of lists, there is no effective limit on the number of candidates running from any party.

While the Uruguayan and Colombian systems share many characteristics, they vary on one important point: unlike Uruguay where votes for the different lists competing under each party's label are summed to generate each party's total, the votes for the different party lists in Colombia are not pooled. This system, known as the single nontransferable vote (SNTV), gives leaders an added incentive to control nominations because, as Cox and Shugart (1995) show, spreading the vote too thinly can result in a party "wasting votes" and losing seats.[17] SNTV was also used in pre-1994 Japan,

[17] As noted previously, in pre-1994 Japan, individual candidates competed while in Colombia closed lists competed against one another. To explain how these systems work, take the example of the Colombian district of Arauca, which elects a single legislator. In 1990, four candidates from the Liberal Party, two from the Conservatives, and one from a party called "The Coalition" competed. The Coalition candidate won the race with 11,766 votes, compared with almost 10,000 for each of two Liberal candidates, a combined total of 5,700 for two other Liberals, and about 2,000 for the leading Conservative candidate. If votes had

but unlike Colombian party leaders, the Japanese leaders were empowered to approve candidacies. The LDP closely guarded the endorsements in order to avoid diffusing the party's vote among too many candidates (Cox and Niou, 1994; Cox and Rosenbluth, 1994; Cox and Shugart, 1995).[18]

One other variant of the open list is the system employed in Ireland, known as the single transferable vote. This scheme allows voters to rank the candidates on the list and generally the votes not used to elect a voter's first preference are transferred to a second or third preference. Unlike other list systems, the Irish rules allow voters to indicate secondary preferences from other than their most preferred party. Because transfers are not always within a party, the parties must concern themselves with the number of candidates they put forward. Unlike Japan, however, Swindle (2002) argues that the Irish parties should not be overly concerned with limiting candidacies because the collective reputation of the party yields transfer rates that are higher within rather than among the parties.

Table 4.2 summarizes this section, predicting nominators' influence as a function of the requirements for leader endorsements and the degree of intraagent competition, taking district magnitude into account. The vertical axis reflects Katz's (1986) study of intraparty (agent) preference voting. It shows two types of general election competition: one in which a single-agent candidate or a closed list competes against other agents and another in which multiple candidates or lists compete against others from the same agent in the same district. Where there is no intraagent competition (i.e., agents are limited to a single candidate or closed list in a given district), the nominator, if one exists, should be able to impose discipline. But, if there is intraagent competition, discipline will be lower since candidates owe only a part of their electoral success to the nominator.

The top row of boxes is subdivided into parts, based on whether there is a closed list of candidates, single-member districts, or both. In none of these cases do members of the same agent compete against one another, but the nominator's influence rises when campaigns are focused on a list instead of a particular candidate. If district magnitude were particularly large or particularly small, the box could be subdivided further.

The horizontal axis portrays requirements for nominations. On the left side are the systems that give the power of officially naming candidates to the agent hierarchy and at the other end of the range are the systems that shut the parties, factions, and alliances out of the nomination process by either

been pooled, as in the open list or Uruguayan-like systems, the leading Liberal candidate would have won the race. But, since the race was run under SNTV rules, the Liberal Party with 26,000 votes lost to The Coalition, which garnered less than one-half as many votes.

[18] In districts where individual factions lost their bids to nominate their candidates, they generally often supported their flag-bearer (with money and sometimes open campaigning) as an independent candidate. If these candidates won (and they sometimes did), they generally shed their independent banner for one with the LDP emblem.

TABLE 4.2. *Effects of Intraagent Competition and Requirements for Agent Endorsements on Strength of Leaders (Lower House Electoral Systems)[a]*

Intraagent competition		Endorsements				
		Required	Required but cannot rank			Not required
		Strongest Nominating Power	All M < 5	Both high and low M	All M > 5	
None	Single closed list	Argentina Costa Rica Paraguay Ecuador (n)[b]				
	Single closed list and single member districts	Bolivia Mexico Venezuela				
	Single member districts					United States
Yes	Open lists or multiple closed lists	Uruguay factions[c]	Chile	Ecuador (p)[b] Uruguay factions[b]	Brazil Peru	Colombia Uruguay parties[c] **Weakest Nominating Power**

[a] Systems in use circa 2000; includes United States, Mexico, and South America.
[b] "Ecuador (n)" refers to the national district; "Ecuador (p)" refers to the provincial lists.
[c] See text for description.

employing primaries to determine general election contestants or allowing
any candidates or list to compete without an official endorsement. In the
middle are the systems that give leaders the power to sanction candidacies,
but the idiosyncrasies of the system remove their power to rank the candidates on a list, thereby diminishing the leaders' power to determine who gets
elected. The middle column is divided according to the district magnitude,
since, as discussed previously, a scarcity of seats and the (generally) concomitant low limit on how many candidates are allowed to compete from a single
agent increases the value of the nomination.

In sum, the strongest leaders should be those where there is no intraagent competition, nominations are required, and district magnitude is large,
while the weakest leaders should be those in systems where there is intraparty competition, and candidates (or, as in the case of Colombia, lists) can
put themselves on the ballot. In Table 4.2, the conjunction of system characteristics in the top left box affords leaders the most power, while the boxes
down and to the right indicate diminished nominating power.

Uruguay presents a classification problem. Party leaders face internal
competition and cannot generally limit participation of different factions.
The party leaders therefore belong in the box with Colombia. It is arguable
that the faction leaders, however, belong in the bottom left box. Recall that
the Uruguayan system gives Senate candidates effective nomination control
over the House candidates and that, until 1999, the presidential candidates
had a similar control over Senate candidates. But the presidential candidates permitted multiple lists of senators, and the senators did the same for
the House lists. As a result, if we take either the presidential or the Senate
candidates as the leaders of the factions, then they officially sanction multiple closed lists of Lower House candidates. This lands them in the lower
left box in the table. On the other hand, because voters determine which
lists win seats, the faction leaders do not rank all the candidates as in other
closed list systems. Their power, therefore, appears more like leaders in open
list systems. As a result of this ambiguous classification, I have placed the
Uruguayan factional leaders in both the bottom left box and, in accord
with the range in country's district magnitude, the middle of the bottom
center box.

Table 4.2 shows that in about half of the Latin American countries the
nominators have relatively clear control over nominations, though three of
these countries (Bolivia, Mexico, and Venezuela) have recently adapted a
two-level system in which voters select a single representative for their district
plus a list of candidates for their region. This should decrease the leaders'
roles somewhat, but unless primaries are adapted to choose the candidates,
the leaders can maintain tight control. In five countries, the leaders have
some ability to name candidates, but the nominators' powers are hindered
by open lists. Of these countries, the Chilean leaders are best off, given the
low district magnitude. Leaders in Peru are the worst off, given that there

is only a single district of magnitude 120. In Ecuador and Uruguay, some district magnitudes are quite small, but the Ecuadorans residing in Guayaquil elect eighteen members and, as noted, the Montevideans elect about forty-five deputies. The Ecuadoran leadership, however, also forms a closed list for their twenty-member national district. Next, the Brazilians cross the line between the high M system, where leaders can name but not rank candidates, and the box indicating that leaders' sanction is not required. This is the result of district magnitudes that vary between eight and seventy, plus the *candidato nato* law. Finally, party leaders in Colombia and Uruguay are in the weakest position because there is intraparty competition and those leaders cannot limit the number of candidacies.

Finally, it is important to note that even though the table makes clear that leaders' power should increase as they move up and to the left, the rate of change is indeterminate. It is unclear, for example, whether a move upward would have an equivalent impact as a move to the left. Thus, the table makes a strong prediction about the northwest and southeast boxes, but there are no clear predictions about the relative power of leaders in other boxes.

Other Limiting Factors

In addition to the intraagent competition, the rules for sanctioning candidates, and the district magnitude, other factors, some of which are not generally considered part of the electoral system, are also highly influential in determining leaders' nominating powers. These include federalism, the legislators' drive for reelection, and agent (partisan) identification. Campaign finance and other powers can also be influential.

Federalism and the Number of Districts. The preceding discussion of nomination control assumes a single leader, or at least a unified group with some level of control over all candidates. In some countries (especially those with federal systems), however, a local leader or group determines the candidate or candidates only for a particular district, province, or state (see Czudnowski, 1975; Gallagher, 1988; Jones, 2002; Desposato, 2002). These leaders, however, may not coordinate amongst themselves, and thus there could be discipline along provincial or district rather than national boundaries (Desposato, 2002). Thus, the geographical distribution of legislators affects not only cohesion (as mentioned in the first section) but also discipline.

In spite of closed lists, Mustapic (2002) argues that Argentina's decentralized elections contribute to internal party conflicts, not partisan unity. The UCR's *Carta Organica*[19] explains how the national party chooses the presidential ticket but not the legislators. Further, the parties have recently begun to experiment with primaries, further diluting leaders' (federal or

---

[19] Available at http://www.ucr.org.ar.

provincial) power over candidate choice.[20] Still, Jones (1997, 2002) allows some weight to national leaders in choosing candidates, explaining that while the provincial leaders determine the ranking of the party's closed list, the national party leaders can still cajole (if not intimidate) provincial leaders through their control of resources, especially for the president's party. Even the opposition party has important influence because it can expel members from the party and even take over the provincial party governance. This latter power may have limited significance, however, because heavy-handedness from the national leaders can put the party's electoral standing at risk and help to germinate successful "provincial" parties. Jones cites an example in which the national Peronist leadership's attempt to change the leadership in the province of Catamarca backfired. In response to the national party's move, some provincial leaders formed a new party and out-polled the remaining Peronists by almost three to one. The new party won a congressional seat, while the Peronists did not, and the division helped the Radicals win the governorship.

Decentralized control over districts would have a similar effect in countries employing open lists, further weakening national party leaders. This has been an important issue in Brazil, where some state leaders have exercised their influence in the national legislature (Ames, 2002; Samuels, 2002).

Reelection. In a very few cases, reelection of legislators is limited by statute, but even where it is allowed, the degree of – and the drive for – reelection varies greatly. In the United States, around 90 percent of lower house members seek reelection and at least 90 percent of them win, justifying the assumption that most U.S. legislators are reelection-minded. In most of the Latin American cases, however, this assumption does not hold. Chile provides the closest approximation to the U.S. pattern, as 76 percent of the incumbents were renominated and 78 percent of these people won in 1993.[21] The overall turnover rate there, however, is more than twice that of the United States (41 percent versus 17 percent). A step down the ladder are Brazil and Uruguay where in the mid-1990s about two-thirds of the candidates ran for reelection, but only half of these were successful. In Argentina, even fewer are reelected, under 20 percent through the 1990s, and in Mexico immediate reelection is prohibited.[22]

[20] Jones (2002) explains that in some districts the primaries are competitive but that in others leaders present a single slate of candidates.
[21] The data here only refers to a single election, but averages over the past few elections are very similar.
[22] A party rule creates extra hurdles for incumbents seeking reelection in Argentina's UCR. In their regional primaries, they use a list proportional representation system, but primary lists that contain incumbents must receive two-thirds of the vote for their candidates to gain a place on the general election list. Most lists, therefore, are "pacted" to ensure such a high vote total, but the legislative leader of the Radicals (Jaroslavsky) was dumped owing to this

The low rates have obvious importance for nominators' influence over those legislators who are not seeking to continue their legislative careers. They may even indicate a problem for nominators in regards to the reelection-minded legislators because the low overall rates may imply the availability of attractive alternatives to legislative offices. Further, if there is a lack of qualified or popular candidates, instead of candidates begging leaders for a nomination, leaders may have to beg candidates to run. At the same time, because leaders who have the power to nominate legislators often hold the keys to other offices, the low rates do not necessarily imply that the nominators lose influence after a legislator decides not to run for reelection (as in Mexico). Thus, while high reelection rates certainly signal that nominators guard desired gates, low reelection rates will not necessarily be associated with a diminution of the nominators' powers.

Agent Identification. The most limited notion of nomination control is the formal power to grant or deny a potential candidate the right to participate in an election using a particular group's name or label. This presupposes a high value of an agent's label because presumably candidates could compete under an alternative label or even form a new agent. Existing labels are valuable, however, because they provide voters with cues about the candidates. Thus, the more highly tied voters are to existing agents (i.e., the stronger is the agent [partisan] identification), the more valuable the right to use an electorally successful agent's label becomes. In short, if a candidate's agency (partisanship) is not an important voter cue, then control of nominations loses its importance. The party jumping discussed in Chapter 3 suggests that this could be a concern for some agent leaders in Brazil.

Other Leadership Powers. Aside from control over nominations, leaders may have other tools to affect candidate selection and behavior formally or informally. Formally, the Panamanian Constitution allows parties to remove legislators who are unfaithful to their party's ideology, program, or policies (Article 145). Informally, leaders in many countries help voters distinguish among intraparty candidates by offering finance, campaign speeches, and photo opportunities. Campaign finance is a particularly important issue because the costs are exorbitant. In Uruguay, for example, the legislature passed (over an executive veto) a law to finance publicly the 1994 campaigns at a rate of $7.00 per presidential vote.[23] In Chile, one legislator complained to a newspaper that while he had spent 13 million pesos (around US$31,000) in

rule in the mid-1980s, and overall the Radicals only return 13 percent of their legislators to Congress. The Peronists also prefer fresh faces in the legislature. They only reelected 17 percent of their legislators.

[23] As explained, the presidential candidate is tied to Senate and lower House candidates. The $7.00 was distributed among the three levels of candidates.

1993, his cross-coalition rival had spent 150 million pesos (US$360,000) and his intracoalition partner had spent 100 million pesos (US$240,000).[24] In Venezuela costs for each vote in the 1970s were estimated at $23 (US$104 million in campaign spending divided among 4.5 million voters) and the 1983 costs were twice as high (Martz, 1988). And in Brazil, Mainwaring (1999, p. 151) reported an estimated cost of $600,000 for a Brazilian lower house seat in 1986, based on declared campaign donations, and Samuels (2003) reports expenditures of "just" US$94,000.[25]

These high expenses suggest that if leaders controlled campaign resources, they would have a valuable tool to later discipline their rank-and-file. The Uruguayan case provides a good example of the importance of control of finance and other forms of campaign support. Even though dozens of candidate lists for the Senate and House compete in general elections under each party's (and faction's) banner, presidential candidates (faction leaders) often designate an "official" group that they support openly. In the 1994 election, though Sanguinetti (the winning presidential candidate) was supported by twenty-three different groups, his "official" list garnered 45 percent of the total won by these lists.

In most cases, however, where the electoral system endows agent leaders with significant control over nominations, that leader also controls campaign resources, and vice versa. That is, in countries where the electoral system suggests a weak nominator, the control of campaign resources is generally decentralized, and in countries where the electoral rules suggest central roles for leaders in nominating candidates, leaders also control the campaign funds. For example, even though U.S. party leaders are able to direct some campaign funds to needy candidates, Mayhew (1974) quotes a legislator as saying that no U.S. legislator could get elected by relying solely on the party (pp. 26–7). For Brazil, Mainwaring quotes a former party treasurer of the PMDB saying: "'The party does almost nothing in campaign finances'" (1999, p. 150).[26] In accord with the prediction, control of finances in Uruguay belongs to the faction rather than party leaders. In an interview, a Blanco diputado explained that financiers support faction leaders, who in turn help lower-level candidates with the campaigns "as they see fit." Legislators also explained that few supporters would donate money to

[24] Reported in Huneeus (1998).

[25] Though the volume edited by del Castillo and Zovatto (1998) is a great advance, little is known about campaign finance for Latin America owing to lax reporting requirements and generally limited legal requirements. Zovatto's summary chapter is particularly noteworthy, as it offers comparative information about finance laws with details about whether funds are from public or private sources, how funds can be spent, spending limits, and accountability, without explaining whether candidates or their leaders control the funds. The chapter studies, then, offer some information about whether candidates or leaders control the funds. The chapter studies in Alcántara Sáez and Freidenberg (2002) offer further details.

[26] Desposato (2002) notes that though the campaign finance system and other factors limit their influence, state political parties control media access during campaign times.

anyone but the leader. Rial (1998, p. 555) adds that the public financing is distributed to the list (faction) leaders.

At the other end of the spectrum, the Argentine system endows their party leaders with significant control over nominations. The system is also extraordinary for its concentration of campaign finances in the hands of the party leaders (see Sabsay, 1998).[27]

The relationship of electoral-system-based nomination control and control of campaign finances is perhaps weakest with regard to Chile. There, party and coalition leaders have an important degree of control over nominations, though it is diluted by intraparty competition. Huneeus (1998) states, however, that Chilean "candidates have the principal responsibility to finance their electoral campaigns, they must make personal efforts to collect the resources that they need. The candidates' parties help with some wall banners as well as some general party propaganda, but they do not give each candidate important monetary resources to develop their campaigns" (my translation, p. 87).

In addition to patrolling the gate to a legislative job, leaders may have control of other sought-after jobs or income sources. In Costa Rica, legislators are limited to a single (consecutive) term in office; therefore, leaders cannot threaten the rank-and-file by the prospect of withholding future nominations.[28] The prospect of executive appointments, favorable committee assignments, staff support, policy support, prime office spaces, and access to pork-laden budgets, however, can also conjoin disparate philosophies. Carey (1996) explains how the Costa Rican party leaders try to assure legislators future jobs to gain loyalty, but since they cannot guarantee that their party will retain power, the parties cannot guarantee access to future jobs. This explains why, in spite of using very similar electoral laws, Costa Rican party discipline is low, while in Venezuela, which does not employ term limits, discipline has been iron-clad. Mexico is one of the few other countries that imposes term limits on its legislators.[29] But owing to the PRI's (Partido Revolucionario Institucional; Institutional Revolutionary Party) seventy-year continual rule, which only ended in the Congress in 1997 and the presidency in 2000, Mexican legislators had little doubt about the PRI's continued access to government jobs. The PRI's credible claim to control future political careers of their legislators, which was coupled with

---

[27] Sabsay (1998) mentions very little about individual candidates in his study. The most pertinent note discusses how some of the most important candidates are able to raise their own funds, thus implying that most candidates do not do this.

[28] Zuckerman (1979) explains how continued access to power affects factionalism within Italy's Christian Democrats. "The DC's successes in all spheres of political competition have given the party enormous amounts of government resources – the food for the presence and growth of clientelist factions" (p. 82). That is, the Christian Democrats are more clientelistic than the other Italian parties since the DC's continual presence in government affords them the resources necessary to maintain the clientelistic links.

[29] The others are Ecuador (until 1996) and the Philippines.

tight control over candidacies, helps explain their much greater success in enforcing discipline in comparison with the Costa Rican parties (de la Garza, 1972; Smith, 1979; Weldon, 2002).

In sum, in addition to nominations, leaders may control other resources that affect a legislator's election or future career. The electoral system may allow leaders sufficient control, and when they have nomination control, they are likely to control these other resources as well. But, where the electoral system fails to endow leaders with these powers, some agent leaders do gain control over these alternative resources and thus gain control over their membership. As will be explained in a moment, the PT provides a particularly clear case of this alternative path. This leads, again, to the conclusion that without additional context, electoral rules are usually an insufficient explanation for unity rates.

Ins, Outs, and the Electoral Cycle. Finally, the weight of leadership sanctions, ideological attachments, and other factors that bear on legislators' voting decisions depend on the timing of the vote and the legislators' association with the president. Legislators who belong to the same group as the president face different incentives to join with the president and, hence, other members of their group, than do opposition legislators. Two separate factors work in favor of unity of the opposition, but the sum of the forces yields an ambiguous expectation for unity of the "Ins." On the one hand "Outs" may find utility in binding together in opposition to the president, while Ins must weigh support for the group and the legislative success of the president versus their individual interests. But, the level of unity among the Ins is supported by the president's greater ability to "buy" the support of In legislators (see Carey, forthcoming). In parliamentary systems, executives are able to influence back-bench coalition members with their control of the agenda and the threat of dissolution (Huber, 1996; Heller, 2001). In presidential systems, executives cannot threaten new elections, but they are more able to influence votes of legislators who are not part of the president's party or coalition. Presidents' access to electoral and other resources, such as policy concessions, bureaucratic jobs, public works projects, and travel junkets, allow them to influence legislators of all stripes. It was well publicized, for example, that President Clinton not only called many members of Congress from both sides of the aisle for support of the North American Free Trade Agreement but also offered them direct benefits in exchange for their votes.[30] Peru's President Fujimori and numerous politicians in Argentina have recently been implicated in the direct exchange of monetary payments

---

[30] Mayer (1998) discusses the creation of the North American Development Bank (NADbank) as a way that Clinton won the support of a California representative. Valverde Loya (1997) details a long list of pay-offs that were given to specific members of Congress in efforts of secure votes.

to legislators for switching votes or changing parties.[31] But because Outs do not receive the benefits from holding office, the price of their votes in terms of policy concessions, bureaucratic jobs, public works projects, and travel junkets (if not bribes) should be higher. This too should support unity of the opposition.

These cost and benefits vary across the electoral cycle. Though concern with presidential success may help hold the Ins together generally, as elections near, individuals' interests may overtake the interest in solidarity. Members of the In-group must all take a stance on the president's record and all face incentives to differentiate themselves in order to gain votes relative to other Ins. The infighting should be particularly pronounced if the president is not willing or able to run for reelection. While Outs also face incentives to differentiate themselves, their first priority is to beat the incumbent agent. For them, choosing amongst presidential candidates should be secondary to winning office. Thus, the unity of the opposition should improve as elections near, while the campaign or at least the primary season should drive wedges into the Ins.

The electoral cycle also affects the president's ability to buy votes. At the beginning of a term, presidents are most powerful because they can promise future budget provisions, cabinet positions, bureaucratic jobs, and policy concessions. But as the end of the term nears, presidents' stocks of goodies dwindle considerably, especially if they cannot run for reelection. Thus, legislators who are willing to vote with the president early in the term may be less willing to do so toward the end. The expectation, again, is that this will aid opposition unity and harm unity of the agents associated with the president.

Finally, while there are several factors working against unity for the Ins as elections approach, the leadership sanctions may carry more weight at the end of the term than the beginning, thus reinforcing unity. Presumably leaders who control candidate nominations view a legislator's whole record in determining loyalty. But, when crucial votes come up toward the end of a term, legislators who hope for reelection will surely be wary about nomination procedures and the support of the leadership for the campaign.

In sum, the expectations are that the opposition will maintain higher unity overall and that the unity among the Ins will be most problematic toward the end of the term. The forces working on both the Ins and the Outs, however, are in conflict; thus, the differences between the two groups may not be particularly clear.

[31] The implications for Peru, which were even reported in *The Economist* (July 29, 2000), had little effect until Fujimori's security adviser was caught on film handing a then-opposition candidate a thick wad of bills. After the legislator switched parties and the film was exposed, Fujimori resigned.

Assessment and Alternative Explanations

The electoral system, in sum, can endow leaders with an important degree of control over nominations. But, few leaders have unambiguous control over nominations because, in most cases, it must be shared with regional leaders or the voters. Further, in many cases, the control has a limited value because legislators put limited value on being nominated by a particular party, and often even less on the renomination after having served a term in the legislature. Still, there are important differences in terms of the power that different leaders have over nomination control, and these differences should help explain different average unity rates among countries. But, by itself, nomination control is an insufficient explanation of unity rates, and the factors bearing on cohesion must determine whether agent members are united on a particular vote.

To this point I have not discussed the sources of cohesion nor other potential sources of an agent's unity, both of which are themes that could be the basis for additional studies. As an example of how these issues could bear on unity, consider Brazil's PT, which has used alternative means to support the power of leaders in the face of an electoral system that works agent unity against leader control. Unlike other Brazilian parties, the PT's organizational structure, internal rules, and ideological image help bind legislators through cohesion and discipline. First, the party socializes its members (most are union members already) through party activities that occur continuously, not just around election time. Further, because the party is tied so closely to the unions, legislators are concerned about their leaders' influence in future career moves. Mainwaring (1999, pp. 165–6) explains that this is a serious threat because the PT has used its power to expel legislators who fail to follow the party line. Additionally, the party's high level of unity and its noteworthy leftist position help to reinforce the party's image among the voters, who identify with the PT to a greater degree than they do with other parties (as evidenced by the much lower rate at which PT voters exercise their right to choose particular candidates). Whether the unity is a cause or consequence of the other leadership powers, the higher degree of partisan identification reinforces the leaders' power.

This type of explanation separates the PT from other Brazilian parties, but it is too specific to the case to allow for a variable-oriented intercountry analysis. Figueiredo and Limongi (2000) offer another explanation for what they view as high unity in Brazil based on the president's legislative powers.[32] Though the possession by all presidents of formal and informal powers that allow them to influence the legislative process would complicate any attempt to differentiate among the countries, theoretically the variable would be

---

[32] See also Carey (forthcoming) who discusses how presidents use different resources to influence legislative voting.

applicable to an intercountry analysis (but it could not explain intracountry differences). Like the explanation regarding the PT, their explanation is only necessary to explain a case where unity is high in spite of expectations based on the other variables for low levels. Further, while this variable would be consistent with the higher unity scores in Brazil than in the United States, it would fail to explain why many Brazilian parties score lower on the unity scales than agents in the other Latin American cases.

Figueiredo and Limongi's (2000) other important point is that centralized legislative procedures help party leaders to overcome the divisive pulls of the electoral system. In this assessment, they are supported by the numerous studies of House rules in the United States. Their contention faces two challenges, however. First, Aldrich and Rohde (2001) contend that the U.S. House rules reflect the level of agreement among the majority party's members. The rules, in short, are endogenous to the level of cohesion. Other variables, such as the composition of the majority that approved the rules, also come into play here, but the important point is that the origin of the rules requires explanation. Second, their variable is insufficient to explain the very low unity score of the PMDB, a principal party of the legislative majority. They contend that the PMDB did maintain high unity on a large number of votes (as I show as well), but as Ames (2002) has contended, leadership recommendations are generally unrelated to the Brazilian parties' unity. Cohesion, therefore, seems a better explanation of the unity on this subset of votes.

In sum, though other variables are clearly related to unity scores, the most important alternatives appear to suffer from either limited variance (at least in Latin America) or a strong endogenous relation with either the cohesion variables or whether the agent is a member of the president's coalition. For these reasons, as well as the importance of working toward a parsimonious explanation and the maintenance of a comparative structure, I will continue to focus on the more limited set of cohesive and disciplinary variables discussed throughout this chapter.

A NOTE ON THE FORMATION OF FACTIONS

In Chapter 3, I argued that, at least in Uruguay, factions operate as agents, and voters can identify the faction labels on their ballot. This chapter has further argued that the Uruguayan electoral system gives factional leaders the power to discipline their members. To a degree, this succinct explanation of factionalism clashes with Coppedge's (1994) identification of over thirty sources of factionalism. This section, therefore, explores this issue in a bit more depth, explaining how the electoral system can create the opportunity and often the means to form factions or alliances with strong enough leaders to ensure at least a modicum of discipline. The argument is based on the idea that while competition for leadership always leads to some level of factionalism, leaders' control over candidate nominations plus intraparty competition or regionalism create the necessary intraparty rivalries and the opportunities for organization that can give rise to institutionalized factions.[33]

Before beginning the discussion of those electoral variables that affect institutionalized factional formation and continuance, it is important to dispense with alternative explanations and arguments that electoral systems do not impact on such formation.

First, those who argue against any relevance of the electoral system often cite cases of factions predating the systems in which they thrive (see D'Amato, 1965; Zariski, 1978). While some factions undoubtedly trace their roots to periods preceding current electoral laws, the electoral system is still vital to our understanding of factional formation in such cases because it determines the degree to which factions can continue participating in campaigns. For example, though the Uruguayan factions predate the electoral system, the system was set up precisely to facilitate continued factional competition in the general elections (see McDonald, 1978). If the parties could not run multiple candidates for the same office, factions would be relegated to competition for nominations to a party list instead of competing openly in the general elections. Thus, though the causal arrow is bidirectional, the roots of continued Uruguayan factionalism lie largely in the electoral system.

Second, Coppedge's (1994) literature review uncovered explanations that included not only the electoral system but also cultural norms, clientelism, a lack of a charismatic leader, financing schemes, federalism, internal party rules, and presidentialism as causes of factional formation. He explains that this long list of causes is the result of the wide variety in factional types, and he thus concludes that there can be "little profit in the comparative analysis of [the causes of] factions." However, he continues, "one can draw some useful conclusions about the consequences of factionalism, which are fewer in number and lend themselves more easily to generalization" (p. 96). Though he and the authors he cites are undoubtedly right about the multitude of causes and range of faction types, Coppedge overstates the inability to generalize about factional formation. Political phenomena are always affected by numerous variables; the goal of analysis is not always to explain all the variation in a model but to isolate the impact of one or more substantive

---

[33] Even though I have not previously used the term "institutionalized" here, I mean little more than the routinized means to act collectively. This generally necessitates a defined organization that will likely have regular meetings and identifiable leaders who can reward or sanction followers, but I am not concerned with institutionalization in Huntington's (1968) sense of complexity, adaptability, and the like. My only purpose is to distinguish those factions that continually vote together from temporary voting blocs that can form out of common interests on a given issue. These latter groups, such as the various issue-specific caucuses in the U.S. Congress, may have regular meetings, but they generally lack powerful leaders.

variables. Thus, the key to my analysis is isolating a particular type of faction – those that are sufficiently organized or unified to act as agents – and determining whether the electoral system has a systematic effect on formation of this factional type. If other variables also have systematic effects, then they too should be subjected to cross-country analyses.

Electoral Laws, Nomination Control, and Factions

A typology of factions would have to separate those that operate nationally from those that operate regionally, and those that are fleeting and unorganized factions from those that are hierarchically organized and longstanding. To fit the definition of an agent, a faction could be either regionally or nationally based, but it must be relatively well organized and unified. Leaders will have the opportunity to organize factions when they, rather than party leaders, can provide legislators with a means to some valued end (e.g., access to electoral ballots). Electoral systems contribute to the formation of such factions by requiring official sanctions for candidates and either (a) promoting intradistrict rivalries or (b) fostering regional powerbrokers.

I have argued here that control over the nomination process gives leaders an important tool with which to discipline the rank-and-file. As such, if nomination control is disbursed among district-level leaders, then each of these leaders has the potential to form a regionally based faction. The primary question is whether the local leaders can wrest this control from the national leaders.[34] A comparison between Argentina and pre-1993 Venezuela highlights this issue.

Until Venezuela changed its system in 1993 (to a German-style mixed system), the electoral systems in Venezuela and Argentina were very similar, with each employing closed lists systems with about equal average district magnitudes (6.2 in Argentina and 7.6 in Venezuela).[35] Since their respective turns to democracy (in 1958 for Venezuela, 1983 for Argentina), both countries have also had two primary political parties, though those systems have begun to break down.[36]

The countries differ, however, in the role of regional leaders in naming candidates. Unlike the Argentine provincial leaders who, as discussed previously, have retained an important power in the naming of local leaders, Venezuelan provincial leaders had a very limited role in naming candidates in the pre-1993 system (and the new system does not seem to improve their lot). It seems no coincidence that while the Argentine local leaders

[34] I use the terms "local" and "regional" interchangeably.
[35] Venezuela also had a fifteen-member national district (Jones, 1995).
[36] In the most recent presidential elections, neither of the two main Venezuelan parties won the presidency and a strong fourth party emerged as well. In Argentina one of the two traditional parties won the presidency, but a strong third party also competed.

have been central to Argentine national politics (see, for example, Eaton, 2002), the political role of the pre-1993 Venezuelan regional leaders is hardly discussed.[37]

In explaining the weakness of the Venezuelan state or local leaders, Martz (1988, p. 167) states that though "the recommendations of loyal and state party officials must be reviewed . . . [they are] often overridden by the national leadership." Crisp (1997) continues that

leaders at the state level [for the AD party] submit to the National Executive Committee (CEN) of the party lists of potential candidates for the Chamber of Deputies and the Senate. These lists must contain three times the number of seats available, and the candidates must not be ranked. The CEN, a group of 20–30 leaders, chooses which candidates will run and rank orders them. What is more, it has the right to replace half the list submitted by the state level leaders with candidates of its own. That is more than enough names to fill all the available seats. (p. 170)

In contrast to the situation in Argentina, this description of Venezuela implies that the importance of party labels, at least until the mid-1990s, helped prevent unhappy local leaders from forming their own independent lists as has happened in Argentina. The recent changes in the Venezuelan electoral laws, in which half of the seats are elected in single-member districts and the other half in closed lists, concomitant to the devaluing of the party labels, which has aided the rise of new parties, may therefore lead to the end of the AD's central control over their candidate lists and their (now much less numerous) legislative delegation (see also Wells, 1980; Coppedge 1994; Carey 1996). The loss of central control should also mean a strengthening of the legislators' ties to their districts and possibly an increased role for regional leadership.

Second, electoral systems can help breed hierarchically organized but nonregional factionalism (or allow factions to continue) by allowing intraparty competition. By forcing voters to choose among the candidates for reasons other than their party affiliation, these systems diminish the importance of the party label. And, since voters cannot rely on party labels to choose among candidates, factions may be able to provide the voters the needed voting cues. Further, while most systems include an element of intraagent competition, at least for leadership contests in primaries or caucuses, ceteris paribus, those systems that allow such competition in the general election are more likely to produce permanent and unified factions. This results from the greater ability of potential leaders to gather widespread support and define their organizations by competing in general elections rather than just the less-publicized primaries.

[37] Neither Crisp (2000) nor Coppedge (1994) discuss the regional leaders' political role, except to show how insignificant they are in the candidate nomination process.

Recall from a previous discussion that there are two types of systems in which general elections feature intraagent competition while leaders retain nomination control: open list systems (especially those with a small district magnitude) and those in which multiple officially sanctioned candidates compete in the general election. The multiple list systems are particularly prone to factionalism, if leaders can gain control over the makeup of the lists. In Uruguay, since each of the multiple lists of lower house deputies must be attached to just one of the relatively few groups of senators (and prior to 1999 to presidential candidates), the lead senators (and previously the presidential candidates) had control over deputy candidate lists throughout the country, and factions formed around these personalities. In pre-1994 Japan, where multiple candidates (rather than lists) from each party ran in each district, factional leaders gained a similar level of control by divvying up the limited nomination spots in each district (Shiratori, 1988; Cox and Rosenbluth, 1993, 1994, 1996). Finally, the Chilean case suggests that open list systems can also sustain hierarchically organized factions, at least if the district magnitude is small enough to put a high value on nomination control. As I argued earlier, the relation between Chile's alliances and its parties is akin to a system of factionalized parties. And, like the pre-1994 Japanese factions, the parties that make up the Chilean alliances bargain with each other for the right to name their favored candidate in propitious districts. This has arguably helped the parties retain their central role within the bi-alliance system.

In sum, while a popular leader or idea can encourage the development of factionalism based on cohesion, the electoral system can help breed and maintain factions based on discipline. In addition to the unity that the discipline implies, these types of factions have the potential to institutionalize by developing organizations that are relatively independent of the parties and, in turn, maintain themselves over a long period of time. In short, the electoral system can help build factions that operate as agents.

CONCLUSION: DISCIPLINE, COHESION, AND UNITY

Unity, I have argued here, is a function of discipline and cohesion. In determining the restrictions on access to labels – be they party labels as in most countries, alliance labels in Chile, or faction labels in Uruguay – the electoral system can endow leaders with a powerful disciplinary tool. As argued here and in Chapter 3, the electoral system also affects the agent system by determining whether voters will be able to choose specifically among candidates or will be directed toward factional groupings, parties, or coalitions. By themselves, then, the electoral systems yield very different roles for leaders and the consequent unity among alliance, party, or factional members. The electoral system, however, fails to provide unambiguous power to most agent leaders, and thus an explanation of unity requires a consideration of variables, which I grouped under the term "cohesion." The electoral system can also influence some aspects of cohesion, but common beliefs and interests also arise from separate forces.

The next chapter shows the validity of these hypotheses through statistical testing. It highlights the generally strong positive relationship between nomination control and agent unity, while also providing evidence that different aspects of cohesion are sufficient to support unity for other agents.

5

Explaining Voting Unity

Democracy is a function of policy and process. Thus, to continue on their path toward consolidation, governments in Latin America must not only provide economic opportunities and social progress, but also generate these outcomes through a representative, open, and competitive process. The extent to which a country has achieved these procedural goals is particularly evident in the legislature. That is, a legislature's multiple elections, open debates, and competition of ideas among representative groups lay bare the inner workings of a democracy.

Legislators' voting records are key indicators of the patterns of competition. They can help show which groups form coalitions, whether parties are unified or factionalized, and the issues on which groups divide. This chapter tests the theory of agent unity discussed in Chapter 4. That chapter suggested that an agent's unity is a function of both cohesion, which is the result of electoral or ideological affinities, and discipline, which is the power of leaders to enforce voting decisions. The explanation of voting unity thus requires two sets of variables. These variables, in turn, must help to explain two sets of differences: among and within countries.

Electoral systems must play a key role in explaining intercountry variation. This system-level variable structures legislators' incentive systems through its assignment of varying degrees of power to agent leaders over the naming of candidates. When agent leaders have significant power to nominate candidates, the rank-and-file legislators should owe loyalty to the "nominators." Thus, the primary system-level hypothesis is that electoral systems that grant leaders nominating power should increase unity through their impact on discipline.

Although the electoral system acting through its impact on nomination control plays a key role in my explanation, that variable applies equally to all agents within a country, and thus it cannot explain the differences in the AWU scores among a country's agents. Furthermore, factors other than the electoral system can affect the power of leaders to impose discipline, and where discipline is weak, other cohesive factors can support unity. Chapter 4 noted five specific categories of these variables. First those agents that attract a heterogeneous group of legislators in terms of their ideological beliefs will have difficulty in maintaining unity. Concomitantly, ideological beliefs that clearly separate or polarize one group from others should increase unity. Second, when legislators' electoral fates are tied together (i.e., they are concerned with their group's national results), the legislators should be more willing to subordinate their individual preferences to the group's goals. Third, cohesion and perhaps discipline should increase when the agent's members are concentrated geographically. Fourth, agents that are allied with the president face different incentives to coalesce than others. I also argued, however, that both the Ins and Outs face conflicting incentives, thus yielding ambiguous expectations for the effect of this variable on unity. These pressures interact with the final variable, the electoral cycle. While agents may join together early in the term to take advantage of presidential largesse or to fulfill electoral pacts, such agreements should come under strain as the campaign season nears.

In this chapter, I operationalize nomination control and the other variables and subject them to both bivariate tests for their impact on the agents' average weighted unity scores. As will be discussed, the data do not lend themselves to a multivariate analysis, but the bivariate tests do provide general support for all hypotheses.

NOMINATION CONTROL

The external theory posits that agents form around nominators, and that the level of an agent's discipline is tied to the strength of the nominator. As argued in Chapter 4, countries can exhibit nominators at the individual, factional, party, state or provincial delegation, and/or coalition levels. At whatever level, however, the strength of these nominators also varies. I argued, specifically, that the leaders' nominating power is affected by the degree of internal party competition, the district magnitude in combination with the type (open or closed) and number of lists, and requirements about whether candidates need approval to participate in a campaign. Potentially powerful nominators can be undercut or weak nominators supported, however, by factors such as legislators' interests in reelection and the leaders' control over postlegislative careers, the strength of voters' loyalties to existing agents, federalism, and campaign finance rules. These confounding issues left in doubt whether the electoral system sources of nomination control are sufficient to explain unity rates.

Table 4.2 classified nominator strength according to the leaders' ability to rank-order candidates, the level of intraagent competition, and district magnitude. The table posits that agents in the top-left box will have the highest unity scores and those in the bottom-right box will have the lowest.

Movements up and to the left in the table imply increased nominating power, but the rate of change is indeterminate. If this variable is strongly associated with an agent's unity, then AWU scores should follow the same pattern. Table 5.1 tests this hypothesis.

As predicted, the Argentine parties do separate themselves from other agents in this sample by exhibiting the highest unity scores. Recall, however, that the electoral system hypothesis only relates to nomination control of the provincial, not national, leaders in Argentina. Unity at the national level, therefore, must be predicated on either cohesion among the parties' provincial delegations or national party leaders' ability to control nominations in each province. To a lesser extent, the Chilean parties and Uruguayan factions also fit the prediction, in that they have higher unity levels and are located to the left of the Brazilian and Uruguayan parties. Further, disaggregating the Uruguayan factional scores yields an improved fit, in that four of six factions have AWU scores above 85. But, the conflicting incentives of the Uruguayan electoral system forced the ambiguous placement of the factions in the table (in two alternative boxes), and the reason why factions differed was more closely related to differences in electoral support than to the electoral system. In sum, these cases provide only moderate support for the hypothesis.

Table 5.1 also fails to foretell other agents' unity scores. The U.S. parties have much lower AWU scores than others in the sample, yet they are not in the box that predicts the lowest scores. The Chilean coalitions, Brazilian parties (excepting the PT) and the Uruguayan parties (excepting the Frente Amplio) have essesntially equivalent AWU scores, but they are placed in different boxes. Further, the leaders of Brazil's PT and Uruguay's Frente Amplio clearly have more control over nominations (and higher unity rates) than others in their respective countries, but that power emanates from factors other than the electoral system.

Overall, then, the nominator variable does only a fair job of explaining variance in AWU scores. Thus, at least where the electoral system fails to provide nominators with clear control, unity rates must depend on other factors that either boost the leaders' power or induce the agents' members to vote together.

COHESION

Volatility and Common Electoral Fates

Leaving aside discipline, Chapter 4 described several factors that support cohesion, and thereby voting unity. The first of these was the degree to which legislators see a need to consider the reputation of their group when making their voting decisions, which results when they see the agent label as important to their own electoral fates.

TABLE 5.1. *Nomination Control and AWU Scores*

		Endorsements			
		Required but cannot rank			
	Required	All M < 5	Both high and low M	All M > 5	Not required
	Strongest Nominating Power				
None					
Single closed list	Argentina parties 90.1				
Single closed list and single member districts					
Single member districts					United States parties 58.2
Intraagent competition					
Yes					
Open lists or multiple closed lists	Uruguay factions 81.2	Chile coalitions 75.4 Chile parties 84.3	Uruguay factions 81.2	Brazil parties PT 96.1 Others 73.7	Uruguay parties FA 98.0 Others 74.3
					Weakest Nominating Power

Measuring voters' affinity toward parties or other agents through a survey is problematic because it is difficult to separate a voter's preferences for a particular candidate in a recent or forthcoming election from that voter's preferences for a particular party or other group over a longer time period. Scales of electoral volatility, however, provide a good proxy of such loyalties. If voters are strongly tied to extant parties, factions, or coalitions, then electoral competition should be more stable than where voters do not habitually vote for the same group. As a result, lower levels of volatility should be associated with higher levels of voting unity.

Several recent studies have focused on volatility in Latin America, generally settling on the Pedersen (1979) index as their statistical measure (Coppedge, 1998; Roberts and Wibbels, 1999). The index is a measure of the collective change in parties' (agents') support across two elections.[1] The values that the index produces vary, of course, depending on which set of elections is included in the analysis. Roberts and Wibbels, therefore, use the average over a set of elections, while Coppedge argues that using the end points of the period of interest provide a better description of the electoral changes. There is also some question about how to account for coalitions among parties, which leads Coppedge to group the parties into party families in order to conduct his calculations. The studies all agree, however, that Brazil has experienced much greater volatility than the other countries. At the same time, if we restrict the index to the elections in the 1990s, Argentina and Uruguay show more signs of volatility than does Brazil.

The Pedersen index provides a straightforward view of the changing support levels for parties or (or other agents), but it has two important problems. First, because it generates an aggregate statistic for the country, it can disguise variance among agents within a country. Second, Potthoff and I (Morgenstern and Potthoff, 2003) have argued that the Pedersen index conflates several issues related to changing support levels. We therefore advocate a components of variance model that separates volatility from other effects and yields a measure of volatility for individual agents. Our model cannot easily deal with agents that do not run in all districts in each year; therefore, in what follows, there are statistics for Chilean coalitions but not parties. Further, the analysis is run on Uruguayan parties and not factions due to a lack of information about factional support at the district level. Still, by allowing disaggregation to the party level in Uruguay and the coalition level in Chile, this method provides more detail than the Pedersen index.[2]

---

[1] Specifically, volatility $= 0.5 \sum |P_{i,t+1} - P_{i,t}|$ (summed from $n = 1$ to i), where $P_{i,t}$ is the percentage of the vote won by party i in year t.

[2] Two-agent systems are a partial exception, since the results for one agent necessarily mirror those for the other. The results for both Chilean coalitions and U.S. parties, therefore, are the same. For the United States, the analysis considers only those districts where the two main agents competed in every year. Note that even though the analysis could not be applied to

Our results reveal some important differences in the interpretation of volatility in our five countries. Before detailing the model and the results, however, it is necessary to discuss the question of tied electoral fates, since our model also speaks to that issue.

As discussed in Chapter 4, Cox and McCubbins (1993) follow Stokes (1965, 1967) in arguing that when legislators' electoral fates are tied, legislators have an interest in building the group's collective image. This requires that the electoral success of the group has a direct bearing on the members' individual electoral success.

While membership in a faction, party, or coalition certainly ties all legislators together, the degree to which their fates are tied varies greatly. By implication, where the binds are relatively loose, legislators should be less concerned with the collective reputation than where all legislators rise and fall together. The variance among an agent's vote across district lines provides the data to construct a measure of the strength of these ties. Specifically we can measure the degree to which a change in an agent's national vote share is consistent across electoral districts. If all districts move together, there is an important national element to the elections. If, however, the change in the districts' vote shares is highly variable, then district-level factors (including candidate characteristics) must play an important role in determining electoral outcomes.

Potthoff and I term this the district-time (DT) effect, to capture the idea of movements of an agent's vote shares in a particular district at a particular time. Its relation to agent unity scores is based on the premise that if changes at the district level reflect national movements (which yield a small district-time effect), then legislators should be concerned with national-level politics and should thus pay heed to the national leaders. If, alternatively, swings at the local level are unrelated to national developments (i.e., the district-time effect is large), then legislators would have less concern about how their voting patterns affected their party, faction, or coalition's electoral results. In sum, the district-time effect should be inversely related to agent unity scores.

The components of variance model we apply captures this district-time effect as well as the degree of electoral volatility over time (see Appendix 5.1 for details).[3] The model, based on district-level electoral returns, assumes

Chilean parties because no party competed in all districts, and many districts had to be cut from the U.S. analysis where one of the parties declined to participate, this is not a serious problem for straightforward proportional representation systems. In Brazil, for example, two small parties failed to compete in all districts, but because their support levels were less than 5 percent in some districts where they did compete, winning zero support could be considered normal variance.

[3] A simple measure of this concept could be based on the standard deviation of the change (swing) of the electoral returns across districts. If all districts move together, then the standard deviation would be small. This type of analysis, however, suffers from the same problem as the volatility studies in that it would conflate several sources of variance in one statistic.

that an agent's electoral support varies across districts and across time. It also includes a residual that captures variance across time within districts. The measure of over-time variance provides us with a proxy for volatility, and the residual, which provides our measure of the district-time effect, indicates the degree to which the districts move together, taking account of the other effects. As such, it gives a measure of the degree to which candidates' (or agents') electoral fates are tied together. (A large district-time effect implies that the districts are not moving together, and a small residual would imply that there is very little variance explained by the particularities of a given district at a given time.) The remaining component, the district-heterogeneity effect, is akin to studies of nationalization (see Jones and Mainwaring, 2003; Caramani, 2000) in that it captures the diversity of support an agent has across districts. The benefit of the components of variance model is that we can capture each of these effects independently, as opposed to simple analyses of volatility that conflate the different types of variance. Further, as noted earlier, our analysis allows us to disaggregate the data from the country level to the level of agents. We can thus compare volatility and the other effects not only among countries but also within.

The results of the components of variance analysis offer an important clarification of the volatility analyses and an interesting first view of the electoral ties among agents in Latin America (Table 5.2).[4] First, our analysis shows that over time volatility has been quite low in Brazil, at least for the three elections in the 1990s. What was quite variant was the amount of support the parties had in particular electoral districts (in this case demarcated by states). In other words, the variance in Brazilian elections is primarily accounted for by differences in the average support of parties across states and the changes in support of parties in each state. Over time volatility accounts for almost none of the overall variance, save for the case of the PSDB. What this suggests is that, in accord with the analysis defining agents, volatility in Brazil is not a party phenomenon but rather a state-party phenomenon. Further, the data clearly separate the PT from the other parties. The second column indicates that the PT has more consistent support across districts than the PMDB, the PFL, or the PSDB, and the final column indicates that the PT's support rises and falls in a much more consistent manner across states. This implies that in comparison with the other parties, the PT's popularity is based less on personalities and district-level issues than on its national image.

The results also suggest different interpretations for the other countries. Foremost, once accounting for the district-time effect, electoral volatility was

---

[4] Both ratios and the raw figures can be useful in a comparison. Table 5.2 details the raw figures, which allow a comparison of the actual amount of variance inherent in the system. For more detail, including a comparison with European cases, see Morgenstern and Potthoff (unpublished manuscript).

TABLE 5.2. *Components of Variance Analysis*

	Time (volatility)	State/district heterogeneity	District-time (tied fates)
Argentina, 1991–1999			
PJ	10.6	86.0	54.9
UCR/Allianza	50.5	77.2	61.8
Brazil, 1990–1998[a]			
PMDB	1.6	77.0	53.9
PT	1.4	24.7	10.3
PFL	2.1	87.0	76.3
PSDB	19.8	46.1	24.8
PTB	−0.6	31.4	31.4
PDT	1.3	20.2	17.5
PPB	1.0	38.6	43.4
Chile, 1989–1997[b]			
Concert. & Rt.	−0.4	33.8	48.9
United States[b]			
1952–1960	10.2	126.9	19.6
1974–1980	8.8	217.2	61.9
1984–1990	2.1	242.8	51.3
Uruguay (1990–1998)			
Colorados	31.5	26.7	3.0
Blancos	21.5	47.3	5.2
Frente Amplio	24.3	48.3	2.7

[a] The PTB and PPB did not compete in all districts in all years. Unlike the Chilean parties, this appears as normal variance, since these Brazilian parties frequently win just a few percentage points in several districts. The PPB was the PDS in 1986 and 1990 and the PPR in 1994.

[b] For Chile and the United States, the figures are identical for both parties or alliances, because there are just two competitors.

lower for most parties in Brazil than for any party in Argentina and Uruguay. In Argentina the PJ was relatively stable, but the rise of the Frepaso and then the Alianza (which joined the Frepaso and the UCR) drove a relatively high level of over-time volatility in the UCR.[5] In Uruguay the statistics reflect the Frente Amplio's continual rise.

[5] The analysis was conducted using data for the UCR for 1991–5 and then for the Alianza for 1997–9. This process probably reduces the total amount of variance that would be produced if we used solely the UCR figures, since its decline is offset by the amalgamation of the new parties. If we use just 1991–5 for the analysis, the time volatility figures for the PJ are considerably higher (45.7), but lower for the UCR (24.4). The district-time effect for the period 1991–5 is somewhat lower for both parties: 44.0 and 29.4, respectively.

The district-time effect is surprisingly large for both parties in Argentina, where the closed-list electoral system should generate a relatively low personal vote. This is not the result of different "normal" levels of support across the provinces, as this is accounted for by the district-heterogeneity (DH) component. What it perhaps suggests, therefore, is that although individual candidates may have limited roles, the quality of the list (or the head of the list) does play an important role in determining the outcome of particular races. As such, it suggests that state-level party leaders in Argentina can claim some independent electoral strength, which in turn could help them sustain some independence from national leaders.

While unexpectedly high for Argentina, the district-time effect is surprisingly low for all the Uruguayan parties. Only Brazil's PT approaches any of the Uruguayan parties in term of this effect. We cannot unfortunately consider the factional level, but we must conclude from these statistics that the electorate moves among the parties in a relatively consistent manner across the country. Again, this suggests an orientation toward national policy as opposed to local issues. As such, it should support the unity of the Uruguayan parties.

Finally, for Chile, while the small negative number in the first column highlights the remarkable consistency of electoral returns at the coalition level over the first three postdictatorship elections,[6] the third column shows that there was significant movement at the district level. In each of these three elections, the average vote across the districts for the Concertación was between 59 percent and 60 percent. But, in eleven of the sixty districts in 1993 and thirteen of the districts in 1997, the coalitions experienced swings in support levels of at least 10 points, and some of the changes were significantly greater. Thus in spite of very low levels of overall volatility, the ties among coalition members' electoral fates do not appear much stronger than those among party members in the United States.

I have combined the scores for volatility and district-time effects under the hypothesis that either a low degree of voter identification with an agent (as suggested by the volatility) or weakly tied electoral fates among an agent's legislators (as indicated by the DT effect) is sufficient to weaken AWU scores. By combining the variables, I am also assuming that, if both factors point in the same direction, the effect will be reinforced. (DH is less relevant to this analysis.) Higher values on this combined variable should thus correlate with lower AWU scores, and the resulting Pearson's correlation is −0.47. There is some danger of the extreme values biasing this correlation, and thus I have also tested the relation of the AWU scores with the log of the sum of the two components of variance. That correlation is even stronger, −0.51.

---

[6] The small negatives can be interpreted as zero effect. Other versions of components of variance models avoid producing negative results, but they appeared very seldom in our analysis.

Federalism and Geographic Concentration of Legislators

The next factors that Chapter 4 discussed as affecting unity were federalism and the geographic dispersion of an agent's legislators. To review, in federal systems, national leaders must share their nomination control with state or provincial leaders, thus reducing the power of the national leaders and potentially creating disciplined groups at the state/provincial level but not at the national level. A related idea was that where legislators are concentrated in a limited number of districts, leaders will generally have more power (since they control a greater percentage of the agent's members) and the group will likely be more cohesive as well.

To address this issue, Table 5.3 displays the geographic dispersion of legislators for parties and coalitions in our five countries. The first column of statistics shows how many different constituencies the agents must appeal to. In the United States, an agent's members must direct their campaigns towards 435 distinct groups of voters, while the number is under 30 in Argentina, Brazil, and Uruguay. The second column shows how many seats the agents won in a recent election, and the third column starts the analysis by showing over how many districts these seats were distributed. The final two columns show the degree to which these seats were concentrated. The fourth column gives the number of districts required to make up 50 percent of an agent's seats and the final column sets the cut-off at 75 percent. That is, to reach half of the PMDB's 107 seats, they required only six districts, and to reach three-fourths of their total, they required twelve districts. The PT's seats are more highly concentrated; half came from just three districts, and three-quarters were concentrated in seven districts.

While there are a few significant outliers, geographic concentration is significantly correlated (−0.65) with the AWU scores.[7] This result reflects the findings from Chapter 3 that some state party delegations are highly unified in spite of very low party scores overall. This suggests, therefore, that the large number of districts in Chile and the United States – and not just the personal voting systems – hinders agent unity.

Ideology

While there seems to be general consensus that ideology has a direct impact on legislative politics, there is considerable debate regarding how the concept should be measured. Many studies have long used the readily available interest group rating scores, such as the Americans for Democratic Action (ADA), which base their scores on the votes each legislator casts. Poole and

---

[7] The high concentration and low AWU for Uruguay's Colorados and Blancos are unexpected, as are the opposite statistics associated with Chile's UDI.

TABLE 5.3. *Geographic Concentration of Legislators*

	No. districts	No. seats	No. districts where agent won at least 1 seat	No. districts to yield > 50% of agent's seats	No. districts to yield > 75% of agent's seats
Argentina (1989)[a]	24				
PJ		120	24	5	12
UCR		90	23	4	10
Brazil (1994)	27				
PMDB		107	23	6	12
PFL		89	23	5	9
PPB		52	19	5	9
PDT		34	15	4	8
PTB		31	14	4	7
PSDB		62	18	3	7
PT		49	16	3	7
Chile (1997)[b]	60				
Concertación		70	59	24	47
DC		39	39	20	30
PS		11	11	6	9
PPD		16	16	8	12
Right		49	48	24	36
RN		23	23	12	18
UDI		17	17	9	13
Uruguay (1994)	19				
FA		31	9	1	2
PC		32	18	3	11
PN		31	18	4	12
United States (1995)	435				
Dems		204	204	102	153
Reps		230	230	115	173

[a] Number of seats in legislature election following midterm election in which half of seats are renewed.
[b] Small parties are excluded from table and thus coalition totals do not sum to party totals.
Sources: Molinelli, Palanza, and Sin (1999) and Marconi (1998).

Rosenthal (1985; 1991; 1997) argue that these scales are misleading, becuase they are based on a limited set of votes. Their alternative is to generate ideological positions in one or more dimensions based on the totality of controversial votes. Londregan (2000) also devised a vote-based system to impute the ideological positions for his study of the Chilean legislature, with the advantage that it is applicable to small groups (such as committees). These vote-based scales have been strongly criticized by Krehbiel (1993), Jackson and Kingdon (1992), and Scully and Patterson (2001) among others for using actions (votes) to impute ideology and then using that same scale to predict the very votes that were used to create the scale. Further, in some sense, ideology measured through votes reverses the causality because in cases where leaders can impose voting discipline, a vote-based measure would impute identical ideological scores to each member.

These critics, it should be emphasized, do not doubt the role of ideology in influencing legislative behavior. Jackson and Kingdon say: "We do not contend that ideology is unimportant. Indeed, we are convinced it is central to decision making and to policy outcomes" (1992, p. 814). The implication, as they state it, is that in order to "assess the impact of ideology on behaviors such as legislative roll call votes, measurements of ideology that are constructed independently of the roll call votes themselves are required" (1992, p. 815). The obvious source of this type of independent information would be a survey, as are commonly used to read the ideological predispositions of the general public. Unfortunately, similar soundings of legislators' opinions have not been common. For Latin America, however, a team of researchers, led by Manuel Alcántara in Salamanca, Spain, has conducted such surveys and have generously made their data available.[8] The team has conducted several rounds of these surveys for eighteen Latin American countries, and I am using the data collected between 1994 and 1997, which allows a reasonable approximation of the legislators' beliefs at the time of the votes for which I have roll-call data.[9] The surveys do not include every legislator, but they do include a significant sample of legislators from all the major agents. The specific number of responses is listed in Appendix 5.2.

These surveys asked a very broad range of questions ranging from policy positions to personal characteristics. The surveys are not, however, without their weaknesses. In particular, some surveys were carried out over a greater period of time than others, some have higher response rates for some parties than others, and the timing of the interviews, in terms of the electoral cycle, varies across borders. Maybe most importantly, the dates of the surveys do not all align with the data on legislative voting against which I am comparing them. Still, the surveys provide an excellent view of legislator opinions,

[8] The survey project is formally titled "Elites Parlamentarias en América Latina," conducted by the Instituto Interuniversitario de Estudios de Iberoamérica y Portugal. The surveys spurred a group at Duke University, organized by Herbert Kitschelt and including Elizabeth Zechmeister, Guillermo Rosas, Kirk Hawkins, and myself, to begin an analysis of Latin American party elites. Much of the following analysis is based on work conducted by this group.

[9] The Brazilian survey was conducted as a part of the pilot project, and the data are therefore considered unofficial. Because another survey was not conducted of the Brazilian legislators, and because the results coincide with other information about the Brazilian parties, I have continued to use that data.

and unless agent voting and/or ideologies have changed dramatically in a short period of time, the time differences should be relatively unimportant.

The surveys allow numerous possibilities for measuring the ideological cohesiveness of legislators. Particularly interesting, for example, are legislators' responses to questions that probe beliefs about the church, social welfare, and the military's role in society. The multitude of questions offers many potentially useful compound measures of cohesiveness, but here I present just one simple measure, based on the spread (standard deviation) of legislators' responses about their own and their agents' placement on a left–right scale. The scale has different meanings to different people and across country boundaries, but among elites within a country there should be a general consensus about the terms. Where the spread of responses among a group's legislators is small, we can conclude that the group is cohesive, at least on the particular issue that the question is testing. If the spread is wide, then the group is not cohesive.

The ideological data allow a direct test for the hypothesis that ideologically cohesive groups should have higher voting unity. The data also allow a test of the hypothesis that the groups on the ideological fringe should be more unified than centrist groups. Within each group, the standard deviations of the legislators' responses speak to the first hypothesis, and the mean responses of the group's legislators speak to the latter. If correct, we should find that the agents that (a) have mean scores closer to the end points of the spectrum or (b) have small standard deviations in their scores should be highly unified in their voting patterns. Other more centrist or diverse parties must rely on other mechanisms, if available, to assure voting unity.

The statistics largely bear out this prediction. In Table 5.4, three of the four agents that are relatively extreme but internally cohesive (the southwest box)

TABLE 5.4. *Extremism, Cohesion, and Unity*

		Relative extremism	
		High	Low
Internal differences	High	PTB$_B$, PPB$_B$, Conc$_C$, Right$_C$, UDI$_C$,[a] RN$_C$	UCR$_A$, PJ$_A$, PFL$_B$, PMDB$_B$, PSDB$_B$, Herr$_U$
	Low	PT$_B$, PPD$_C$, PS$_C$, FA$_U$	PDC$_C$, PC$_U$, PN$_U$, Foro$_U$

Note: Agents in **bold** had AWU > 90. The subscripts refer to the agent's country. "Extremism" is defined as the absolute difference from median left–right self-placement within the country (see Appendix 5.2 for details). The average across countries was an absolute difference of 1.0 from the respective country's mean, and thus agents were classified as "extreme" if they were further than that average. Internal differences are defined by a similar methodology, using the standard deviation for the ideological self-placements. The mean across countries for the standard deviation was 1.1.

[a] The one apparently incorrectly coded respondent was discounted.

have very high levels of voting unity (over 90 on the AWU scale).[10] Brazil's
PT is perhaps the most emblematic, with minimal ideological differences
among its members (standard deviation of 0.65), extreme (self-placement
average at 1.9 on the 10-point scale), and very high voting unity (AWU =
96.1). The only other two agents that have such high levels of voting unity are
the UCR and the UDI. The UDI is somewhat of an anomaly for two reasons.
Though they score high on the extremist measure, they ranked themselves
slightly to the left of their coalition partner, National Renovation (6.08 on
the 10-point scale for the UDI versus 6.70 for the RN). Maybe even more
surprisingly, members of this highly ideological party had the greatest internal disagreement (the highest standard deviation) of any party in the survey
about their left–right position. One explanation for this anomaly is that there
is either a coding error or one of the respondents misinterpreted the scales
or gave misleading answers. When members of other parties were asked to
rank the UDI, they placed the party far to the right of the RN, and the
standard deviation of those responses was quite small. Second, in the survey
conducted in 1998, the UDI members did place themselves to the right of
the RN (and the standard deviation was small). Third, one of the twelve
UDI respondents in the earlier survey answered almost every question as if
he or she belonged to the far left. This person responded that he or she was a
two on the ten-point left–right scale, that the impact of the dictatorship was
very negative, and in contrast to all other UDI respondents, this respondent
was in favor of liberalizing divorce laws. While this respondent seems a clear
coding error, there is one other UDI respondent who chose a self-placement
of two on the left–right scale, in opposition to all the others who ranked
themselves between five and eight. That respondent, however, did seem to
agree with the other UDI colleagues on many other policy issues. This suggests that the party is cohesive regarding some issues but does not have a
unified opinion on others.[11] Interviews with UDI legislative deputies made
plain that a primary goal of the party was to make inroads into areas that
traditionally supported the left, and in fact many had won their seats in
very poor districts.[12] Many UDI legislators were mayors during the dictatorship period and were always sure to highlight their affinity for working on
local nonpartisan issues. One explained his constant meetings with neigh-
borhood groups trying to win money for small public works projects, and
another was inaugurating a new drug treatment in a very poor area of town.
Thus, though the members of the party are almost fanatically aligned on
the right with respect to most social issues (e.g., divorce laws and the role
of the military), on economic issues (e.g., the degree to which the country

[10] The Concertación and the RN were borderline cases, narrowly missing the (arbitrary) cut-off
to move them from high to low internal differences.
[11] See also Hawkins and Morgenstern (unpublished manuscript) who report on the policy
positions of the UDI and other parties using the Salamanca surveys.
[12] Interviews carried out in the summer of 1998.

should privatize state industries) the party houses a wider spectrum of opinions.

Argentina's UCR is the only agent that earned a very high AWU score while scoring low on the extremism and high on the internal divisions scales. Since the UCR is neither coherent nor extreme, the high level of unity appears related to discipline or other cohesive forces.

The behavior of only one other agent failed to substantiate the hypothesis. Chile's RN was relatively extreme, and the members generally agreed on the party's left–right position. Yet, it failed to maintain high unity rates (an average AWU of about 70). This lack of unity is likely the result of the cleavages that the left–right scale fails to capture. The RN has two prominent wings, one tied to the Pinochet regime and another business-oriented group that is considered more pragmatic. These groups are in relative agreement on economic (left–right) issues but divide on other issues. In the summer of 1998, for example, in spite of their free-market platform, many RN legislators joined in a "green coalition" to oppose a reduction of agriculture tariffs. In the surveys, the differences show up in answers to questions about the role of government in providing subsidies for basic services, social security protection, housing for the poor, and education. Their responses about the percentage of the budget that should be spent on social programs ranged from 20 percent to 90 percent![13] Maybe the best indication of the split is on moral/religious questions. While eleven of twelve UDI legislators answered that they attend church every week, oppose abortion in every case, and are in strong opposition to divorce, ten of twenty-three RN legislators seldom attend church, six were willing to admit some legal abortions, and fifteen would allow at least some divorce.

It is also important to note that the agents with significant internal conflicts were unable to solidify for voting. Most emblematic here is the PMDB, which Mainwaring (1999, p. 161) describes as one of the most heterogeneous parties in the world. This party, Mainwaring continues, has had factions from the far left and the far right, but has tried to maintain a centrist position overall. This is borne out in the survey responses (see Appendix 5.2). The PMDB is joined in the northeast box of Table 5.4 by the PFL and the PSDB, parties that traditionally represent the right and left spectrums of the political spectrum. Mainwaring, however, confirms that the PFL is also very heterogeneous, and the PSDB has had to cope with a president (Cardoso) who has prescribed restrictive economic policies.[14]

If we had a similar survey to test the U.S. legislators, the results would likely show low polarization combined with a low degree of internal agreement. Even though I previously criticized the NOMINATE scores as a

---

[13] Other parties also exhibited large ranges, but the RN was the most extreme.

[14] Mainwaring notes that the PSDB did shift toward acceptance of neoliberalism (1999, pp. 314–15), but this change likely generated internal dissension.

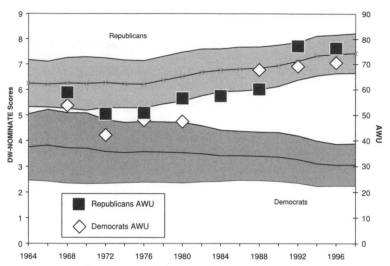

FIGURE 5.1. Polarization, cohesion, and unity in the United States. (*Source of data*: Keith Poole's website, http://voteview.uh.edu/default_nomdata.htm [converted from a –1 to +1 scale to a 1 to 10 scale].)

product not a predictor of cohesion, they do show this general pattern – with more polarization than might have been expected. Figure 5.1 reports the first dimension of Poole and Rosenthal's DW-NOMINATE scores (which they interpret as measuring economic left–right issues) with a one standard deviation band on either side of the averages for the years 1964–97.[15] The wider band around the Democrats indicates that they are less cohesive than the Republicans (most notably in the earlier years), but the graph implies that both parties have an important degree of spread amongst their members. The spread was so great that until about 1970, legislators just one standard deviation away from the mean of their parties almost intersected with one another (Figure 5.1). This implies that about 15 percent of the Democrats were at least as conservative as a similar percentage of the most left-leaning Republicans. This is consistent with the low unity scores recorded for the two parties, shown by the squares and diamonds in the figure. The increased cohesion of the parties (noted by the narrowing bands in the graph) plus their separation from one another overall is also consistent with the impressive increase in U.S. unity scores beginning in the late 1980s.[16]

[15] While highly correlated with the W-NOMINATE scores, the DW-NOMINATE scores are comparable across time and are thus more appropriate for this graph. See Keith Poole's website (http://voteview.uh.edu) for details.

[16] See Aldrich and Rohde (1998; 2001) about these changes. In addition to citing the increased ideological cohesion among House members, they attribute part of the increased unity to changes in House rules that augmented the power of party leaders. I have not attempted

Ins, Outs and the Electoral Cycle

In parliamentary systems, agents associated with the executive face multiple incentives and pressures to maintain high levels of unity. In presidential systems, however, I argued in Chapter 4 that members of both the Ins and the Outs face pressures to dissociate themselves from other members of the agent. In some cases, it may be the Outs, rather than the Ins, that achieve higher levels of unity, but in both cases the countervailing pressures yield rather weak theoretical bases for these expectations. I further argued that both the unifying and repelling pressures should change over the course of the electoral cycle.

The bivariate roll-call data give very limited support for the idea that Ins and Outs act differently in relation to unity, or that the electoral cycle is an important determinant of agent unity. The data sets for Brazil, the Chilean Senate, Uruguay, and the United States all cover at least one full term, thus lending themselves to tests of these expectations. The only country where the hypotheses are clearly upheld, however, is Uruguay.

Three pieces of evidence do suggest that electoral cycles are important to unity in Uruguay. First, after each election, each president has formed a cabinet that united the different factions in their parties (and sometimes parts of the other parties). This unity, however, has not lasted as the different factions have opted out of the cabinet, usually well before the next set of elections.[17]

Second, during election campaigns, when incentives for the In party factions to differentiate themselves are at their highest levels, particularly destructive and renegade candidacies have appeared within the In-parties.[18] In the two elections where there was an incumbent party and no formal primary system (i.e., 1989 and 1994), the incumbent party fielded two centrist candidates. These two internal campaigns were fiercely contested, and in both elections voters rejected the divided (incumbent) party.[19]

Third, the legislative voting data shows clearly that the Out-party becomes (or stays) united in the run-up to elections, while the In-party divides

---

to pursue this line of argument for the other cases here, but Ames (2002) argues that party leaders' weakness in Brazil contributes to the low levels of unity.

[17] See Laurnaga (1993) on the 1989–94 period. As discussed in Chapter 6, the presidents have also offered cabinet posts to members of other parties.

[18] The Frente Amplio presents somewhat of a problem here as they divided previous to the 1989 election with the moderate wing forming a new party, the Nuevo Espacio (New Space) (see González, 1995). Throughout the election period, however, the Frente Amplio and the wing that broke away continued to present themselves as a united front against the traditional parties.

[19] Recall that in 1989 the divisiveness manifested itself in a primary for the incumbent faction of the Colorado Party, while in 1994 the two wings of the incumbent Blanco faction split and fought the election as two different factions.

TABLE 5.5. *Cycles of Party Unity, 1985–1995*

	First four years, AWU scores	Election year, AWU scores
	1985–1988	1989
Incumbent party (Colorados)	99	88
Out-party (Blancos)	99	99
	1990–1993	1994
Incumbent party (Blancos)	59	86
Out-party (Colorados)	45	49

(or stays divided). Table 5.5 breaks the 1985–9 and 1990–4 terms into two parts: the first four years and the election year. The patterns are stark. For the In-party (Colorados 1985–9 and Blancos 1990–4), regardless of their unity during the first four years, unity fell sharply during the election year. The Out-party acted in the opposite manner; regardless of their actions in the early parts of the term, they acted quite unified in the last year. In sum, for both presidential periods, three of the four entries in Table 5.5 support the predictions; only the incumbent party in 1994 failed to follow the prediction. In that election year, however, there were only seven contested votes in the legislature, and the increase to a score of 49 from 45 is meaningless. Further, though Table 5.5 shows only the two traditional parties, the Frente Amplio also fits the pattern. They have always been an Out-party and retained tremendous unity throughout that ten-year period (and later).

While electoral cycles seem to have a clear role in determining Uruguayan unity, their impact is at best murky for the other countries. Amorim Neto and Santos (2001) provide evidence to show that unity rates (what they term "discipline") for Brazilian parties in the 1946–64 period increased in the last part of the electoral cycles. There is scant evidence, however, for this type of pattern in the current period. Focusing on the 1995–8 term in Brazil, the expectation would be for the unity of the PMDB, PSDB, and PFL to drop toward the end of the term, and for it to rise for the PT. Recall that the PMDB had very low unity rates for that term, and that they rose significantly in the last quintile of the term, from about 58 to 73. The final score, however, is still too low to suggest that the effect of the electoral cycle was important enough to generate unity.[20] The PFL, PSDB, and PT, meanwhile,

---

[20] For Brazil, I am relying on the data set supplied by Figueiredo and Limongi here because it covers the full term. That data set is not perfectly coincident with the data provided by Barry Ames that I have used elsewhere.

maintained high unity throughout the term, with little change in the run-up to elections.

The Chilean lower house data does not cover a full term, but the Senate data runs from 1992 to 1998, thus covering the 1993 coincident elections of the president and the legislature, as well as the legislative elections of 1997. The test, however, will focus on just the 1993 election since there are no votes in the database for 1997. The primary expectation would be for the Concertación legislators to show less unity as the elections approached and for the rightist coalition (or its member parties) to increase their level of unity. The Concertación, however, showed almost perfect unity for the last quintile of the electoral cycle (covering thirty-six votes), reaching an AWU score of 95. The UDI showed perfect unity in that period, while the RN split frequently, garnering a Rice score of about 70.

Finally, the data for the United States supported the hypothesis for Reagan's first term and Clinton's second term, but other four year periods (at least since the 1960s) do not help to confirm the hypotheses. During Reagan's first four years, the Democrats controlled the lower house but faced a Republican president. They, therefore, could be seen as the Out-party, seeking to displace the president. Over the four years, the Democrats' average Rice score was about 71. Over the last 10 percent of votes, however, they reached almost 90 percent agreement on average (Rice score just below 80). The Republicans' AWU, as the theory predicts, fell about 10 percent from their average (from 66 to 59) just prior to the presidential election (even though Reagan ran for reelection in 1984). During the 1997–2001 period, the AWU scores of the president's party remained stable over the last 10 percent of the votes (at about 70), but the Out-party's (Republicans') unity rose a significant amount from what was already a relatively high level (moving from an AWU of 76 to 82). Most of that rise, furthermore, can be attributed to the last 5 percent of the votes (over which the Republicans scored an AWU of 91). During the other presidential terms under examination, however, there was no appreciable change in the Rice scores toward the end of the term.[21]

In sum, there is only weak evidence that unity rates differ for the Ins and Outs or vary as the electoral cycle progresses. Perhaps the coincidence of the primary and general election in Uruguay is what leads to the greater effect in that country. In Chile, for example, prior to the 1993 election, the parties of the Concertación came to an agreement on a presidential candidate, and the incentive to bind together in support of that candidate (perhaps in pursuit of the spoils that that candidate was sure to control) may have helped the members overcome the divisive pulls of the legislative elections. That logic might also help explain the sustained unity of Brazil's PSDB and the increased unity of PMDB in the last part of the electoral cycle.

[21] During Clinton's first term, the Republicans' scores increased moderately over the last 5 percent of the votes. There were no evident patterns related to the legislature's two-year cycles.

TOWARD A MULTIVARIATE TEST

Although the bivariate tests presented in the previous pages are supportive of the hypotheses, only a multivariate analysis could show the independent relation of each explanatory variable to the AWU scores. Further, the discussion has provided methods for operationalizing the dependent variable and the independent variables pertaining to discipline (nomination control) and cohesion (the degree of ideological agreement among the agent's members, the extent to which an agent is polarized from the central tendencies in the country, the degree to which there is a personal vote and the electoral fates of an agent's members are tied to one another, the geographic concentration of the agent's legislators, the electoral cycle, and the agent's relation with the executive).

Unfortunately, for two primary reasons, the data are unsuitable for testing the hypotheses in a multiple regression.[22] First, testing the discipline and cohesion hypotheses simultaneously would require a pooled time-series model. Such models that include both cross-time and cross-national data violate a number of assumptions concerning the independence of the error terms. While there are some prescribed methods for dealing with some of these problems, these methods are inapplicable in this case.[23]

---

[22] In addition to the problems that are particular to the analysis, any test of these hypotheses would also have to deal with issues inherent in any regression. For example, there are difficulties in operationalizing nomination control (and the other variable). The operationalization in this chapter suggests an ordinal scale, but in addition to the mathematical issues associated with such scales, it is unclear how different systems should be ranked. A second problem would concern the functional form of the proposed regression. This chapter has explained that either discipline or cohesion is sufficient to achieve unity. As a result, the analysis should not simply posit that an agent's AWU score is a linear combination of the discipline and cohesion variables. This is not an insurmountable problem, but it does complicate the analysis. Third, the regression would have the problem of incomplete data, given that there are no surveys of U.S. legislators comparable to those done in Latin America.

[23] The most widely accepted method for dealing with pooled time series problems is to include a series of dummy variables that allows the slopes and intercepts of the model to vary across countries. These models, termed unrestricted models, require the inclusion of a dummy for each country (less one) in the analysis, and an interaction between those dummies and each other independent variable in the model. (An F-test can then determine if the inclusion of the dummies significantly changes the results.) The "correct" coefficient for an independent variable on a particular country, then, is the coefficient for the base effect plus the coefficient associated with the interaction term for the country and independent variable.

This technique, however, uses a large number of dummy variables, and thus where, as in my case, there is limited variation either within the countries or across the time periods, the unrestricted model can create multiple series of perfectly linear combinations. As a result, a regression would be unable to establish the impact of the different variables.

A second method for dealing with pooled time series data, developed by Beck and Katz (1995), has also gained prominence. Their method, however, requires a consistent number of cases in each time period and makes a number of untenable assumptions about the error terms that are innappropriate for this study.

A second and related problem is that the small number of countries in the regression would provide an insufficient basis on which to determine the impact of the variables that differentiate among the cases. In particular, a regression on so few countries would be unable to differentiate the impact of nomination control from other factors that distinguish the countries. The small number of agents within each country would cause a similar problem.

In sum, the limited number of cases will not allow a statistical test to separate out the independent effects of the causal variables adequately. Thus, until there are sufficient data on a wider range of cases, it will not be possible to validate the hypotheses in a multivariate environment.

CONCLUSION

The degree to which an agent's members vote together affects whether voters can reasonably hold individuals, factions, parties, or coalitions responsible for policy decisions. As such, the factors that determine an agent's unity on roll-call votes have been an important focus of study in both the American and comparative literature.

In this chapter, I operationalized and offered preliminary tests for the impact of agent leaders' disciplinary powers and cohesive elements on unity. Nomination control that results from the electoral system only appeared to have a clear relation with unity rates when the control was quite secure. Further, the electoral system offers few agent leaders undisputed nomination control, and this system-level variable is insufficient to explain intracountry variance. Therefore, in cases where the electoral system affords leaders only low or middling levels of nomination control, unity rates will depend on cohesion and whether the agent leaders can capture nomination control in spite of the electoral system.

This chapter has shown that a number of the factors – both ideological and instrumental – can contribute to cohesion. It has also implied that there is a relation among the cohesion variables because the mostly highly unified agents generally stand apart from others on more than one factor. Further, since the cohesion variables can act as substitutes for one another, agents can attain some unity by relying on discipline or any of the cohesive factors. In addition, the agents that have gained alternative means for controlling their members – in particular Brazil's PT and Uruguay's Frente Amplio – are also quite cohesive. This perhaps suggests a parallel with Aldrich and Rohde's (1997–8; 2001) thesis about conditional party (agent) government, in that when rank-and-file legislators share more homogeneous preferences, they should be more willing to allocate power to leaders.

While this discussion has focused on the relationships among an agent's members, representation and the legislative process also depend on the relationships among agents. Key questions include: Which agents are willing to join others in policy coalitions? Are coalitions stable or shifting? What drives these patterns? The answers to these questions are pertinent to the substance of representation because they determine the decisions that are made in the legislature. They also bear on the form and possibly the stability of democracy because they determine whether the legislature is an inclusive body in which all agents win at least occasionally, or whether it is a majoritarian body that generally excludes certain groups. The next chapter again uses the roll-call data to help answer these questions.

APPENDIX 5.1. COMPONENTS OF VARIANCE MODEL

The components of variance model used in this chapter is based on Morgenstern and Potthoff (2003). In that paper, we develop a model based on Stokes's (1965; 1967) comparative analysis of the nationalization of elections in the United States and the United Kingdom. Stokes's much-cited (i.e., Katz, 1973; Kawato, 1987; Cox and McCubbins, 1993; Cox and Rosenbluth, 1995) model posits that the total variance s^2 in a district's vote is a function of national (s_n^2), state (s_s^2), and district (s_d^2) forces. Since there is only one district per state (province) in Argentina, Brazil, and Uruguay, and district lines are not coincident with state (territory) lines in Chile, the analysis here is based on two levels, the national and the state/district effects. For the United States, the statistics are based on the parties' vote share in a given district. The total variance in the variance components model for these cases is thus $s^2 = s_n^2 + s_d^2$, where these quantities are estimated based on a party's (or agent's) total vote share.

In our version of the model, we rework the model to account for several flaws that we found and rename the different components for analytical clarity. Our model has two variance components. First, what Stokes termed a "national effect," we consider to be a time effect because it captures changes in the agent's average vote totals across time. As it captures changes across time, we use this component to analyze what more recent authors have termed "volatility." Second, Stokes's state effect is really a measure of the heterogeneity across districts. We term this, therefore, the district-heterogeneity effect. We use this awkward term to differentiate it from the residual effect, which Stokes called a "district effect." We argue, however, that it is really a district-time effect because it captures variability across both districts and time (note that the residual subscripts both district and time).

The model that we favor is

$$y_{ik} = \mu + A_k + B_i + C_{ik}$$

where y_{ik} is the percentage of the total vote of an agent in district i at time k, A is the time effect, B is the district-heterogeneity effect, and C is the residual or district-time effect.

The time component is estimated by

$$\hat{\sigma}_A^2 = \frac{M_A - M_R}{I}$$

where M_A is the mean square due to the time or national effect and I is the number of districts. More directly,

$$M_A = \frac{S_A^2}{K-1} \quad \text{where} \quad S_A^2 = I \sum_{k=1}^{K} (y_{.k} - y_{..})^2$$

where K is the number of years in the analysis and . indicates the average over the replaced index. The mean square of the residual, M_R or $\hat{\sigma}^2$, is defined by

$$\hat{\sigma}^2 = M_R = \frac{S_R^2}{(K-1)(I-1)}$$

The component capturing the district-heterogeneity effect is measured by the following equation:

$$\hat{\sigma}_B^2 = \frac{M_B - M_R}{K}$$

where M_B, the mean square, is calculated from S_B^2, the sum of squares reflecting district heterogeneity. The necessary formulas are

$$M_B = \frac{S_B^2}{I-1}$$

and

$$S_B^2 = K \sum_{i=1}^{I} (y_{i.} - y_{..})^2$$

Finally, the residual sum of squares is

$$S_R^2 = \sum_{i=1}^{I} \sum_{k=1}^{K} (y_{ik} - y_{i.} - y_{.k} + y_{..})^2$$

From this analysis, we can draw conclusions about the ratios among the different components or from their actual sizes. Here I have opted to concentrate on the raw numbers, as the ratios can hide intercountry differences in terms of the amount of total variance in the system. In other words, the ratios are misleading when comparing two countries that have very different levels of total variance.

APPENDIX 5.2. AGENTS' LEFT–RIGHT PLACEMENT

TABLE A5.1. *Agents' Left–Right Placement*

	Ideological self-placement (v234)				Placement of one's party (v132)	
	Freq	Mean	Abs[d]	SD	Mean	SD
Argentina						
PJ	22	4.62	0.02	1.36	5.24	1.64
UCR	17	4.50	0.10	1.47	4.53	1.46
Frepaso	10	3.45	1.15	1.91	3.50	1.27
UCEDE	3	7.67	3.07	2.08	8.00	2.00
AVG/TOTAL[a]	67	4.60		1.65	5.02	1.75
Brazil[b]						
PMDB	16	4.63	0.43	1.36	4.53	0.99
PFL	11	5.09	0.89	1.30	5.75	1.76
PSDB	9	4.22	0.02	1.39	4.11	0.78
PT	8	1.88	2.32	0.64	2.00	0.64
AVG/TOTAL[a]	69	4.20		1.97	4.61	2.19
Chile						
Concertación	55	3.96	1.04	1.11	3.98	1.16
DC	31	4.52	0.48	0.93	4.42	0.81
PPD	11	3.60	1.40	0.70	4.36	1.12
PS	13	2.92	2.08	0.95	2.62	0.87
Right	35	6.48	1.48	1.46	6.45	1.46
RN	23	6.70	1.70	1.11	6.48	0.99
UDI[c]	12	6.45	1.45	1.86	6.82	1.54
AVG/TOTAL[a]	93	5.00		1.79	5.02	1.75
Uruguay						
PC	20	4.90	0.69	0.72	5.00	0.56
FORO	15	4.93	0.72	0.80	5.06	0.46
PN	20	4.95	0.74	1.11	5.60	1.05
HERR	9	5.11	0.90	1.27	5.33	1.12
FA	25	3.09	1.22	0.90	2.96	0.84
AVG/TOTAL[a]	73	4.21		1.28	4.38	1.40

[a] Total number of responses includes those of parties not included in the table. The number of responses for the variables is not always identical. The listed number refers to the responses for v234. Averages of other columns are simple averages of included agents.

[b] Mainwaring (1999) reports similar statistics for the 1990 Brazilian Congress.

[c] Eliminating one respondent who is likely miscoded (see text for explanation).

[d] Absolute difference from overall mean.

Source: Manuel Alcántara, dir. *Proyecto de Elites Latinoamericanas* (PELA). Universidad de Salamanca, 1994–2000.

6

Policy Coalitions and Agent Flexibility

In addition to the patterns of unity among agents, legislative politics is defined by the grouping of the agents into majorities for the passage of legislation. Describing these patterns implies a focus on "coalitions," but because presidents do not rely on the confidence of the agents in their cabinet to remain in office, coalitions in presidential systems do not generally take the solid form that they do in countries with parliamentary rule.

Coalition politics, nevertheless, have been central to the histories of much of Latin America (Foweraker, 1998). Deheza (1997) found that more than half of all governments formed in postwar Latin America have included more than a single party and, much like parliamentary systems, there have been multiple examples of governments forming from minimum-winning, super-majority, temporary, and durable coalitions.[1] She concludes, importantly, that these coalitions have helped presidents generate the necessary support to implement their policies. Analyses focused on Argentina, Brazil, and Chile have reached similar conclusions (Figueiredo and Limongi, 2000; Mustapic, 2002; Siavelis, 2002).

In spite of their importance, the definition of presidential coalitions is not yet clear, and a first task of this chapter is to clarify the different meanings of this term. Then, with a focus on "policy coalitions," the chapter demonstrates empirically the proclivity of different legislators and agents to join with one another on roll calls. These two indicators suggest that unlike the polarized 1960s and 1970s, agents have been relatively flexible in the 1990s – except in the United States.

As with unity, an explanation of flexibility rates requires both internal and external variables. Here there is an important commonality, in that the four Latin American countries have all been recently scarred by harsh dictatorships, which have pushed all agents from their staunch ideological postures toward positions that favor greater cooperation. The data show

[1] See especially the first part of Chapter 3. See also Amorim Neto (1998).

that the agents considered to be at the margins of their respective systems have not been ignored as possible coalition partners, thus suggesting that this ideological change has been reflected in legislative politics. Further, through an analysis of Poole and Rosenthal NOMINATE scores for Brazil and Chile, I show that while political battles are frequently fought on the left–right playing field, there is also an apparent range of ideological preferences within the legislatures. This implies that an agent's extremism on one issue will not necessarily translate into exclusion on other issues. This, perhaps, is why the multiagent systems have not tended toward the dangerous polarization that Sartori's (1976) work predicted.

The data also suggest that unity does not necessarily limit flexibility. As Linz (1994, p. 35) suggests, unified agents could be dangerous to democracy if they are less willing to compromise their ideological positions for practical gains. Here I show, however, that even opposition parties and factions sometimes do unify behind negotiated deals; they do not consistently oppose their electoral competitors on roll-call votes.

While ideological moderation aids cooperation among agents, the patterns of cooperation are still driven by political factors. In particular, agents' ideological positions, their relationship with the president and the majority in the legislature, and electoral pressures all affect the legislators' calculus when considering whether or not to support a piece of legislation. This chapter operationalizes and tests these ideas by measuring the influence of the agents' positions on the left–right scale and their membership in presidential cabinets, as well as the timing of each roll-call vote with respect to the electoral calendar, on the formation of the coalitions that form to support legislation.

In addressing these issues, the chapter offers a definition of coalitions in presidential regimes based on policy instead of cabinets. The next section discusses the sources of flexibility, first focusing on the change from the ideologically charged period of the Cold War as the primary reason why agents are working together in the 1990s. It also offers some evidence that politics have been relatively consensual in the 1990s in the four Latin American cases, though it notes a declining level of cooperation between the two parties in the United States. The rest of that section then discusses the hypotheses related to ideology, cabinet membership, unity, and the electoral cycle. The third section then tests these hypotheses by considering the patterns of policy coalitions in the four countries and the United States. It shows that cabinet membership has not been an effective mechanism for cementing relationships among agents, at least not in Brazil and Uruguay. In Chile, however, the electoral alliance appears to play a more important role than ideology in determining the shape of policy coalitions. That section also shows that the electoral cycle also affects the shape of policy coalitions, but the impact is not what might be expected. Instead of increasing left–right tensions, heightened electoral concerns appear to drive wedges into the ruling and/or the opposition camps. As a result, some agents that opposed one another during much of the term find themselves on the same side of votes as elections near. The final section summarizes the findings.

DEFINING COALITIONS AND FLEXIBILITY IN
PRESIDENTIAL REGIMES

While the term "coalition" has a specific and well-understood meaning in parliamentary democracies, for presidential democracies it can apply to electoral alliances, parliamentary-style executive cabinets, or legislative policy coalitions. This chapter focuses on the last of these definitions, but to clarify this focus and avoid a conflation of terms, it is necessary to briefly define each concept.

Electoral alliances are grouping of two or more agents under a single banner for the purpose of electing a candidate (often a president) or list of candidates that all support. Chile's Concertación and the electoral union of the UDI and the RN are the archetypal examples. In this book, I have used the terms "electoral alliance" and "coalition" interchangeably to describe these two groups.

The second definition, based on membership in an executive cabinet, has received new interest among Latin Americanists. Chasquetti (2000), for example, argues about the importance of cabinet coalitions in overcoming the "difficult combination" in presidential systems.[2] Literature on specific cases has also followed suit. For example, Altman (1990a, 1990b, 2000a, 2000b) uses similar definitions – though based on factions, not parties – in investigating the formation, demise, and behavior of coalitions in Uruguay. Amorim Neto's (1998, 2002; Amorim Neto and Santos, 2001) work on Brazil is also very useful in that he addresses the issue of how a party's membership in the cabinet affects presidential support in the legislature. His useful typology of coalitions, however, also focuses on cabinets.

Finally, I define the policy coalitions on which this chapter focuses by the patterns of voting on any given roll call. There are two important indicators of the patterns of policy coalitions or the degree of agent flexibility: the composition of the majority and the frequency with which any two agents join together on the same side of a vote. In majoritarian systems, we would expect to see the same patterns repeated across most votes. In flexible multi-agent systems, however, the policy coalitions can be assembled on an ad hoc basis. The five test cases allow a view of each of these varied types.

Operationalizing the policy coalitions creates new difficulties, especially where the unity of an agent is not extraordinarily high. Therefore, in this chapter, I explore the policy coalitions conditional on varying levels of unity.

---

[2] This expression, which refers to the problem of interbranch stalemate that results from a president's minority support in the legislature, comes from Mainwaring (1993).

THE SOURCES OF FLEXIBILITY IN MULTIAGENT
PRESIDENTIAL SYSTEMS

As with unity rates, an explanation of the patterns of policy coalitions requires a consideration of variables that affect all countries and those that
separate agents within those countries. In what follows, I argue that the
end of the Cold War and the horrible experiences with dictatorships have
worked to encourage more cooperation in Latin America's Southern Cone
than was evident in earlier periods. As a result, there appears more cooperation among legislators from all ideological hues than would be expected
from a winner-take-all view of politics.

Ideological moderation, however, does not account for variation in the
patterns of policy coalition among agents within a country. This section
thus also discusses the hypothesized effects of the ideological positions of
the agents, their membership in electoral alliances and presidential cabinets,
their unity, and the electoral cycle. The succeeding section then provides
support for the hypotheses.

Common External Force: Ideological Moderation

A primary concern about legislative politics is the unwillingness of
"extremist" agents to sacrifice ideological goals for democratic sustainability. Building on Sartori (1976) and Sani and Sartori (1983), Mainwaring
and Shugart (1997, p. 399) argue that ideological distances among parties
make coalition building difficult. This, they continue, determines whether
executive–legislative relations will be characterized by compromise or immobilism. Immobilism, they imply, can result in presidents resorting to decree
powers, which they cite as a serious problem with presidentialism.

Sartori's concern with extremism begins with his classification of agents
(parties) as having either "coalition" or "blackmail potential" (1976, p. 122).
The Italian Communist Party, he argues, had had "for the past 25 years,
virtually zero" potential for joining a governing coalition. Sartori then argues that the existence of extremist parties (which grow in the context of
multipartism) can lead to a "crisis of legitimacy" for the democracy (1976,
pp. 132–3).

Polarized agent positions presented a slightly different problem in Chile.
Until Allende was elected in 1970, the center, dominated by the Radicals
and the Christian Democrats, shared power with the National Party, which
controlled the right end of the political spectrum (cf. Chapters 1 and 3).
There had also been left-center coalitions that led to Radical Party victories
in the presidency in the 1930s and 1940s, and the 1952 victor had support of
both the left and the right (Valenzuela, 1978, p. 5). The problem arose when
the Socialist Party, which had not been a serious coalition partner for the
Christian Democrats or the National Party during the preceding decade,

gained the presidency in 1970. The coalition backing Allende controlled merely one-third of the Congress, and the Christian Democrats and Nationals (the Radicals had splintered) refused to form governing or even policy coalitions. The political stalemate yielded a severe crisis of legitimacy, and as Sartori's feared, this led to the overthrow of the democratic system.

Valenzuela (1978) blames the lack of compromise on the "sharp ideological polarization" of the times (p. 10). He also argues that even before the crisis years in Chile, the constant jockeying for electoral advantage prevented the maintenance of stable coalitions among the parties (p. 7). The polarization was not new to Chile, and Valenzuela argues that its long existence had forced a climate of accommodation in the Chilean legislature. But as he, Garretón (1989), and Shugart and Carey (1992) point out: "The 'clientelism' of electoral politics made [the accommodation] possible" (Valenzuela, p. 19). When constitutional changes of the late 1960s limited the clientelistic opportunities, the accommodation gave way to the politics of polarization.

Cohen (1994) puts these ideas into a game-theoretic form. He argues that parties in Chile and Brazil in the 1960s were caught in a prisoners' dilemma; all would have gained by compromise to avoid the coups, but the structure of preferences voided potential cooperation. The key to his argument is the power of the extremist groups and the fear that moderates had in cooperating with those groups. Further, the moderate right, for example, would fear giving some ground to the moderate left because this could encourage the radicals. As a result, Cohen argues, even cooperation among relative moderates failed.

Over the past decade, however, politics in the region has been less polarized. The Chilean right and left still disagree sharply over military and economic issues, but neither side appears willing to push their disputes to the brink. Speaking of the rightist UDI, Siavelis (2000, p. 118) states that "[i]ndicative of this new orientation [toward democracy] was the party's willingness to reach an agreement with the Concertación to determine Chamber and Senate leadership by engaging in active negotiations and leaving behind the RN." The fall of the Berlin Wall and the experiences with harsh military regimes seems to be at the root of this important change.

A growing literature suggests that groups on the right across Latin America felt betrayed by the military governments (Middlebrook, 2000; Chalmers, de Souza, and Boron, 1992). In earlier periods, the right had seen authoritarian rule as the only way to resolve crises of development; thus, rightist parties and groups invited the military to take power across the Southern Cone. But the economic crises of the 1980s undermined the right's confidence in the military's ability to manage the economy. Some sectors were abhorred by the whimsical use of power by the centralized governments, if not the human rights violations as well. Still, O'Donnell (1992) argues that many of these groups have not developed true "substantive" democratic values; instead, they only support "procedural" democracy in order to win benefits. Recent events, however, suggest that the right has come to accept and perhaps even support democratic rule. Exemplary of this new direction were the right's responses (or lack thereof) in Chile after the arrest in the United Kingdom of Pinochet in 1998 and in Argentina in the wake of the street protests and resignation of President de la Rua in December 2001. Although there was concern about how the right would respond in Chile, there was never a serious threat of upending the democratic government, even after Pinochet was returned to Chile and put under house arrest in order to prepare for a trial. In Argentina, the right was mute, and the threat of military action was hardly even raised. The roll-call data further support the idea of a changed right, as they show the willingness of rightist parties to engage others in democratic deals.

The leftist parties have also undergone a makeover. Unlike their intransigent Marxist forebears, the new leftist parties and other agents are more willing to sacrifice ideological goals in order to participate from within the political system. This is true not only in Latin America but also in Eastern and Central Europe where socialist parties have joined deals with the International Monetary Fund (IMF) to undertake neoliberal economic reforms. In part, the left has changed to respond to new global economic exigencies. Many, however, subscribe to the view that the demise of communist rule in Eastern Europe has deprived the Latin American left of an ideological model.[3] This idea, however, does not explain the continued strength of the Workers' Party (PT) in Brazil, the Socialists and Communists in Chile, and the Frente Amplio, which includes elements of socialists, communists, and ex–guerrilla groups, in Uruguay. The demise of Eastern European communism, then, has not led to an end of leftist political competition in Latin America. It has, however, forced the left to reconsider their ideological positions. Further, the atrocities that leftist leaders suffered under the dictatorships have led the left to revalue their commitment to democracy. Though some revolutionary groups still espouse violence (such as Peru's Shining Path or the Revolutionary Armed Forces of Colombia), these groups are exceptional and lack links to established political parties. This new democratic commitment, plus the move toward the ideological center, has helped end the unwillingness of the left to participate in political deals with the center or even the right.

As evidence for the important level of cooperation, Table 6.1 details the percentage of controversial votes in which at least a majority of each agent supported the winning side of controversial legislative votes.[4] Table 6.1 uses

---

[3] Peeler (1998) underscores how the end of the Cold War left all economic controls in the hands of the West, thus limiting Latin American options (p. 19).

[4] Since votes to change and maintain the status quo are equally important, the tables in this chapter do not discriminate between joining a majority of ayes and a majority of noes.

TABLE 6.1. *Frequency of Agent Voting with the Majority (Contentious Votes)*

Country	%	%	Country	%	%
Argentina	1989–91		Uruguay	1985–9	1989–94
PJ	72.5		Colorados	14.7	93.3
UCR	35.0		FORO		86.7
			C94		93.3
Brazil	1991–5	1995–8	B15		73.3
PDT	52.5	21.8	UCB	20.6	73.3
PFL	78.4	93.3	BU	14.7	
PMDB	92.1	94.1	CBI	20.6	
PPB	63.3	89.1	Nacional	85.3	26.7
PSDB	73.4	95.5	HERR		13.3
PT	38.1	16.2	MNR		60.0
PTB	80.6	91.0	RyV		40.0
			CNH	85.3	
Chile	House	Senate	ACF	85.3	
	1997–9	1992–8	PGP	82.4	86.7
DC	84.9	73.5	Frente Amplio	82.4	86.7
PRSD	76.1	38.6			
PS	82.5	62.7	United States	1965–9	1969–73
PPD	82.9	59.0	Democrats	86.1	77.9
Concert.	86.9	71.1	Republicans	51.6	74.0
RN	47.8	47.0		1992–3	1993–4
UDI	34.7	53.0	Democrats	87.7	29.5
Independent right		47.0	Republicans	34.7	90.1
Right	44.2	47.0			

Note: Majority of the agents, voting with the majority of the legislature; "contentious" defined as votes with at least 10% dissent (weight > 0.2).

this very generous conception of supporting the majority in order to provide a top boundary on the flexibility of the most extreme agents.[5] It shows, importantly, that the leftist parties of Brazil and Uruguay, as well as the rightist UDI in Chile, have won a significant number of legislative battles. It also shows, however, that there has been a sharp decline in the percentage of votes won by the minority party in the United States.

Although all agents win some legislative battles, there are significant differences among the agents within each country. The rest of this chapter focuses on explaining these differences, with a focus on whether membership in electoral alliances or presidential cabinets is an effective tool for generating support. An alternative hypothesis is that policy coalitions are determined

---

[5] Even these statistics underestimate an agent's true flexibility because votes that do not generate the requisite level of controversy are dropped from the analysis.

by the ideological proximity of agents. Each of these hypotheses is then conditioned by unity and electoral pressures that change during the legislative term.

Agent Ideology

If the politics are stripped away, assumptions of rationality expect policy coalitions to form from among ideological neighbors. Legislators, however, must weigh their ideological beliefs against their membership in cabinets, leaders' demands, and constituent interests when deciding how to vote. Even though there are interactions among these variables (i.e., membership in a cabinet often reflects ideological affinities), it is sometimes possible to identify the impact of beliefs independent of the impact of these other factors. If ideology has an independent impact in determining policy coalitions, we should see most policy coalitions among agents that are adjacent or at least close to one another on the left–right scale. The case of Chile, where the parties are grouped into two alliances, will allow us to test whether ideology overrides electoral alliances in driving policy coalitions. If it does, then we should see frequent policy coalitions forming among members of the two parties that are adjacent on the left–right scale but pertaining to different electoral alliances. In Brazil and Uruguay, the use of multiagent cabinets allows tests of whether cabinet membership is effective in agglutinating ideologically disparate (or even similar) agents.

Association with the Executive or Majority Coalition

Next, as forwarded by Amorim Neto (2002) and Amorim Neto and Santos (2001), at least under some circumstances, membership in the executive's cabinet should have a marked effect on the shape of policy coalitions. But, while membership in a president's cabinet should increase participation in majority coalitions, it should not have as stark an impact as in parliamentary systems. Parliamentary cabinets are held together, at least in part, by the coalition partners' knowledge that their support is necessary to ensure continuance of the current executive. When political winds are propitious, agents do withdraw their support and force new elections, but this is a risky political strategy. As a result, agents that participate in parliamentary cabinets are generally expected to compromise on many different issues, and in return they expect some deference with respect to the issues that are most important to their constituents.

In presidential systems, alternatively, the withdrawal of support does not affect the president's tenure or the electoral calendar. As a result, while prime ministers can demand support in all areas in exchange for cabinet portfolios, presidents may have to offer cabinet posts (and the implied access to pork and power) in exchange for support on a particular policy or issue area. The expectation, thus, is that membership in a president's cabinet may improve an agent's support of the president somewhat, but the support level is likely to vary by issue area, and overall it is unlikely to approach the levels expected of agents included in parliamentary cabinets. The corollary is that the different agents with representatives in a president's cabinet will not necessarily vote together.

Unity

In determining the shape of policy coalitions, unity conditions the importance of ideology and cabinet membership, rather than acting as a separate independent variable. The number of votes that the president will sway by offering cabinet portfolios, for example, will decline when unity is low. Likewise, when unity is high, the preferences of the group – which may reflect only the preferences of the leader – will take precedence over the beliefs or interests of individual members.

Further, conditioning individual votes on the unity of the agents can highlight the most salient issues. Even those agents that are not consistently unified do see their members coming together on a significant number of votes. While not all controversial bills are politically salient, those bills that separate unified agents are likely candidates for salient issues. The subset of votes on which the agents are unified, then, allows an analysis of the shape of policy coalitions on particularly salient issues. Frequent cooperation between two agents is a sign of flexibility, but if those same two agents do not cooperate on bills that unite their respective members, then there is evidence that the cooperation only happens on less-significant bills.

Finally, the role of unity is pertinent for those agents that are on the ideological fringe and have not been invited into presidential cabinets. Though other agents have also maintained high levels of unity, Uruguay's Frente Amplio, Chile's UDI, and Brazil's PT stand out for their near perfect unity scores and their continual exclusion from the ruling coalition (though the PT's victory in the 2002 presidential campaign will change this pattern). Are these identifiable agents flexible? Table 6.1 suggested that although these agents are relegated to opposition status on most bills, they at least occasionally show enough flexibility to lend support to majority policy coalitions, an outcome perhaps explained by the prevailing political winds of the 1990s. At the same time, since the sharp ideological differences between these agents and the congressional majorities complicate the formation of policy coalitions, the roll-call data should show that these groups are less frequently in the majority than others.

Electoral Cycle

Since legislators must always concern themselves with elections, the factors that weigh on their voting decisions are all influenced by the electoral cycle. During the honeymoon period, even opposition agents may be more prone to offer a president support than during the run-up to new elections when every decision must be put in the context of electoral support. In the final months of a legislative term, therefore, we should expect heightened tensions, as agents strive to separate themselves from competitors.

For agents grouped into electoral alliances, there are two possible patterns. First, we might expect that In-groups will disperse, in order to gain the upper hand over their intraparty competitors.[6] Out groups face conflicting incentives. On the one hand they might see a value in coalescing in order to present the voters with a united opposition to which they can turn when they are angered with the current bums. But, like the In-group, they also face incentives to disperse in order to defeat their intraalliance partner.

FLEXIBILITY PATTERNS AND TESTS

Argentina: Majority Parties and Unity

The Argentine case presents two main unified parties, holding between them 87 percent of the legislative seats during the period that the data covers. At the time, in addition to the presidency, the Peronists held precisely one-half of the seats in the lower house (plus 54 percent of the Senate seats), and with the assured support of at least some of the smaller provincial parties, the party could act without much concern for the UCR.

This majority position, combined with the high levels of party unity, limited the incentives of the PJ to form cross-party coalitions. The database includes 78 votes that generated at least a modicum (10 percent) of dissent and on 72 of them the PJ and UCR lined up in opposition to one another.

A somewhat more conciliatory spin is also evident. First, there were six controversial votes (8 percent) on which the two main parties did join hands. Second, there were two additional votes that were not controversial. These do not appear to be inconsequential, however. One dealt with protecting workers in banks that were affected by privatization and the other dealt with the sugar industry. Third, though unity was generally high, the parties were not generally 100 percent unified. Thus on about half of the controversial votes (thirty-seven of seventy-eight), at least a few of the UCR members broke ranks and joined the PJ.

---

[6] This is the expected pattern whether or not the In-group expects to win the election. If they expect to win, each group wants to dominate the new government. If they expect to lose, each wants to throw as much blame on the other groups in order to shield themselves for the elections.

Finally, divisions in the PJ, sometimes manifested as abstentions, allowed the UCR to win some important votes. On a bill dealing with protection of the sugar industry, for example, the PJ voted 59 to 10 in favor of the bill, and lost the vote 68 to 78. Dissension also caused them to lose votes dealing with the autonomy of the Supreme Court, sanctions against striking railway workers, and other issues. Abstentions were also costly, as the leaders' inability to muster enough of their members caused the party to lose votes dealing with the privatization of ENTEL (the state telephone monopoly), pensions, and a vote to declare the U.S. ambassador persona non grata. While these votes were losses for the PJ leadership, they were victories for coalition politics, as the minority UCR was able to show some legislative victories.

Brazil: Ideological Positions, Cabinet Membership, and the Electoral Cycle

The Brazilian case allows tests of the effects of ideological positions, cabinet membership, and the electoral cycle and, unlike Argentina, illuminates a case where there is no clear majority and the legislative agents are only weakly tied to the president. In particular, it allows tests of whether leftist parties are included and the importance of cabinet membership to coalition formation. It also allows consideration of agents with varying degrees of unity and ideological predispositions.

Ins and Outs. Brazilian presidents' parties have held very few seats in the legislature. As noted in Chapter 3, in 1985 the vice-president-elect, José Sarney, took power when the president-elect, Tancredo Neves, died. His PMDB (to which he was a recent adherent) did hold a majority of the legislative seats in 1986, but divisions whittled this total down to 21 percent by 1990. When Fernando Collor de Melo won the presidency in 1990, his makeshift party, the PRN, won just 6 percent of the seats. Fernando Henrique Cardoso then came to power with his PSDB holding just 12 percent of the seats in 1994. This lack of a majority has always been exacerbated by the lax party discipline, and together these problems have heightened concern about executive-legislative stalemate in Brazil.

In spite of this lack of legislative support, Figueiredo and Limongi (2000) show that 78 percent of executive bills are enacted, including 825 of 830 budget bills between 1989 and 1997. Foweraker (1998) attributes this type of success to coalition politics.[7] Ames (2002) argues, however, that the statistics are misleading because they do not show the amendments and compromises won by the legislature. Either way, the statistics imply that instead of gridlock, majorities have formed to approve legislation.

---

[7] Foweraker's definition is based on both "participation in the presidential cabinet and party co-operation in the assembly" (1998, p. 665, n 65).

The data set covers most of two presidential terms. The first period pertains to the presidencies of Collor, who was impeached and removed from office, and his replacement, Itamar Franco. Neither of these presidents was an important party leader. Further, instead of composing his cabinet to generate legislative support, Collor filled it with cronies (Amorim Neto, 2002). That cabinet, hence, was dominated by non-partisans (thirteen of thirty) and the PFL (seven of thirty).[8] The PSDB, however, did take a turn in the Ministry of Foreign Affairs, and the PMDB began the administration in the Justice Ministry. Under Franco, independents continued to dominate the ministries, but the PFL and now the PSDB and PMDB were given prominent roles. Franco also gave the PT a job for about four months, in the Ministry of Federal Administration, and he placed a member of the leftist PDT in the Justice Department, though that person abandoned his partisan affiliation. Military personnel rounded out the cabinet membership.

The second part of the data set pertains to the first Cardoso administration, 1995–1998. Cardoso downplayed the independents and gave the predominant share of the ministries to politicians from his own PSDB (twelve of forty-three slots). The PFL got fewer ministries than it had had under Collor and Franco, but they won jobs that probably helped them curry favor with their northern constituents: namely those dealing with environment and water resources, as well as mines and energy. Somewhat surprisingly, they were also given control of the Social Assistance Ministry. The PMDB was given the Justice and Transportation Ministries, and the others were given to the PTB, the PPS, and the PPB (and the military). The two parties that most frequently opposed Collor, the PT and PDT, were shut out of the cabinet.

As explained earlier, while it is expected that cabinet membership should yield more cooperation among the In-agents, the ties among them will not be as strong as among agents included in a parliamentary cabinet. This implies that the PT and the PDT should generally oppose the other parties, but that their degree of cooperation should be higher during the Franco administration. The "cabinet hypothesis" would also predict an increased level of cooperation between the president's PSDB with the PFL and the PMDB during Cardoso's administration.

Ideological Positions. An alternative to the cabinet hypothesis is that ideology drives voting patterns. Lyne (1999) subscribes to this theory, as she found a much higher propensity for parties to form alliances with their ideological neighbors in the postdictatorhsip era than in the 1946–64 period.

The test of this theory will be based on the likelihood of the left and right parties to form coalitions and the degree to which the center votes with its

---

[8] I thank Octavio Amorim Neto for the Brazilian cabinet data. There were fifteen ministries, but most suffered attrition during Collor's shortened reign.

ideological neighbors to the left and the right. Deheza (1997) (and others) divide the Brazilian parties into three groups: including, among others, the PT and PDT on the left, the PSDB and PMDB in the center, and the PFL, PTB, PDS, and PL on the right. Hawkins and Morgenstern (unpublished manuscript), using the same database, show that none of the parties, including the PT, is especially cohesive when considering particular issues (where cohesion is defined by the degree of agreement among party members on important issues). This would suggest that while the PT might not be the most common partner in policy coalitions, there may be many issues on which the party would be a willing partner, at least if decisions were taken based on policy preferences alone.

Unity and the Electoral Cycle. While Chapter 3 concluded that the only Brazilian party that has been a consistently unified agent is the PT, other parties reached unity frequently. If these others unite on issues that are ideologically charged or that have a particular political relevance, we should expect to see a clearer separation of the left and the right, or the Ins and the Outs on unified votes. As elections near, however, there will be increased pressure on In-groups to separate from each other, thus leading to fewer accords among In-agents in the last part of the term. If, alternatively, the external hypothesis is false and left–right divisions continue to predominate, then the PT should join few coalitions with center or rightist parties, especially as elections near.

Tests. In order to discuss the multiple hypotheses, the first part of this section concentrates on which agents vote with the majority, leaving the issue of the composition of different policy coalitions for the second part. In addition to validating the external hypothesis, the primary conclusion is that while ideology clearly shapes policy coalitions, the composition of cabinets also plays a role in building support for legislation. I also find evidence for the role of electoral cycles in Brazil, in that cabinet membership is a more important determinant of the shape of policy coalitions at the beginning of the presidential term. As elections near, however, there appears to be more posturing among the agents represented in the cabinets, especially among those that are ideologically distinct. There are thus fewer, rather than more, policy coalitions that clearly separate the In-agents of the right from the Out-agents of the left as elections approach.

While interagent fights yield greater headlines, the data suggest that most bills generate substantial support, and that even those bills that are controversial enough to generate some opposition do not always divide the left and right. In the first time period, there were 211 votes of which 142 votes generated at least 10 percent opposition, while 357 of the 421 votes reached that level of controversy in the second period. Further, many of the votes reached the 10 percent opposition threshold but without generating

TABLE 6.2. *Likelihood of Voting with the Legislative Majority, Brazil*

Agent	Total in party[a]		No. joining majority on less than 60% of votes		No. joining majority on more than 80% of votes	
	1990–4	1995–8	1990–4	1995–8	1990–4	1995–8
Left						
PDT	31	20	3	19	0	0
PT	35	42	25	42	1	0
Center						
PMDB	109	83	1	20	94	32
PSDB	47	91	0	4	20	57
Right						
PFL	80	73	1	4	40	52
PTB	45	31	0	1	25	16
PPB	64	64	0	15	15	17
TOTAL	411	404	30	105	195	174

[a] Number of legislators identified in the database (at beginning of term).

Note: Those who voted fewer than ten times and those for whom the database does not include party identification were discounted. Placement of left, center, and right parties follows Deheza (1997) and Mainwaring (1999).

minimal winning coalitions, as the average (and median) margin on those bills was well over 100 votes. A focus on the PT provides further evidence. Across the two periods, at least 90 percent of the PT members supported 111 votes (55 in the first period, 56 in the second; about 22 percent of the total), lending around 27 votes on average. For these 111 votes, the average margin of victory was about 86 votes, implying that 30 percent of the legislators dissented from the majority. On many votes, however, there was much more dissension[9] thus showing that the PT sided with the majority on some very controversial decisions. These votes included issues such as price indexing, minimum wages, energy rates, constitutional plebiscites, and agricultural reform.[10] It does not appear correct, therefore, to label the PT inflexible.

These patterns are evident in Table 6.2. Discounting legislators who voted fewer than ten times, the table shows that few legislators consistently vote in opposition to the legislative majority. In the first time period, all but thirty Brazilian legislators voted with the majority on least 60 percent of roll-call votes. Since twenty-five of those thirty legislators belonged to the PT,

[9] In the second period, for example, ten of the fifty-five votes had a margin of victory of fewer than twenty, and twenty-two had a margin of fewer than fifty votes.

[10] The information on the content of the votes comes from the data provided by Figueiredo and Limongi (2000), which was cited in Chapter 5.

that party's members appear less flexible than others. Still, the average PT member did join the majority on 58 percent of bills. In the second period, the PT legislators were more frequently in opposition, as their average legislator voted with the majority on one-quarter of the controversial votes. In sum, the PT legislators are the least likely to join majority coalitions; they do join the majority on an impressive subset of bills.

Since the PT has been both removed from the presidents ideologically and generally excluded from cabinets, it is difficult to detect the independent impacts of ideology and cabinet membership. The important change in the PT's behavior between the two periods, however, may signify an independent impact of the cabinets to policy coalitions. Though the PT only served briefly in Franco's cabinets, the short inclusion implies that it was not eschewed in the same way it was during Cardoso's government. Amorim Neto (2002) argues that Cardoso used the cabinets to generate support, while this was not the prime concern of Collor and Franco. As such, while Cardoso may have built some support among the included parties, he may have undercut any support that the PT may have been willing to give.

Neither ideology nor cabinet membership, however, fully determined the shape of policy coalitions. During the Collor/Franco period, the PMDB was the largest party in the legislature, though it held just 22 percent of the seats. The rightist PFL was the next largest with 17 percent; thus, if the two parties could have maintained unity, they could have formed a solid center-right bloc and dominated the agenda. The PMDB had reasonable success in this exercise, as shown by the fact that 91 of their 109 legislators joined the majority on over 80 percent of the votes. The PFL was less solid, as only forty of their seventy-three members found themselves on the winning side that often. These numbers, of course, suggest that legislators from other parties were frequently in the majority also.

Though Cardoso's cabinet was more reflective of his ideological leanings, his attempt to construct a parliamentary-style cabinet was not completely successful, as the policy coalitions did not always reflect a government versus opposition framework. More members of his own PSDB supported the majority position than not, but divisions were frequent. The patterns were similar for the other two parties represented in his cabinet. In particular, only fifty-two of seventy-three members of the PFL and thirty-two of eighty-three members of the PMDB voted with the majority on 80 percent of the controversial bills.

While not particularly strong, this record stands in contrast with the two leftist parties that were excluded from Cardoso's cabinet, as none of their members are found in the far right column of the table. Still, one of the twenty members of the PDT did join the majority frequently, and the average PDT member joined the majority on about 30 percent of the votes. As noted, the average PT member also joined the winning side of about one-quarter of the controversial votes. This may indicate that the left is frequently excluded for

TABLE 6.3. *Voting with and against the Legislative Majority,*
Highly Unified Brazilian Parties

Party	With majority on contentious votes (% of votes)		Against majority on contentious votes (% of votes)	
	1991–95	1995–98	1991–95	1995–98
PDT	39.4	11.2	21.8	49.3
PT	39.4	15.4	54.2	82.1
PSDB	47.2	65.0	9.9	0.6
PMDB	55.6	19.0	0.7	0.0
PFL	49.3	74.2	9.9	2.0
PPB	45.1	11.5	9.2	0.0
PTB	40.8	58.0	4.9	0.6

Note: Percent of all contentious votes in which at least 90% of agent
members (i.e., Rice > 80) voted with and against the legislative majority
($n = 142$ for 1991–95, 357 for 1995–98). "Contentious" defined as votes
with at least 10% dissent (weight > 0.2).

ideological reasons, but because the leadership of the PT had not changed,
there is some evidence that the change in how cabinets were constructed
in the two periods had an independent effect on the shape of the policy
coalitions.

The next test changes the unit of observation to unified parties, considering only those votes on which either enough of a party's members were in
agreement or the leaders of those parties were able to bring enough pressure
to bear to yield Rice scores of at least 80. Table 6.3 gives further support
to the cabinet hypothesis by again showing a difference between the two
periods, especially with regards to the left. While in the first period, the PT
and the PDT were frequently unified and supportive of the majority, the PT
was unified and opposed to the majority on almost two-thirds of the votes in
the second period. For the parties of the center-right, there were also some
important changes, though not all in the expected direction. Neither the PFL,
PSDB, nor PMDB opposed the majority on a significant percentage of the
votes in either period, and Cardoso's strategy seemed to pay off with the
PFL and the PSDB, as these two parties were more likely to be unified and
supportive of the legislative majority in the second period. But, the other important party included in Cardoso's cabinet, the PMDB, was much less likely
to offer their unified support to the majority than during the Collor/Franco
period.

Turning now to which parties joined with one another in policy coalitions,
Table 6.4 reports the percentage of controversial votes in which a majority
of one party voted in the same direction as the majority of other parties. The

TABLE 6.4. *Two-Party Policy Coalitions*

	PT	PDT	PSDB	PMDB	PFL	PTB
			1991–1994			
PT						
PDT	18.8					
PSDB	60.9	57.2				
PMDB	37.7	77.5	73.2			
PFL	67.4	36.2	56.5	51.4		
PTB	22.5	89.1	57.2	78.3	39.9	
PPB	17.4	76.8	46.4	59.4	28.3	75.4
			1995–1998			
PT						
PDT	88.8					
PSDB	15.1	20.7				
PMDB	15.4	21.6	91.0			
PFL	9.8	15.7	92.4	89.9		
PTB	9.2	16.8	88.8	88.2	93.0	
PPB	9.5	17.9	85.7	87.4	89.1	90.8

Note: Defined as majority of each party voting in the same direction, on votes that generated at least 10% legislative dissent ($n = 139$ for 1991–94; $n = 357$ for 1995–98).

table shows that every party has found itself on the same side of issues with every other party; there are no pariah parties. This again supports the idea that all parties are participating in the decision process and voting in favor of bills that, in their view, improve the policy position.

Still, as previously, these data indicate an important change in the two periods with respect to the PT. During the first period, the PT was on the majority side frequently and even voted with the rightist PFL on 93 of the 139 controversial votes (67 percent). While the PT continued to find itself voting with all comers in the second period, it joined the PFL on only one of every ten controversial votes and was not consistently voting with any of the other In-parties either.

Tables 6.5a and 6.5b consider the two-party policy coalitions taking unity into account. Table 6.5a shows little difference between the two terms with respect to the PT–PFL relationship, in that when the two parties were both unified (Rice > 80), they wound up on the same side on only 3.6 percent of the controversial votes in the first period and 2.5 percent of the controversial votes in the second. The number of policy coalitions between the PT and the PSDB, however, drops precipitously from one term to the next. Among the parties represented in the cabinet, there is a notable increase in the frequency of PFL–PSDB policy coalitions, but because the PMDB was unified so

TABLE 6.5a. *Unified Two-Party Policy Coalitions, Brazil*

	% of votes					
	Unified	PT	PDT	PSDB	PMDB	PFL
			1991–1995			
PT	95.0					
PDT	62.6	48.2				
PSDB	56.1	36.7	29.5			
PMDB	55.4	17.3	22.3	29.5		
PFL	59.0	3.6	7.9	17.3	32.4	
PPB	53.2	5.0	10.8	13.7	25.2	36.7
			1995–1998			
PT	98.3					
PDT	61.6	57.1				
PSDB	66.4	3.9	5.3			
PMDB	19.3	1.7	3.4	18.2		
PFL	76.8	2.5	3.6	58.8	17.9	
PPB	12.0	1.7	2.2	9.8	4.2	10.6

Note: The first column indicates percent of contentious votes in which the party achieved a Rice score of at least 80. Other entries are the percentage of all contentious votes in which the two parties were unified and voted in the same direction. "Contentious" defined as votes with at least 10% dissent (weight > 0.2) (*n* = 139 for first period, 357 for second).

TABLE 6.5b. *Unified Two-Party Conflict, Brazil*

	% of votes				
	PT	PDT	PSDB	PMDB	PFL
		1991–1995			
PDT	10.1				
PSDB	16.5	9.4			
PMDB	33.8	10.8	6.5		
PFL	51.1	28.8	13.7	0.7	
PPB	45.3	23.7	12.2	4.3	0.7
		1995–1998			
PDT	4.2				
PSDB	60.2	35.3			
PMDB	17.1	7.8	0.0		
PFL	72.8	44.3	0.3	0.0	
PPB	9.8	3.4	0.0	0.0	0.0

Note: The entries indicate the percentage of all contentious votes in which the two parties were unified and voted in opposing directions. "Contentious" defined as votes with at least 10% dissent (weight > 0.2) (*n* = 139 for first period, 357 for second).

infrequently in the second period, there was a decrease in the number of policy coalitions that joined the PMDB with either the PFL or PSDB. As a result, though these three parties always voted together when they were unified, this only happened on 60 of the 357 controversial votes.

Table 6.5b gives another window on this dynamic by displaying data where two unified parties lined up against one another. It shows that while the PT and PFL only opposed one another on half of the votes in the first period, they were in opposition to one another on over 70 percent of the votes in the second. Similarly, the percentage of votes in which the PT and PSDB opposed one another rose from 16.5 percent to 60.2 percent across the two time periods. There was a concomitant decrease in the percentage of votes that generated conflict with the alliances. That is, unlike the first period, in the second period there were almost no votes in which members of the PSDB, PMDB, or PFL unified and found themselves voting against one of the other unified parties represented in the cabinet. Likewise the percentage of votes in which the PT and PDT opposed one another fell from 10.1 percent to 4.2 percent.

While there is an obvious interaction between ideology and the makeup of cabinets (at least in the Cardoso period), the data suggest that these two variables also have independent impacts on policy coalitions. On the one hand, the marked difference in behavior across the two terms, which is especially apparent in the patterns of conflict among the parties (Table 6.5b), suggests that cabinets can play an important role. But, since even under Cardoso the frequency with which even two parties represented in the cabinet unified and voted together was rather small (Table 6.5a), it appears that interests and ideology generally trump cabinet membership in explaining voting patterns.

One other piece of evidence points to the importance of ideology in structuring the policy coalitions in the Brazilian legislature. Using Poole and Rosenthal's static model (W-NOMINATE scores), the Brazilian data proved surprisingly organized along a left–right dimension, as graphically demonstrated in Figures 6.1a and 6.1b.[11] For the first period, 87 percent of the legislators' responses were correctly classified by a single dimension.[12] Organizing the legislators by their individual scores clearly shows a partisan division, with the PFL at one extreme and the PT at the other. The data do

[11] For more information on W-NOMINATE scores, see Keith Poole's "data download page" at his website, http://voteview.uh.edu/. I thank him for the great assistance in generating the data discussed here and in the Chilean section. The W-NOMINATE scores spatially locate legislators within a particular legislature, as opposed to the dynamic model, which I applied to the U.S. data in Chapter 5, that is comparable over time. The Brazilian and Chilean data series are too short to apply the dynamic model, but Poole and Rosenthal (1997) note that the two scales are highly correlated.

[12] In the analysis, 462 of 543 legislators and 179 of 212 votes were scalable. The proportional reduction in error (APRE) = 0.481 and the geometric mean probability (GMP) = 0.762. See Poole and Rosenthal (1997) for details.

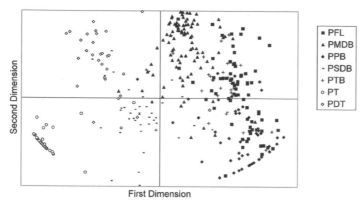

FIGURE 6.1a. W-NOMINATE scores for the Brazilian House, 1991–1994.

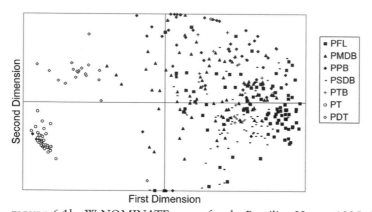

FIGURE 6.1b. W-NOMINATE scores for the Brazilian House, 1995–1998.

show, as expected, that there are inconsistencies within the parties. The PFL, for example, has some legislators who earn W-NOMINATE scores at close to the absolute extreme (−1) and others who are much closer to the center of the scale (0). Similarly, the PSDB members range from −0.86 to +0.11 and the PMDB from −0.79 to +0.4. Again, only the PT maintained its legislators in a short band, from +0.76 to +0.91.

The patterns were quite similar for the second period, with perhaps more heterogeneity at the right end of the scale. Now the PFL shared the extreme spaces with a number of PPB legislators. The PMDB was still spread about, but a good number of them were concentrated just to the right of the center mark. The PSDB now looks like the centrist party, with scores ranging from −0.4 to +0.4 (median 0.15, s.d. 0.2).

It is important to note that the data indicate a second dimension to Brazilian politics as well. Although some parties do cluster on either the top or the bottom of the graph, this dimension cleaves most parties.

Until we have more information about the actual votes, it is not possible
to determine the substantive meaning of this division.

Multivariate Test: Cabinets, Ideology, and the Electoral Cycle. As a final test of the hypotheses about ideology and cabinet membership, as well
as a check of the role of electoral cycles, I conducted a multivariate test.
The test consists of a logit analysis, with the dependent variable equal
to 1 when two parties, at a minimum of 90 percent unity (Rice > 80),
voted together on a particular bill, and 0 if they opposed one another.
Votes where either of the two parties did not achieve 90 percent unity, or
where there was not at least 10 percent of the full legislature in opposition, were thrown out. This resulted in 3,384 dyads (1,750 positive and
1,634 negative) from which to test the importance of the three independent
variables.

    In order to test the importance of alliance membership, each vote was
coded for the parties' membership in the cabinet. This yields two variables,
Both In and *Both Out*, the first of which is set to 1 if both parties were in the
cabinet and 0 otherwise and the second is equal to 1 if neither party held a
cabinet post and 0 otherwise.[13] To test the importance of ideology, I coded the
difference in the average left–right ideology scores of the parties as discussed
in Chapter 5. The expectation is that these two variables would work in
opposing ways; ideological differences should decrease the likelihood of a
policy agreement, but including or excluding both agents from the cabinet
should increase it.

    Finally, as a test of how electoral tensions affect the likelihood of policy
coalitions, I coded when in the electoral cycle each vote was taken. The
first hypothesis was that the Ins and Outs would separate themselves in the
run-up to elections, and the alternative was that the In-groups would break
apart at that time. This hypothesis thus required that the timing variable be
interacted with cabinet membership. Further, because the hypothesis does
not imply a monotonic decline in interalliance policy coalitions (after the
initial period when the president consolidates power there may be a relatively
stable period before the expected decline in the run up to elections) I have
used two dummy variables to indicate whether the vote took place in the
first quintile of the electoral cycle (Honeymoon) or the last quintile (End
of Term). If the polarizing hypothesis is correct, the regression should yield
positive coefficients for the interactions of End of Term with Both In and Both
Out, to indicate a greater likelihood of policy coalitions between parties that
are both in or both out of the cabinet at that time. If, alternatively, either the
Ins or the Outs break apart as elections approach, the coefficient would be
negative.

---

[13] I also ran a model in which there was just one dummy variable, equal to 1 if either both
were in the cabinet or both were out. The results were very similar.

TABLE 6.6a. *Logit Estimates of Brazilian Policy Coalition Formation*

Variable	Coefficient	Std. Error	Z–Score
Both In	3.73	0.18	20.80
Both Out	2.47	0.14	17.60
Ideological Distance	−0.84	0.05	−17.86
Honeymoon * Both In	1.56	1.03	1.51
End of Term * Both In	−1.66	0.61	−2.72
Honeymoon * Both Out	−0.79	0.39	−2.01
End of Term * Both Out	−0.14	0.48	−0.29
Honeymoon	0.40	0.16	2.51
End of Term	0.41	0.23	1.82
Constant	0.44	0.10	4.47

Note: $n = 3,384$; log likelihood, −1354.6; correctly predicted = 80.6%; model chi-squared 1978.11, $p < .0001$; pseudo $R^2 = 0.42$.

TABLE 6.6b. *Substantive Impacts*

Variable	Values								
Both In	0	0	0	1	1	1	0	0	0
Both Out	0	0	0	0	0	0	1	1	1
Ideological Distance	.2	1.7	4.45	0.2	1.7	4.45	0.2	1.7	4.45
End of Term	1	1	1	1	1	1	1	1	1
Constant	1	1	1	1	1	1	1	1	1
P(Policy Coalition)	.665	.360	.053	.940	.816	.305	.953	.853	.366
Both In	0	0	0	1	1	1	0	0	0
Both Out	0	0	0	0	0	0	1	1	1
Ideological Distance	.2	1.7	4.45	0.2	1.7	4.45	0.2	1.7	4.45
End of Term (& Honeymoon = 0)	0	0	0	0	0	0	0	0	0
Constant	1	1	1	1	1	1	1	1	1
P(Policy Coalition)	.568	.272	.036	.982	.939	.605	.940	.815	.305

Tables 6.6a and 6.6b portray the logit results. They show the validity of the first two hypotheses, indicating that policy coalitions and membership in the executive cabinet are strong predictors of policy coalitions. Converting these coefficients into substantive impacts implies that the two alliance variables are highly influential (Table 6.6b). When either Both In or Both Out is equal to 1 (i.e., either both parties have cabinet ministers or neither has one), the probability of the two parties forming a policy coalition is over 80 percent when the ideological distance is set at its mean (1.7). This more than doubles the probability of a coalition between two parties that have a

similar ideological division but only one holds a cabinet seat. The ideological distance variable also has a large impact, especially at the upper end of the scale. As it moves from 0.2 to 1.7 (the minimum value to the mean), the probability of a policy coalition drops by about 10 percent when the two parties are on the same side of the cabinet, but by about 30 percent if they are on opposite sides. As the ideological divide between the two parties grows from the mean to the maximum value, the probability of a coalition drops sharply, even if both parties are included in the coalition. The table only shows the maximum value (4.45), but this effect becomes quite noticeable when the ideological distance is set at anything over two (for which there are over 700 cases in the data set). Further, the importance of ideology relative to cabinet membership grows if we take into account the finding that the End of Term variable is only statistically significant when interacted with Both In. Recalculating the probabilities of a policy coalition with the assumption that the coefficient on End of Term is 0 yields a much greater change as the ideological distance value moves from 0.2 to 1.7 (going from 0.90 to 0.72 if End of Term * Both In is set at 1). In sum, the statistical analysis suggests that cabinet membership boosts cooperation somewhat, but it is insufficient to overcome the divisive pulls between ideologically disparate parties.

The time variable has a very limited effect, except in the cases where both parties are in the coalition and ideology is at its maximum (or anything over 2). The sixth column of the table indicates that the probability of a coalition between parties with the maximum level of ideological difference is only 30 percent at the end of the term, but 60 percent during the middle of the term. This indicates that to the degree that cabinet membership helps to overcome ideological differences, it is only effective until electoral pressures mount. On the other hand, parties that are not far apart ideologically are slightly *less* likely to vote together as elections near, which, as the alternative hypothesis suggests, could result from the parties trying to distinguish themselves from their intracamp rivals for the elections. This refutes the polarizing hypothesis that would predict greater intraalliance voting as the elections approach.

This finding is also evident in simple bivariate relationships. Throughout the seven-year period, the PT and PMDB teamed up 30 times and opposed one another 108 times (with the requisite amount of partisan unity and legislative opposition). Seven of these 138 votes took place in the last quintile of the electoral cycle, and two of the seven votes found the two parties cooperating.

These numbers are similar for the PSDB–PT dyad. The only dyad where the ideological polarization does manifest itself is between the PT and the PFL. Those two parties voted together on 14 of 345 votes, none of which took place in the last 20 percent of the electoral cycle. Because the probability of a PFL/PT alliance is so small generally, this is scant evidence that the electoral cycle leads to a marked increase in left–right polarization.

Chile: Ins, Outs, Ideology, and the Electoral Cycle

The Chilean case allows further tests of how ideology and membership in the president's governing coalition weigh on policy coalitions. It also provides another example of a country where a mood of political conciliation and cooperation have seemingly taken hold.

As argued previously, this political moderation is a stark change from the pre-Pinochet period. As Scully (1995) describes, in that period "ideological escalation made compromise extremely unlikely, paving the way for an eventual breakdown of democracy" (p. 121). But in contrast to the "inflexible and polarized party system [of the 1970s], the late 1980s see the right seeking (albeit haltingly) political legitimacy, the left recommitted to procedural democracy, and the chastened political center searching for alliance partners" (pp. 127–8). The main expectation, therefore, is to uncover a general commitment to compromise and inclusion.

While the external hypothesis expects an important level of cooperation among legislators of all stripes, the continued division of the political system into two visible electoral alliances each with identifiable parties, leads to further hypotheses about the shape of the policy coalitions. First, the importance of the electoral alliances in Chile suggests that, unlike Brazil, there should be a more defined pattern of Ins versus Outs. As argued in Chapter 3, there are potentially great electoral costs in leaving the electoral alliances, and adhesion to the governing alliance has also meant representation in the cabinet. This suggests that membership in the Chilean electoral alliances necessitates a greater degree of compromise than simply joining a president's cabinet as in Brazil. The implied hypothesis is that membership in the electoral alliance should generally override ideological concerns in determining policy coalitions.

Second, while the primary hypothesis is that membership in the In-group should dominate over ideology in determining policy coalitions, the Chilean case allows a direct test of the importance of ideology. In particular, since the In-group is more clearly defined, the data allow us to observe the proclivity with which the ideological adjacent parties from across the alliance lines (i.e., the DC from the Concertación and the RN from the Right) form coalitions.

The ideology and electoral alliances variables are, of course, conditioned by the level of unity. The alliance unity scores of around 75 first imply that there are an important number of policy coalitions that form across the alliance boundaries. At the same time, the higher unity scores for most of the parties indicates that it is not always just a few legislators that jump ship, but that unified parties sometimes vote against their alliance partners. The data here allows us to test which legislators or unified parties are most prone to cross alliance lines. As indicated previously, when the parties are unified the expectation is that the DC and the RN will be more prone to break with their electoral partners than others. We might also see alliances of the DC and UDI, as their members align on religious matters. When the parties are unable to maintain unity, we should expect that members of these same three parties will be those that are most tempted to join their ideological neighbors from across the aisle.

Third, while the time period covered by the Chilean House data set is short, it does cross a presidential and a legislative election, and thus both the House and Senate data allow another test of the impact of electoral cycles. The Brazilian case belied the hypothesis that elections increase interalliance tensions and showed instead heightened intraalliance tensions. We might also expect greater tensions within, instead of among, the left and right alliances in Chile, at least in the run-up to legislative elections. Finally, while not part of the general hypotheses, the data allow an investigation of the role of the "institutional" senators, who were created by Pinochet to help the right maintain a majority in the Senate.

Data and Tests. Before turning to whether ideology or membership in the alliances takes precedence, the first part of this section provides evidence in support of the external hypothesis, that a spirit of inclusiveness frequently prevails in the Chilean legislature. The subsequent discussion then turns to the issues of membership in the electoral alliances, ideology, and electoral cycles. The primary conclusions are that membership in the electoral alliances is a more important determinant of the vote than is left–right ideology, but there is a substantial degree of cooperation among legislators and unified agents from across the alliance lines as well. These conclusions are clearest with regards to the lower house, but the same general patterns appear to shape voting in the Senate as well.

Perhaps the best evidence for the spirit of inclusiveness is the preponderance of highly consensual votes. Of the 547 issues that were put to a voice vote and gained the requisite quorum[14] in the House, 308 yielded near unanimity, and most of these do not appear to be simple procedural questions. A chance sample of three of these votes yielded bills covering the "constitution and function of religious organizations," a regional development project, and economic benefits for military personnel and the reorganization of the interior (hacienda) ministry.[15]

Tables 6.7 and 6.8 show that while there is a pattern of Ins versus Outs on the other 239 House votes, many of these bills did not separate the majority Concertación from the minority rightist alliance. Table 6.7 first shows that

---

[14] Though certain types of legislation require greater attendance, the quorum for voting on regular legislation in either house in Chile is just one-third of legislators.

[15] Bill numbers: 340-20-01, 339-34-03, 339-48-01. The first two numbers indicate the session number and the last is the vote number of the particular day.

TABLE 6.7. *Likelihood of Voting with the Legislative Majority, Chile*

Agent	In analysis		No. joining majority on less than 60% of votes[a]		No. joining majority on at least 80% of votes	
	House	Senate[b]	House	Senate	House	Senate
Concertación[c]	70	33	1	0	61	13
DC	37	20	1	0	32	10
PS	15	5	0	0	14	1
PPD	16	4	0	0	13	1
Others	2	4	0	0	2	1
Right	50	27	42	15	1	2
RN	30	11	24	5	1	0
UDI	14	9	13	6	0	1
Other	6	7	5	4	0	1
Institutionals/Life		17		4; 3		0; 3

Note: $n = 73$ contentious votes for House that had quorum; 81 for the Senate. "Contentious" defined as votes with at least 10% dissent (weight > 0.2). Data here include only May 22, 1997, to January 21, 1998, for House and full Senate series (1992–98).

[a] The denominator in the calculations is the number of votes in which the legislator participated. Abstentions, absenteeism, etc., are excluded.

[b] Includes different senators across two time periods. For the institutionals, the first number indicates the votes during the period 1992–97 and the second indicates the votes in 1998.

[c] Two Concertación legislators changed parties, one from the PS to the PPD and one independent joined the PS. The statistics reflect their final party affiliation.

TABLE 6.8. *Voting with and against the Legislative Majority, Highly Unified Chilean Agents*

Agent	With majority on contentious votes (% of votes)		Against majority on contentious votes (% of votes)	
	House	Senate	House	Senate
Concertación	62.8	59.3	0.8	18.5
DC	68.2	63.0	2.5	19.8
PS	72.4	60.5	7.1	28.4
PRSD	73.6	38.3	10.9	17.3
PPD	65.7	59.3	5.4	21.0
Right	21.3	24.7	35.6	13.6
RN	29.7	25.9	36.8	17.3
UDI	26.4	50.6	55.6	33.3
Institutionals[a]	23.3; 12.5		8.2; 0	

Note: $n = 239$ contentious votes in House, 81 in Senate. "Contentious" defined as votes with at least 10% dissent (weight > 0.2).

[a] Statistics indicate periods before and after the new senators took office in 1998; $n = 73$ for first period (including two ties), 8 for second period.

while almost 90 percent (61 of 70) of Concertación diputados voted with the majority on at least 80 percent of the bills or motions, 16 percent (8 of 50) of the rightist members were on the winning side on at least 60 percent of these votes. At the party level, Table 6.7 shows that members of the RN were more likely to vote with the winning side than the UDI, and members of the PS were less likely than members of other Concertación parties to vote with the losers. Moving to the level of unified parties, Table 6.8 shows that at least one of the rightist parties was on the winning side on about 30 percent of the votes that had enough political content or leadership pressure to both generate some dissent and unite the members of one or both of the rightist parties. The parties of the Concertación were both unified and on the winning side about twice as often.

Recall that unlike the House where the Concertación has held a clear majority (though it dwindled significantly in 2001), the right has had an advantage in the Senate where the institutional senators have held the balance of power. This contrasting agent system has resulted in distinct voting patterns. At one level, the inclusive spirit does not seem as prevalent in the Senate, as only eleven of eighty votes were highly consensual, and more than half of the remaining votes had very small winning margins.[16] At the same time, however, the votes did not as clearly divide the Concertación and the rightist alliance. While over 80 percent (forty-two of fifty) of the rightist diputados failed to support the majority on at least 60 percent of the votes, almost half of the rightist senators (twelve of twenty-seven) found themselves in the majority on 60 percent or more of the votes. Likewise, while almost 90 percent of Concertación diputados voted with the majority on most votes, the comparable figure in the Senate is under 50 percent (thirteen of thirty-three).

The search for cross-alliance cooperation seems to have broken down somewhat after the new designated senators took office in 1998. This date marked an important change, since the senators who served until 1998 were appointed by Pinochet and those serving the succeeding term were appointed by President Frei.[17] Frei did not have free rein in his choice, as the Chilean Constitution still allowed Pinochet into the Senate and mandated that the other designees include two ex-Supreme Court justices, an ex-comptroller general, four ex-military generals, an ex-university president, and an ex-cabinet minister.[18] Most of the people who qualified had been appointed to their original posts by Pinochet, but Frei was successful in moderating the rightist influence.

[16] High consensus defined as weights of less than 0.2; narrow margins defined as weights greater than 0.8. Weighting system defined in Chapter 3.

[17] Because these senators are given eight-year terms, Patricio Aylwin, president from 1990 to 1993, was unable to make any appointments.

[18] As noted, Frei then joined the Senate as a life-member in 2000.

The time series is very short for the post-1998 transition in the Senate, but if the few votes are indicative, they show that at least a few of the institutionals are much more willing to join legislative majorities than before. Further, the statistics also indicate an important shift in the other parties. Ten of the fourteen members of the DC supported the majority position on every vote in which they participated in 1998 (that is in the database), three UDI members lost on every vote, and five of six RN members were on the losing side at least 60 percent of the time.

Table 6.8 again considers the likelihood of joining the legislative majority but changes the unit of analysis to the unified agent. For the House, it again shows that while the divisions among the electoral alliances are quite evident, there is also a substantial degree of cooperation among House agents on different sides of the electoral alliance lines. First, when united, the UDI proved willing to vote with members of the governing coalition on 26.4 percent of the controversial votes, and the fact that the PS, PRSD, and PPD only united on about 70 percent of the votes implies that many of their members crossed the electoral alliance border on multiple occasions. Moreover, these extra votes helped a united (but minority) right to win 21 percent of the votes that had at least a modicum of controversy. A small sample of these votes showed that they were not insignificant bills.[19] In short, at least on some issues, all parties look like potential partners for policy coalitions. At the same time, when their members unify, the Concertación parties seldom find themselves on the losing side of an issue. The rightist parties, alternatively, are much more frequently found on the losing side, but they also unite to support the majority on about one-quarter of the roll calls.

The Senate, again, provides a slightly different picture. As a result of the institutionals holding the swing votes, the Senate parties of the Concertación lost a significant number of votes. The alignment of the right and the institutionals against the Concertación did not emerge frequently, however, as no united Concertación party lost more than 28.4 percent of the votes.

In focusing on the political affiliations of the individual legislators, Tables 6.7. and 6.8 also provide the first clues about the roles of ideology and membership in the electoral alliances. It is difficult to separate these two variables because the four parties in the Concertación are all ideologically situated to the left of the UDI and RN. But, we can begin to separate the two variables by focusing on the DC, as it holds the strategic median policy

---

[19] The four that I sampled dealt with an investigatory commission dealing with forest fires (339-40-11), debts of mayors and municipal corporations (339-40-09), scholarships (339-54-02), and the convocation of a special session to deal with exchange and interest rates (339-59-02).

position both in terms of the left–right scale (as displayed in Chapter 5) as well as its generally accepted economic and religious positions. The ideological hypothesis would thus predict that members of the DC should be more prone to join the rightist parties than members of the PS and PPD. Further, according to that hypothesis, as the party at the ideological median, the DC should always be a part of winning coalitions. Alternatively, if pork, regionalism, or other concerns override left–right ideology, then members of the other Concertación parties should frequently cross the alliance lines as well. In finding that a greater percentage of DC legislators were commonly found in the minority than were PS legislators (13.5 percent versus 6.7 percent), and that the proportion of PPD legislators who crossed into the minority was about the same (18.8 percent), Table 6.7 gives more support to the alternative. Table 6.8 yields a similar story. While the DC won virtually all votes on which it unified, so did the other parties of the Concertación. If left–right ideology was driving these votes, then the PS and PPD should have lost frequently to policy coalitions joining the DC, RN, and UDI. These statistics, in sum, suggest many votes counterpose the two electoral alliances, and that left–right ideology is a poor predictor of the policy alliances on other occasions. Thus, while we cannot discount the importance of ideology in the formation of the alliances, there is evidence that membership in an alliance can override ideological considerations.

Again, the picture is murkier in the Senate where the evidence is scant for either the left–right or the electoral alliance hypotheses. Although the designated senators who served until 1998 held the swing votes and were hand-picked by Pinochet, that group did not usually form a unified bloc and seldom helped the right to control voting outcomes (as evidenced by their having united and won only 23.3 percent of the votes and lost on another 8.2 percent during that period). The two electoral alliances are somewhat apparent in that the percentage of votes in which the Concertación parties (excepting the PRSD) joined the majority was consistent, but the percentage of votes in which they opposed the majority showed some variance, and the two member parties of the rightist alliance showed quite distinct patterns. As a result of its members maintaining unity more often, the UDI was more frequently opposed to the majority than the RN, but the UDI also joined the majority much more often than did its electoral partner. Next, while either the left–right or the electoral alliance hypothesis would predict that the RN, UDI, and institutionals should have shut out the Concertación parties, the Concertación parties formed a part of many more majorities than did the institutionals or the parties of the rightist alliance. Last, while the left–right hypothesis would predict that the DC would more easily find voting partners with which to form majorities than would the PS or PPD, these latter parties were as frequently in the majority as was the DC.

These same patterns are apparent when considering the other indicator of flexibility, the propensity for an agent (parties or electoral alliances in this case) to join with other agents in policy coalitions, thus bolstering the conclusions about the factors driving the trends. If membership in either electoral alliance helps structure the vote, then most policy coalitions will form within the two electoral coalitions. If, alternatively, ideology structures the vote, then ideological neighbors should be as willing to join with one another as vote with their electoral partners. Again, the key party is the Christian Democrats, which is a member of the Concertación but ideologically adjacent to the Renovación Nacional on economic issues and the UDI on religious matters.

When considering the voting coalitions of the majority of a party's members, Table 6.9 first gives more evidence of the willingness of Chilean legislators to reach accords regardless of party or coalition affiliation. Even the two parties from the extreme sides of the ideological spectrum, the PS and the UDI, joined together on about 20 percent of the controversial votes in the House and 30 percent in the Senate. With relation to the importance of left–right ideology in determining the voting patterns, Table 6.9 shows that there is no greater propensity for the DC to join with the rightist parties than for the other Concertación parties to form such policy coalitions. The table shows, in particular, that each of the Concertación parties has joined with the RN on about 30 percent of the votes and with the UDI on about 20 percent. At the same time, because the RN is a more frequent coalition partner for members of the Concertación than is the UDI, there is some evidence that the UDI's more extreme policy position does render it a less-likely policy coalition partner.[20]

When unity is added to the equation, there is a more apparent pattern of policy coalitions forming within the electoral alliances. As Table 6.10a shows, on about 60 percent of the controversial House votes, at least one party in the Concertación was both unified and paired with at least one other unified Concertación party. In the rightist alliance, the RN and the UDI were both unified and in agreement on about 50 percent of the votes. And, on only between 10 and 15 percent of the votes did a unified Concertación party join with a unified party of the right.

Table 6.10b shows, however, that the spirit of inclusiveness is still evident, as the infrequent cross-alliance policy coalitions did not always translate into cross-alliance conflict. On half of the votes, a united Concertación aligned against the UDI, but the two electoral alliances faced off on only one-third of the votes.

---

[20] As explained in Chapter 5, the UDI does not display a more extreme position on the left–right scale in the survey, probably as a result of their members' attempts to portray their party as appealing to the poor and generally centrist. On specific questions regarding economic policy or religion, however, the UDI generally comes out more extreme than the RN.

TABLE 6.9. *Policy Coalitions and Majority of Agents, Chile*

	Conc	PS	PPD	PRSD	DC	Right	RN	UDI
				Lower House (% of all votes)				
Concertación								
PS	88.3							
PPD	90.8	85.8						
PRSD	84.1	77.0	81.6					
DC	93.7	83.3	84.5	79.9				
Right	29.7	28.0	28.9	26.4	27.2			
RN	33.5	32.2	32.2	30.1	31.0	85.8		
UDI	21.3	20.9	20.1	16.7	19.7	87.0	73.2	
				Senate (% of all votes)				
Concertación								
PS	85.5							
PPD	73.5	74.7						
PR	51.8	43.4	34.9					
DC	97.6	83.1	71.1	50.6				
Right	21.7	20.5	19.3	15.7	24.1			
RN	24.1	19.3	18.1	15.7	26.5	84.3		
UDI	31.3	30.1	26.5	18.1	33.7	63.9	59.0	
Institutionals	32.5	26.5	24.1	16.9	34.9	71.1	62.7	62.7

Note: Percent of all contentious votes (at least 10% dissent) in which the majority of each agent voted together; *n* = 238 where *weight* = 0.2 in House, 03 in Senate (including two ties).

Though there are many interelectoral alliance policy coalitions, these tables confirm the preceding findings that left–right ideology is less important than membership in the electoral alliances in determining policy coalitions. As Table 6.9 also shows, the DC was not only far more prone to side with other Concertación members than with parties on the right, but the PPD and the PS were also slightly more likely to wind up voting with the RN and UDI than was the DC.[21]

The patterns are largely borne out in the Senate as well. Tables 6.10a and 6.10b show that while the degree of cooperation between the UDI and RN was not particularly high (joining one another on only 28 percent of the votes and opposing one another on 10 percent), the PS, PPD, and DC almost always sided together when they were unified (though again the small PRSD was less friendly to its coalition partners).[22] As in the House, the DC

[21] Taking the 173 votes on which the DC was unified, the DC's 24 coalitions with the RN and 20 with the UDI convert into coalitions on 14 percent of the votes with the RN and 12 percent with the UDI. This compares to 18 percent and 14 percent for the PS, 15 percent and 11 percent for the PPD, and 13 percent and 17 percent for the PRSD.

[22] There were two PRSD diputados from 1994 to 1997 and four thereafter.

TABLE 6.10a. *Unified Two-Agent Policy Coalitions, Chile*

	% Unified	Conc	PS	PPD	PRSD	DC	Right	RN	UDI
			Lower House (% of all votes)						
Concertación	63.6								
PS	79.5	59.4							
PPD	71.5	57.3	62.8						
PRSD	89.5	57.3	63.6	61.5					
DC	70.7	59.8	57.3	54.8	60.7				
Right	56.9	0.0	7.1	4.2	8.4	3.8			
RN	66.5	6.7	14.6	11.3	15.9	10.0	52.7		
UDI	82.4	3.8	11.3	7.5	11.7	7.9	54.0	51.0	
			Senate (% of all votes)						
Concertación	78.3								
PS	95.2	73.5							
PPD	97.6	68.7	73.5						
PRSD	100.0	39.8	43.4	34.9					
DC	83.1	75.9	73.5	66.3	42.2				
Right	38.6	1.2	1.2	1.2	3.6	1.2			
RN	43.4	4.8	6.0	6.0	4.8	6.0	32.5		
UDI	88.0	18.1	20.5	20.5	16.9	22.9	33.7	27.7	
Institutionals	31.3	3.6	4.8	3.6	3.6	7.2	15.7	13.3	25.3

generally voted with other members of the Concertación. It very seldom voted with a united RN, but it did vote with the UDI on about 18 percent of bills, which in part reflects the greater degree of unity of the UDI, but may also reflect the common religious base. The infrequency of RN-DC alliances, however, again suggests that left–right ideology does a poor job in explaining policy coalitions. A final sign of the importance of the electoral alliances is the almost complete lack of votes in which unified parties separated from their electoral partners. For example, a unified RN joined most of the Concertación (Rice > 80) on only four votes, three of which yielded significant abstentionism among the UDI members and the remaining vote split the UDI members almost in half.

The conclusions about the predominant importance of the electoral alliances rather than ideology are supported by an analysis of the W-NOMINATE scores, but those statistics also offer some evidence for ideology-based voting. The graphs in Figures 6.2a and 6.2b for the Lower House break the time series into two pieces based on the legislative election of 1997.[23] They clearly show a divide between the two electoral alliances, as

[23] The elections were held in December 1997, and new legislators took office in January 1998. The first graph is based on 216 votes; the second, on 370 votes.

TABLE 6.10b. *Unified Two-Agent Conflict, Chile*

	Conc	PS	PPD	PRSD	DC	Right	RN	UDI
			Lower House (% of all votes)					
Concertación								
PS	1.7							
PPD	0.4	1.3						
PRSD	0.8	5.0	1.3					
DC	1.3	3.3	2.1	2.9				
Right	33.5	37.2	33.9	39.3	36.8			
RN	34.3	38.1	35.1	40.6	37.7	3.3		
UDI	50.6	55.2	50.2	59.8	54.0	3.3	6.3	
			Senate (% of all votes)					
Concertación								
PS	1.2							
PPD	1.2	2.4						
PRSD	1.2	3.6	3.6					
DC	2.4	3.6	6.0	2.4				
Right	31.3	34.9	28.9	18.1	31.3			
RN	30.1	34.9	28.9	20.5	31.3	1.2		
UDI	44.6	53.0	47.0	32.5	44.6	7.2	9.6	
Institutionals	19.3	25.3	24.1	19.3	19.3	0.0	2.4	2.4

Note: See description following Table 6.5b. In the bottom part of Table 6.9 for cases such as DC–Concertación or RN–Right, the figures indicate the votes in which a unified party voted against all other members in their alliance. $n = 239$ for House, $n = 83$ for Senate, including two ties.

all but one member of the Concertación are far to the left of all members of the rightist alliance. But, at least in the first period the DC legislators separate themselves from the other members of the Concertación, and the RN and UDI maintain clearly separable voting patterns. The UDI members parallel DC legislators on the vertical axis, and the RN is clearly more centrist on the horizontal axis.

The graph of the Senate data in Figure 6.2c is based solely on the 1992–7 data. As in Figures 6.2a and 6.2b, the data considers only those legislators who voted with enough frequency to determine their coordinates; thus, for example, there are only three UDI members and six institutionals in the graph. The remaining fifty-one senators, however, clearly divided on left–right lines, with not one member from either electoral alliance landing on the "wrong" side of the graph, and all the institutional senators siding with the rightist alliance. Within the alliances it is possible to detect spatial positions that separate the parties, but there is a significant degree of cross-over.

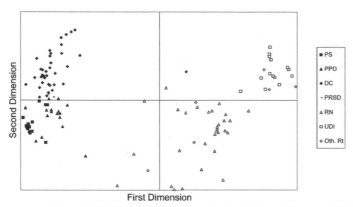

FIGURE 6.2a. W-NOMINATE scores for the Chilean House, 1997–1998.

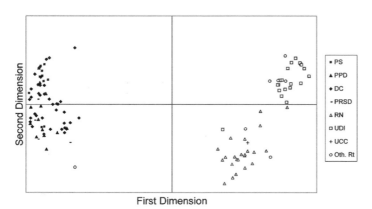

FIGURE 6.2b. W-NOMINATE scores for the Chilean House, 1998–1999.

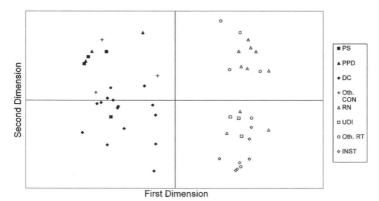

FIGURE 6.2c. W-NOMINATE scores for the Chilean Senate, 1992–1998.

The NOMINATE scores, in sum, provide some evidence that the parties do maintain independent ideological positions within the electoral alliances, particularly in the House. The data also suggest, however, that there is a much clearer divide between, rather than within, the two alliances.[24]

The final hypothesis to be tested regards the impact of electoral cycles on interalliance policy coalitions. Chilean presidential and congressional terms are not co-terminant, thus complicating the definition of the electoral cycle. But since the question is whether elections increase tensions on coalitions, I have demarcated the end of a cycle by any national election, be it for the president or congress. As such, the data that covers the period in the run-up to the December 1997 congressional elections were coded as pertaining to the end of the term, as were the votes that were taken close to the December 1999 presidential election. It is unfortunately not possible to reliably test whether the pattern is different before each type of election, since the data series ends a few months before the 1999 election and therefore contains few votes that pertain to the final quintile of a period before the 1999 presidential election.[25]

Recall that for Brazil I found an increase of intraalliance squabbles as elections neared, signifying that alliance members were staking out independent positions for the election. Prior to presidential contests in Chile, we might expect a different pattern because the members in each alliance must all support a single presidential candidate. They do not need to unite, however, for congressional elections. This may explain why, as shown in Table 6.11, there was an increase, rather than a decrease, of interalliance agreements in the last part of the term. These numbers are still too low to suggest an important impact of the electoral cycle on the patterns. However, the sharp decrease in the number of RN-UDI alliances in the last part of the term is evidence that these two electoral partners did jockey for position as the elections neared. The Senate data (not shown) have a complementary pattern. Again comparing the first 80 percent of the term with the last quintile, while the percentage of policy coalitions that joined the UDI with the DC almost doubled, moving from 17 percent to 31 percent, the percentage of DC-RN policy coalitions remained stable (6.3 percent and 5.7 percent).[26]

---

[24] Because of the very strong correlation (0.85) between the agents' left–right placement and their membership in one of the two alliances, it is not possible to test their separate impacts in a multivariate model. A logit model, however, does substantiate either a highly significant impact of coalition status or ideology on the propensity of an agent to form a policy coalition with another agent.

[25] As noted earlier, in the run-up to Brazilian presidential elections and Chilean congressional elections, the expectation is for intraalliance squabbles as each party tries to position itself for the election. But, in the Chilean presidential race, the parties in each alliance are tied together by a common presidential candidate. This should aid, rather than hinder, intraalliance cooperation in the run-up to the election.

[26] The percentage of RN-UDI policy coalitions remained relatively stable, moving from 25 percent to 31 percent.

TABLE 6.11. *The Electoral Cycle and Policy Coalitions in the Chilean House*

Within electoral alliances			Between electoral alliances		
Policy coalition	Rest of electoral cycle	End of electoral cycle	Policy coalition	Rest of electoral cycle	End of electoral cycle
	(% bills in policy coalition)			(% bills in policy coalition)	
CONC-PS	58.1	63.3	DC-RN	7.8	16.7
CONC-PPD	55.9	61.7	DC-UDI	4.5	18.3
CONC-DC	62.6	51.7	DC-RT	2.8	6.7
DC-PPD	56.4	50.0	PPD-RN	8.9	18.3
DC-PS	59.2	51.7	PPD-UDI	3.9	18.3
PS-PPD	58.7	75.0	PPD-RT	3.4	6.7
			PS-RN	11.7	23.3
RT-RN	57.0	40.0	PS-UDI	7.8	21.7
RT-UDI	58.1	41.7	PS-RT	6.1	10.0
RN-UDI	55.9	36.7	RN-CONC	5.0	11.7
			UDI-CONC	1.7	10.0
			RT-CONC	0.0	0.0

Note: Agreement scored when Rice score is at least 80 for each party. If either party were less highly unified, scored as no agreement. $n = 79$ for end of cycle; 160 for rest of cycle.

Finally, to test the hypotheses simultaneously, I ran a logit model similar to that performed on the Brazilian data.[27] This logit, however, ran into the problem of a very high level of multicollinearity (-0.86) between coalition membership in an alliance and the difference in mean ideological scores. The model thus returns statistics that indicate that alliance membership dominates all other concerns. The time variables are small and insignificant, and though the ideological variable gains statistical significance, the substantive impact is negligible.[28]

Uruguay: Electoral Alliances, the Electoral Cycle, and Ideology

Power sharing has long roots in Uruguayan politics. As described in Chapter 3, the father of democratic politics, José Batlle y Ordóñez, left a legacy of collegial executives and power sharing to Uruguay. Since that time, for good and for bad, Uruguayan politics have been defined by cross-partisan agreements among factions from the "traditional" parties. To review, Uruguay's coup in the 1930s was made possible by a conspiratorial

[27] The logit does not use "endogenous" policy coalitions, such as CONC-DC or RT-RN.

[28] Further, the sign indicates that as ideological distance grows, the prospect for alliances grows as well. This probably reflects the reversal of the RN and UDI on the ideological scales (see Appendix 5.2).

coalition between the lead Blanco and Colorado factions. In the 1970s, Colorado president Juan María Bordaberry lacked support in his own party but won a deal with conservative Blanco factions to support his government before succumbing to the nation's second coup in 1973. Then, the democratic transition was largely negotiated by the Colorados (under the leadership of future president Julio María Sanguinetti) in concert with the Frente Amplio (under General Liber Seregni).[29]

In the postdictatorial period, the spirit of cooperation has manifested itself in the presidents' attempts to form cross-partisan cabinets. Though all the postdictatorship presidents have met with some resistance, each has had some success with forming cross-party coalitions. The Colorados have won three of the four presidential elections since the restoration of democracy in 1984, twice behind Julio Maria Sanguinetti (1984 and 1994) and most recently (1999) with Jorge Batlle. In Sanguinetti's first term, he tried to form a governability pact (entitled the "Gobierno de Entonación Nacional") with the Blancos and sought participation of the Frente in his cabinet as well. Two Blancos (who were not particularly prominent in their party) did join, but the Frente charged that Sanguinetti was trying to co-opt them, instead of showing a willingness to negotiate substantial issues (Barahona, 2002, p. 23). Still, the two opposition parties did take charge of a number of autonomous state enterprises (Lanzaro, 2000). In his second term (1995–9) Sanguinetti succeeded in bringing the Blancos into his cabinet, giving them important ministerial posts including those of Defense, Foreign Relations, and Social Security (Barahona, 2002, p. 25).[30] Further the PGP (Party of the People's Government), which had run with the Frente in 1984, and then as an independent party in 1989, joined the Colorados for the 1994 election, with their leader named as Sanguinetti's running mate. Current president Batlle has followed Sanguinetti's example, though he kept most of the primary ministries for the Colorado party.[31]

The sole Blanco-elected president since 1984 was Luis Alberto Lacalle (1990–4). Like the Colorado presidents, Lacalle invited Colorado factions into his cabinet. His "Coincidencia Nacional," however, fell apart after just two years, as all but the smallest Colorado factions (the UCB) and even the most prominent Blanco faction (the MNR) aside from the president's (the Herrerristas) dropped out (Laurnaga, 1993).

[29] The Blancos sat out of the negotiations in protest of the proscription and arrest of their leader, Wilson Ferreira.

[30] The last of these was a particularly important position because privatization of social security was an important topic of the day. Since the policy change was going to mean some important societal resistance, many Blancos opposed the MNR's acceptance of that cabinet post.

[31] The Blancos were given Industry, Energy, and Mining, Work and Social Security, Education and Culture, Housing, and Sports (Barahona, 2002).

Though the culture of power sharing may help to explain the proclivity of presidents to invite opposition groups into their cabinets, politics and political institutions still play key roles in determining voting patterns. Particularly important are the shape of the agent system – that is two centrist, factionalized, and noncohesive parties in combination with a rising leftist electoral threat – and electoral politics.

First, the Colorado and Blanco parties' heterogeneity and centrism contrast with the Frente Amplio, which, while also somewhat heterogeneous, is positioned far to the left of its main rivals. The data from the Salamanca surveys indicate that on a 10-point scale, the Blanco and Colorado legislators placed their parties, on average, at 4.90 and 4.95, respectively, while the average Frente Amplio members positioned their party at 3.09. The standard deviations of these means indicate that almost no members from the Frente Amplio would overlap ideologically with members of the other parties.

Second, the presidents' minority position has encouraged the presidents to seek cross-partisan cabinet and policy coalitions. Cooperation at the party level has been encouraged by ideological proximity of the two traditional parties as well as the growing electoral threat from the left. As described in Chapter 3, the Frente Amplio first showed its electoral power just prior to the military coup of 1973 when it won 18 percent of the vote in 1971. Then, after twelve years of repression, it won a virtually identical vote share in the first election in the restored democracy. Its growth has since led it to the brink of taking the presidency from the two traditional parties. This rising threat incited the Blancos and Colorados to work toward a reform of their electoral system and it has also been a force in helping the two traditional parties to sustain (albeit shaky) bipartisan cabinets.[32]

Factionalism contributes to the presidents' weak position, leading presidents to have to worry not just about cross-party support but also about generating support from rival intraparty factions. I have argued that the relationship among factions in Uruguay is akin to the relationship among parties in the electoral alliances in Chile, and because the electoral alliances proved to be an important variable in tying parties together in Chile, a first hypothesis for Uruguay is that intraparty factions should be prone to supporting one another. There is, however, an important difference between Chile and Uruguay. In Chile, the presidential candidate is chosen independently from the legislature after the parties have agreed on a unique presidential candidate for their alliance. All alliance-member parties have then rallied to support the alliance's chosen leader in the general elections. Until the 1999

---

[32] Among other changes, the 1996 reform created a run-off system for the presidential race. This was in response to the fear that the Frente Amplio could out-poll the traditional parties in a three-way race; however, in a second round the two traditional parties could still out-distance the Frente Amplio.

election in Uruguay, however, the factions competed with separate presidential candidates in the general election. A competing hypothesis, therefore, is that the factions will withhold support from presidents who belong to different factions of their own party in order to increase their own identifiability, especially as the pressures of the electoral calendar begin to grow.

The Uruguayan case, then, presents five alternative hypotheses. First, given the presidents' minority positions, we might expect a gridlocked situation where the president and his faction are opposed by all other groups. A second possibility is the formation of policy coalitions that coagulate parties. This would imply that the president would gain the support of all factions in his party, and perhaps other parties as well. Third, if the composition of the cabinet is important, then the factions or parties with representatives in the cabinet should support the presidential bills. This should be particularly evident in the veto overrides. Fourth, the traditional parties might form a solid voting bloc against the Frente Amplio, regardless of the cabinet makeup. Finally, the more centrist groups from the Colorados and Blancos could form a voting bloc in support of the presidents' vetoes, with opposition coming from more extreme wings of the traditional parties and the Frente.

The following evidence suggests, first, that while there has been an important level of Blanco-Colorado cooperation when voting on legislation, the forces driving the two parties together have neither overcome the interparty differences nor overwhelmed the forces driving the organization of factions. Thus, as in Brazil, the main conclusion must be that offering cabinet posts to electoral rivals has only limited effects in generating legislative support. Second, the data for Uruguay give the best support the hypotheses related to the electoral cycle, showing that the likelihood of cooperation among the In-groups declines as elections near.

Data and Tests. Because the roll-call data for Uruguay is rather limited, it is important to note other evidence as tests of the hypotheses. First, there is very limited evidence for widespread gridlock because many important political, economic, and social bills have passed through the legislative process. In my review of the budget process, I found hundreds of amendments submitted by all parties and a great degree of cooperation among the committee members in working through the proposals. I also found that the legislators were able to bargain with the president to avoid constitutional restrictions on their ability to increase budget line items.[33]

In considering the vetoes, it is clear, however, that the relations between the branches are not always smooth. First, the large number of vetoes suggests an important degree of interbranch conflict or gridlock. But, because most of

---

[33] When the legislators wanted an increase, they "asked" the president to send his own amendment, threatening cuts in other areas if the president failed to respond.

the vetoes eliminate only individual articles (i.e., line items) rather than entire bills, the number of vetoes may overstate the degree of conflict somewhat. On at least one occasion, however, the partial veto meant a complete change in the orientation of the bill. At the end of 1994, the president and the legislature could not come to an agreement about the degree of autonomy for the Central Bank. President Lacalle therefore vetoed the article of the Organic Law that the Congress had approved and sent the bill back to the legislature with a "suggested" alternative version of the crucial article. This showdown occurred toward the end of the electoral campaign season, and the Congress was unable to muster a quorum to debate the veto. Then, owing to an ambiguous article in the Constitution, the published law included the president's substitute article – an article that had never been voted on by the legislature.

Next, it is clear that the power sharing – or at least understanding – between the Colorados and Blancos has had important repercussions for the policymaking process. Most evidently, many economic bills, including the annual budget, as well as other important reforms including the military amnesty and the major change of the electoral system (both of which were finally approved in referendums), have joined the traditional parties against the Frente Amplio. In interviews, some Frente Amplio legislators complained that they were excluded from legislative decisions by the traditional party legislators. One Frente Amplio legislator even alleged that the other parties held committee meetings without informing the Frente Amplio legislators. That legislator further alleged that he was not privy to sensitive material about government operations that the others were using in their deliberations.[34]

Turning now to the roll-call data, there is more evidence that (a) at least in the second term the president could not count on his own party for support; (b) neither president has been able to count on the factions from opposing parties in spite of their inclusion in the cabinet; (c) the Frente Amplio always opposed the presidents' vetoes, and the party was sometimes successful in its overturn attempts; and (d) presidential support has dwindled as elections have approached. The data also suggest, however, that the Ins have not been able to dictate terms, and that the Outs have been able to record some important victories.

The data in support of these conclusions, as explained earlier, are votes in the combined House and Senate (the General Assembly) on the legislature's attempts to override vetoes between 1985 and 1994. While the number of votes is rather small, since the votes all involve veto overrides, they explicitly divide the president and his supporters against an opposition. For the 1985–9 period, there were forty-one veto override votes and another twenty-two between 1990 and 1994. While the nature of these votes implies some

---

[34] Interview with a diputado of the Defense Committee, 1994.

level of controversy, seven votes in the first period and eight in the second aligned at least 90 percent of the whole legislature. While I will continue to use the 10 percent level of dissent as a cut-off for inclusion in the discussion, it is important to note that six of the eight votes in the second period that did not generate 10 percent dissent among the legislators favored overriding the veto.

The Uruguayan data also require a modification of the definition of flexibility because veto override attempts require a three-fifths majority to succeed. As a result, an agent "wins" if it is either part of a group comprising at least 60 percent of the legislature that favors overturning the veto or votes to sustain the veto and is part of group comprising at least 40 percent of the legislature.[35]

The first conclusion is that the presidents have faced rather significant opposition at the party level. Recall from Chapter 3 that during Sanguinetti's presidency the parties were unified, but that during Lacalle's presidency the Frente Amplio as a party and the factions in the traditional parties commonly voted in almost unitary fashion. Table 6.12 shows that, during Sanguinetti's presidency, the Colorados were unified on thirty one of the thirty four votes, and because the party held enough seats to sustain vetoes by itself, the outcome of the vote coincided with the Colorados' wishes on twenty-nine of these decisions. The Blancos and Frente Amplio opposed the Colorados on most of these votes; as a result, the Blancos won just six of thirty-three votes on which they unified, and the Frente Amplio won just five of thirty-two. Tables 6.13a and 6.13b confirm these patterns, showing that on over 90 percent of the votes the Blancos and Frente Amplio aligned against the Colorados, in spite of the cooperative agreement between the Blancos and Colorados.

While the factions grouped in the electoral alliance under the Colorado label maintained enough unity to support Sanguinetti on his vetoes, the Blanco factions were unable to do the same for President Lacalle. Unlike Sanguinetti before him, Lacalle's party did not control the requisite 40 percent of the legislature needed to sustain vetoes. Perhaps in recognition of this problem, he offered more cabinet posts to the Colorados, and at the outset was successful in forming a biparty cabinet with the Colorados. He was not successful, however, in bringing all the Blancos together, and the factionalism that had been suppressed during the first postdictatorship presidential term resurfaced. Further, as they had done with Sanguinetti, the Frente continued to oppose the president's faction on every override attempt (Table 6.13a). As a result, the multifaction and cross-party cabinet was not long-lived, and Lacalle was unable to translate the power-sharing arrangement in the cabinet into support in the legislature.

[35] Of the thirty-four controversial votes in the first period, thirty-two were sustained; in the second period six of fourteen were sustained.

TABLE 6.12. *Flexibility of Highly Unified Agents, Uruguay*

Party/Faction	Avg. no. of voters		Winning on contentious votes (No. of votes)		Losing on contentious votes (No. of votes)	
	1985–1989	1990–1994	1985–1989	1990–1994	1985–1989	1990–1994
Colorado	47.3	28.0	29	6	2	1
B15		7.9		5		0
C94		6.5		8		4
FORO		7.6		10		3
UCB		5.7		5		0
National	38.7	36.1	6	2	27	2
HERR		18.9		5		6
MNR		11.8		10		3
RyV		3.9		7		3
Frente Amplio	24.3	25.4	5	8	27	6

Note: "Highly unified" defined as Rice scores > 80. "Contentious" defined as votes with at least 10% dissent (weight > 0.2). Winning requires 60% of the voters to overturn a veto or 40% to sustain it. $n = 34$ for 1985–89, 14 for 1990–94, where weight > 0.2.

TABLE 6.13a. *Unified Two-Agent Policy Coalitions, Uruguay*

1985–1989 (% of votes)

	Unified	COL	NAL	FA
COL	91.2		2.9	0.0
NAL	97.1			91.2
FA	94.1			

1989–1994 (% of votes)

	Unified	COL	B15	C94	FORO	UCB	NAL	HERR	MNR	RyV
COL	40.0									
B15	40.0	26.7								
C94	86.7	40.0	26.7							
FORO	93.3	40.0	33.3	73.3						
UCB	40.0	25.7	20.0	40.0	26.7					
NAL	13.3	0.0	0.0	0.0	0.0	0.0				
HERR	80.0	5.7	20.0	6.7	13.3	6.7	13.3			
MNR	86.7	33.3	20.0	53.3	53.3	26.7	13.3	13.3		
RyV	73.3	13.3	26.7	13.3	20.0	13.3	13.3	60.0	20.0	
FA	100.0	33.3	20.0	80.0	73.3	33.3	0.0	0.0	73.3	6.7

TABLE 6.13b. *Unified Two-Agent Policy Opposition, Uruguay*

1985–1989 (% of votes)

	COL	NAL	FA
COL			
NAL	85.3		
FA	85.3	0	

1989–1994 (% of votes)

	COL	B15	C94	FORO	UCB	NAL	HERR	MNR	RyV
COL									
B15	0.0								
C94	0.0	0.0							
FORO	0.0	0.0	0.0						
UCB	0.0	0.0	0.0	0.0					
NAL	0.0	0.0	14.3	14.3	0.0				
HERR	21.4	21.4	57.1	57.1	21.4	21.4			
MNR	7.1	14.3	21.4	28.6	7.1	42.9	64.3		
RyV	0.0	0.0	42.9	42.9	7.1	0.0	7.1	42.9	
FA	7.1	14.3	7.1	14.3	7.1	14.3	78.6	14.3	64.3

Note: n = 34 for 1985–9, 15 for 1989–94. See notes for Table 6.5a.

182

The data show that the Blancos were united very infrequently in that period, winning just two and losing two votes as a unified group. More telling in terms of the weakness of the Blanco-Colorado agreement is the finding that the president's faction, the Herreristas, was so unsuccessful in generating cooperation that it was rolled on six of the eleven votes on which its members were unified. These six votes, moreover, were all to sustain a veto, implying that the president was unable to generate the support of even 40 percent of the legislature on more than half of his controversial vetoes.

The president's overall weak support was not significantly bolstered by offering cabinet posts to the electoral opposition. The main Colorado faction, Sanguinetti's Foro Batllista (FORO), was in the cabinet for six controversial votes but voted to sustain the veto on the first two occasions only. The rightist UCB stayed in the cabinet for the duration of Lacalle's term but supported just five of the fourteen vetoes. Lacalle's inclusion in the cabinet of factions of his own party did not help him either, as the MNR voted to sustain just two of eight vetoes while it was a member of the cabinet (and only once, on a divided vote, thereafter).

Finally, the electoral cycle did seem to play an important role in the Uruguayan flexibility patterns. In the first period, Sanguinetti won very high levels of support from all the Colorados until the last three votes in the data set, all of which occurred just weeks before the election. In the second term, the most notable change was the sharp drop in Lacalle's support following a short honeymoon. The Colorados' FORO cooperated with the Blanco president's Herrerista faction only on the first two override votes of Lacalle's *quinquenio* and the Colorados' C94 voted with the Herreristas only on the first vote. Further, it was clear that the Herreristas were breaking apart at the end of the cycle, as their unity declined precipitously (and abstention inclined sharply).

In sum, neither cabinet membership nor even a rising electoral threat was sufficient to overcome tensions among electoral rivals on a consistent basis. The electoral threat did lead to a major change in the electoral laws on which the two traditional parties cooperated, but the veto data suggests that this type of cooperation was not always assured.

While these findings may imply frustrated presidents, they have at least one positive aspect in terms of a flexibility scale. The Frente Amplio opposed both presidents on every vote. But, because Lacalle seldom controlled enough seats to sustain his vetoes, and a few Colorado legislators stayed home or defected on a few votes during Sanguinetti's term, the Frente Amplio could claim not-infrequent legislative victories. Likewise, the rightist UCB could be seen neither as an intransigent oppositionist nor as a predisposed vote for the president because during Lacalle's term they unified only on six votes (once in favor of the president and five times against), and on each of these occasions they were on the winning side.

United States

Patterns of flexibility in the United States are conditioned by the two-party system, coupled with low levels of unity. The data support the notion that the majority party does take advantage of its position, but there are some notable changes in the patterns of cross-party cooperation over the thirty year period.

The low levels of unity have meant that there are relatively few votes on which 90 percent of either party found themselves on the majority side of the vote. As a result, the Democrats, a majority party until 1994, unified on the winning side only between 11 percent and 17 percent of the votes between 1965 and 1980 (Table 6.14). Then, in Reagan's first term, that number increased to 31 percent, and then to over 50 percent in his second term. The majority party's success rate went up to almost 70 points after the Republicans gained control of a majority of the seats in 1995 before falling back to just under 60 points for Clinton's second term. These figures represent a great change from the 1960s and 1970s, when the minority Republicans had about as good a record as the Democrats in terms of the likelihood of unifying on the majority side of an issue (even surpassing the Democrats between 1965 and 1973). Further, over time there has been a tremendous increase in the number of votes in which the parties stood unified and in opposition to one another, rising from under 5 percent to about one-quarter of all votes.

Given the low levels of unity, it is also useful to consider the statistics in terms of simple majorities of the parties. In most years, the majority party voted with the winning side of the vote about 75 percent of the time, and the opposition party won about 55 percent of the votes (implying that on about 20 percent of the votes a majority of both parties voted with the winning side). There were, however, some anomalous sessions. In particular, the 1969–73 session stands out as the two parties overlapped much more than during other years, with a majority of Republicans voting on the winning side almost as often as the Democrats (on about 75 percent of the controversial votes).

The other exceptional period was Clinton's first administration, where polarization rather than accommodation was evident. In the 103rd Congress (1993–4), a majority of the Democrats voted with the majority of the legislature almost 90 percent of the time, and the Republicans reached a slightly higher figure for the 104th Congress. The Republicans' score fell to "just" 84 percent for the 1997–2001 period. Further evidence that this period was an important departure from the congenial coalitions of the previous thirty years was the drop to only 21 percent of the votes on which a majority of the two parties joined together on bills that still generated at least 10 percent opposition. In most other periods, this was the case in over one-third of the votes, and it grew back to 29 percent in Clinton's second term. Finally, as

TABLE 6.14. *Flexibility of Highly Unified Parties, United States*

Year (sessions)	Unified Dems. in majority (%)	Unified Reps. in majority (%)	Unified Reps. vs. unified Dems. (%)	No. of contentious votes
1965–68 (89–90)	15.2	15.9	3.7	574
1969–72 (91–92)	11.2	17.1	1.3	707
1973–76 (93–94)	17.2	13.2	1.9	1668
1977–80 (95–96)	16.7	14.7	2.2	1865
1981–84 (97–98)	31.3	14.1	4.2	1174
1985–88 (99–100)	52.3	11.3	9.3	1395
1989–92 (101–02)	49.7	11.8	11.3	1383
1993–94 (103)	53.9	15.5	24.3	906
1995–96 (104)	7.4	68.7	27.9	1109
1997–2000 (105–06)	18.1	58.9	25.3	1642

Note: High unity implies Rice > 80. "Contentious" defined as votes with at least 10% dissent (weight > 0.2).

is also evident in Table 6.14, while the minority Democrats had a terrible experience in their first two years as a minority (winning just 7.4 percent of votes between 1995 and 1997), over the next four years the Democrats' success rate climbed up to a level even higher than the minority Republicans had experienced in recent decades. At the same time, the Republican major-ity continued to unify and win a significantly higher percentage of the votes than was the norm during the years of Democratic majorities.

SUMMARY

This chapter has had three goals. It first considered the concept of a coali-tion in a presidential system and argued for a focus on policy coalitions. Throughout the chapter, I operationalized the concepts of policy coalitions and flexibility by considering the frequency with which an agent joined the majority and the proportion of roll-call votes on which any two agents joined forces.

The second goal of the chapter was to demonstrate empirically the level of flexibility in the four Latin American countries and the United States. Patterns of Ins versus Outs or left versus right splits were evident, but so too were signs of cross-alliance flexibility. Even in Argentina, where the PJ was a highly unified majority party, there were a number of issues on which the parties cooperated and others where part or all of the PJ lost important votes. Similarly, the Chilean Concertación did not shun the right. Frequently it was members of the center-right RN or the center-left DC that crossed the palpable electoral chasm, but there were also many other forms of policy coalitions. In Brazil, the leftist parties have clearly been Outs, but neither side is glued by tight electoral arrangements, and several parties lack consistent unity. As a result, the leftist parties vote with a range of partners and score an important number of victories. In Uruguay, a pattern of Ins and Outs developed on the votes to overturn presidential vetoes, with the president having some difficulty in winning support from other factions in his own party, let alone from other agents. Still, most vetoes were sustained, so the lack of support on these votes was inconsequential. We would need data on other votes to compare the level of flexibility of the agents in Uruguay with the other countries accurately. Finally, in the United States, when the minority party has been unified, it has been able to win a significant number of votes owing to defections from the majority. Further, there has been a large volume of legislation that passed with bipartisan support.

The important conclusion from the descriptive section is that the common interagent alliances appear propitious for democracy. Voters supporting agents that can show legislative victories are differently represented than are voters supporting agents that are always in the opposition. While voters in the former situation can attribute gains to their favored agent, opposition supporters must be contented with promises and policy proposals as opposed to real benefits. These latter voters may thus begin to question the efficacy of the representative process. Democracy, therefore, is vouchsafed if agents are not always left in the opposition. Further, when an agent votes with the majority, that agent must defend a democratic decision, which again forces an emphasis on the positive benefits of democracy. In short, agents' willingness to participate in winning coalitions favors democratic stability. While we have no statistics from the 1960s, it is likely that they would show much more strident competition between the left and right than was shown here, with Out-agents seldom voting on the winning side. Curiously, the case of the United States yielded the opposite result, with a dramatic move toward less accommodation between the parties during the Clinton administration.

The third goal of this chapter has been to explain the patterns of policy coalitions. I first argued that the recent and fearful experience with dictatorial rule has moderated the legislative agents' ideologies and has given them all an added incentive to work together instead of against one another. This factor probably explains why the empirical data did not turn up any pariah agents, and why there were so many different forms of policy coalitions. Still, politics lives, and coalitions were more likely among some groups of agents than others.

The rest of the explanation focused on cabinet membership and ideological distance, both conditioned by unity and the electoral cycle. The data provide some support for the notion that cabinet membership can help a president to shore up support in the face of ideological differences, but the effect appears quite limited. In Argentina, the PJ dominated the cabinet and held a near-majority in the Congress for the period under consideration; as a result, it won about three-quarters of the controversial votes. But, defections or abstentions cost the party an important number of legislative victories. In Brazil, the PT held a cabinet post for a short time during the Collor-Franco period and joined the majority coalition much more frequently than it did in the succeeding term when it was shunned from the cabinet. Still, cabinet membership proved to be a much weaker variable than ideology in explaining patterns of policy coalitions in Brazil. In Uruguay, the evidence for the importance of cabinet membership was also weak, as the included agents frequently opposed the president on veto override attempts. Only in Chile, where the cabinet-style government is reinforced by an electoral alliance, did membership in the cabinet seem to override ideology and other factors in determining which agents joined the policy coalitions. Even then, however, there were notable examples of parties or their members defecting from their electoral alliance partners.

7

Conclusion

With apologies to E. E. Schatschneider (1942, p. 1), "modern democracy is unthinkable save in terms of" agents. The agents that we have explored in this book take many different forms, ranging from highly unified (identifiable) collective actors to relatively independent legislators grouped into loose conglomerations of parties, factions, delegations, or coalitions. I have argued here that the agents' different forms, and the interactions among them, define the patterns of legislative politics and thus have important implications for representation and democratic governance.

Earlier theorists have also been concerned with flexibility and identifiability. Madison's worry was that "factions" would generate rigid barriers, excluding minorities. More recent theorists have been concerned with accountability, especially in multiagent systems. Stokes (2001b), for example, focuses on the particular requirements that allow voters to identify the hero or villain responsible for the given economic situation. The first characteristic she notes is a clear ruling majority, because "people may have difficulty attributing responsibility under coalition, minority, or divided governments" (p. 14). Powell (1999) finds that concentrating power in a majoritarian system "is necessary, although not sufficient, for citizen control" (p. 5). At the same time, he follows J. S. Mill in arguing about the importance of multiple "representative agents ... [that] bargain with each other in a flexible and accommodative fashion" (p. 6).

Powell is concerned that these two goals of democratic governance are incompatible because they imply two different views of the citizen-legislator link. One vision assumes a general will and that citizens then hold an identifiable agent accountable for providing that good. In the other, citizens are heterogeneous, and representative government should therefore seek to ensure that many different voices are heard. The cases in this book, however, suggest that the choice is not dichotomous; as I discussed in Chapter 1, individual agents can be both identifiable and flexible, thus yielding a coalitional style of legislature. The interaction of agents showing different levels of identifiability or flexibility yields either a polarized noninclusive legislature or a legislature characterized by inclusiveness based on the vote trading among legislators rather than recognizable groups of legislators.

In this conclusion, I first summarize the questions that motivated this book and the primary conclusions. I then provide a comparative view of the patterns of legislative politics in the four Latin American countries and the United States and discuss the main explanatory variables and their limitations. The final section then discusses unanswered questions and avenues for future research.

A SUMMARY OF FINDINGS

The key questions for this book have been: Who are the legislative agents? What explains their level of unity? and To what degree have different agents cooperated with one another on policy decisions? These questions redound to the fundamental issues in legislative politics, as the shape of the agent system determines how citizens, interest groups, the bureaucracy, and executives relate to the legislature. Thus, in order to develop a comparative and theoretical understanding of legislative politics, it is necessary to first generate a comprehensive description and model of agent systems.

Answering theoretical questions about legislative politics is particularly important to Latin America, given their continuing effort to sustain and deepen their democracies. Issues such as money in campaigns, different lobbying practices, coalitional politics, constituency services, and the general legislative process all have a dramatic impact on the types of policies that a system will produce. As such, macro-outcomes, such as economic growth, the distribution of income, international relations, civil–military relations, and the level of support for the democratic process are all functions of legislative politics.

This book has attempted to create a framework from which to explore these larger questions. It has thus sought to describe the agent systems and explain why the levels of unity amongst legislators and coalition formation amongst groups of legislators vary both across and within borders. Towards this goal, this book began in Chapter 2 with a critique of theories of governance based on parties. By their very name, studies of the "party system" neglect or obfuscate the centrality of different political actors in a system. Identifying the number of parties in a system can be irrelevant because the parties can be either highly factionalized or grouped into tight alliances. Further, it is not clear that voters necessarily view parties as their primary representatives. Sometimes voters choose among parties and see parties as responsible for policy outputs (or outcomes). Under other electoral systems, however, the voters can select individual candidates, factions, or alliances – and in these systems these groups become as highly salient to the political realm as do parties. The "party system," in short, is a misleading term.

In its place, I suggest the phrase "agent system," which captures two aspects of legislative actors. First, it conjures an idea of voters holding accountable their delegates in a principal–agent style relationship. This image would provide a theoretical framework for important questions about voter–representative relationships. The principal concern in the principal–agent literature is the ability of the former in controlling the actions of the latter. In other words, how do principals avoid "agency slack" – the propensity of agents to use their hidden knowledge of how they spend their time in pursuing their own interests instead of working as desired by the principals? Roll-call data provide key information to voters and watchdog groups that want to oversee the actions of their agents. This, in addition to the screening mechanisms (i.e., campaigns) that voters employ, could be the basis of a principal–agent-style theory about accountability.

The second meaning of the term "agent" implies the ability to take independent action. In this study, I have tried to identify which groups of legislators act as coherent units on a consistent basis. Roll-call voting, again, aided this effort. Where legislators are voting together repeatedly, it is reasonable to ascribe agency to that group. If, however, a larger group (say a party) votes together only out of the chance agreement of smaller agents (say factions), then only the smaller group has agency.

Recognizing which legislative groups have agency is, again, important to studies of legislative politics generally. If parties are unified in their voting patterns, then studies can employ unitary actor assumptions about parties in their analyses. Generally, however, parties are complex organizations that must work to maintain unity. Therefore, studies should identify unity levels before attributing decision-making authority to parties or other legislative groups.

In an effort to discuss the identifiability of the different agents, Chapter 3 profiled the balloting systems that determine how voters are able to target their praise or anger, and the relationship between those systems and the agents' behavior. I argued that there was a consistent relationship between the electoral systems, the context of politics, and the level of voting unity in the United States and the four Latin American countries.

First, for Argentina, voters choose parties, and elections have revolved around the split between the Peronists and the anti-Peronists (frequently the UCR) since the 1940s. This partyism is consistent with very high levels of party voting unity in the Congress.

The standard story in Brazil is that the electoral system contributes to a system of disorganized and undisciplined parties. The individualism of Brazilian legislators, coupled with a continued focus on parties and state-party delegations rather than nonregional factions or alliances is consistent with the voters' abilities to specify their preferences for individual candidates as well as parties on their ballots. The unity data gave evidence of this tension. It showed, in particular, that while voters' ability to judge their agents was challenged by low levels of unity and limited allegiance of many legislators to their parties, voting patterns still did provide voters a basis on which to judge parties, state delegations, and left–right coalitions. Several of the parties exhibited high or at least relatively high unity rates, especially in comparison with those of the U.S. parties. Further, even the party that showed the weakest level of average unity, the PMDB, could be seen as structuring many votes, and sometimes state-party delegations achieved high levels of unity; hence, they can be identified as agents as well. Also important for accountability in a multiagent system, the NOMINATE scores (shown in Chapter 6) revealed a clear left–right split that separated two groups of parties. Thus, in spite of the multiagent system and the lack of tight unity inherent in some of these agents, voters could reasonably attribute macrolevel outcomes to a recognizable majority.

Historically Chilean politics was defined by a three-way split in the agent competition, with presidential candidates and their supporting parties and factions clearly delineating the left, center, and right. Since the refounding of democracy, this three-way competition has been forced into a two way split, with support of Pinochet as the primary dividing line. The tradition of multipartyism, however, has not disappeared, and thus Chilean legislative politics has two types of agents. The left and right coalitions are clear actors, but coalition membership does not explain a large number of votes. Further, though the parties frequently show the ability to act both collectively and independently, some of the parties (in particular the DC and RN) are not always successful in congealing their members. In sum, the reasonably high values on unity at the party and coalitional levels suggest that while voters have a basis on which to choose coalitions and parties within the coalitions, there is also room for voters to identify the independent actions of particular legislators.

This agent system is again consistent with the theory about the ballot structure in congressional elections. The Chilean ballot identifies coalitional and party affiliations for every candidate, and those two groupings gain prominence in discussions of that case.

The Uruguayan system offers further evidence of this theory. There the double-simultaneous vote system allows voters to choose factions and parties, and this is the only case where the factions have been institutionalized agents. That is, while factionalism has raised its head in all countries, only in Uruguay do the factions maintain a consistent membership and operate as distinct and coherent groups in the legislature (as well as in elections). During the two terms under analysis, the factions did unify under their party labels for one term, but this apparent aberration broke down in the subsequent period.

Following the exploration of the levels of unity among different potential agents in the different countries, the next two chapters sought explanations for why unity rates varied both across and within borders. I argued that unity can result from discipline (the enforcement of behavior by authorities) or cohesion (the ideological or instrumental agreements among legislators). The discussion about discipline focused on how the electoral system endows some leaders with extraordinary power to name candidates. I argued that while a single closed list at the national level would generate agent discipline, such a system does not exist in Latin America. Argentina has closed lists, but they are operated from the provinces. The other systems under investigation dilute the leaders' power through intraparty competition. When candidates must compete against others from their same party, faction, or coalition, they cannot rely solely on the agent label to win an election. Because these systems lead candidates to run individualistic campaigns, the legislators have an incentive to seek independence from the leaders in the legislature. The statistical tests then showed that, as predicted, where the electoral system provided leaders with high levels of control over nominations (i.e., Argentina), unity rates were also high. But elsewhere, where the electoral system did not grant such unambiguous control, that variable was unable to explain the differing unity rates clearly.

Where the electoral system does not create a strict disciplinarian, unity must result from either cohesion or other factors that support leaders' powers. I argued that cohesion can have ideological or electoral bases. Two aspects of ideology – an agent's degree of polarization on a left–right scale and the degree to which an agent's legislators were in agreement with one another about that placement – showed themselves as able to signify an agent's unity level. It was also clear that when most of an agent's legislators were concentrated in just a few districts, unity rates were higher. The importance of electoral politics also showed in a variable measuring the consistency of voting patterns across electoral districts. Based on ideas first proposed by Stokes in the 1960s, the hypothesis was that when districts move together electorally, legislators have common interests in supporting the agent's policies. Finally, I suggested that, as Aldrich and Rohde's theory of conditional party government predicts, the leaders of the most cohesive agents in a given country were also the most powerful.

The tests were also interesting for what they did not find. For example, neither the agents' association with the executive (Ins versus Outs), nor the electoral calendar, proved to have a strong relationship with unity rates in all cases. Still, the strong theoretical foundation of these variables combined with their prominent roles in the changing unity rates in some cases suggests that a multivariate model could uncover the significance of these variables.

The final substantive chapter returned to the question about how identifiable agents fit into a realm of legislative politics where coalition making is crucial. The chapter first discussed the definition of coalitions in presidential systems and argued for a focus on policy coalitions instead of cabinets. The chapter then displayed and sought to explain the patterns of policy coalitions among the agents in each country. In addition to evaluating the role of ideological positions and cabinet membership in explaining the voting patterns, an important motivational question for the chapter was whether the most unified agents were flexible enough to join policy coalitions. The chapter was motivated by two concerns. First, Linz and Mainwaring argue that multiagentism, when combined with presidentialism, is dangerous to democracy because it can generate stalemate between the branches. Second, Sartori was concerned that if agents are consistently left out of policy coalitions and thus benefit little from the system, they could come to support antisystems of revolutionary action to bring about change.

The premise of exclusion leading to turmoil may be correct, but Chapter 6 suggested that no agents in these countries have been consistently excluded. Of course, some agents are less frequently in the majority coalition than others, but even the relatively extremist and unified agents of the left (in Brazil and Uruguay) or the right (in Chile) joined the winning side of a substantial number of controversial votes. These presidential democracies, thus, seems to be working better than what Linz and his followers might have expected.

In sum, this book has undertaken an extensive examination of roll call voting to identify and explain prominent patterns of legislative politics. The following section charts the two main patterns, identifiability and flexibility, to provide a final comparative view of the five countries. It also offers a final discussion about the explanatory variables and their limits.

PATTERNS OF LEGISLATIVE POLITICS AND
LIMITED EXPLANATIONS

To provide a comparative view of the legislatures under study here, Figure 7.1 provides a schematic view of the agent types, based on one measure of their identifiability and flexibility. The horizontal axis on the graph shows the agents' unity scores and the vertical axis is a measure of the agents' willingness to compromise with others from across the governance borders. That is, the vertical scale measures the degree to which agents from within the governing coalition have formed policy coalitions on controversial votes (weight > 0.2) with agents considered to be in the opposition. To use Chile's UDI as an example, the measure is calculated by computing the percent of votes in which a majority of UDI members voted in the same direction as the majority of either the DC, PS, or PPD. The scale is then inverted (in order to coincide with Table 1.1) by subtracting that figure from 100. For Brazil, the calculations are based on the PT on one side of the divide and the PMDB, PSDB, and PFL on the other. For the United States and Argentina, where there are just two agents considered, the flexibility represents the percentage of controversial votes in which a majority of the two main parties voted together. Uruguay presents a problem since the Frente Amplio always voted against the president on the veto overrides and thus could be placed at the

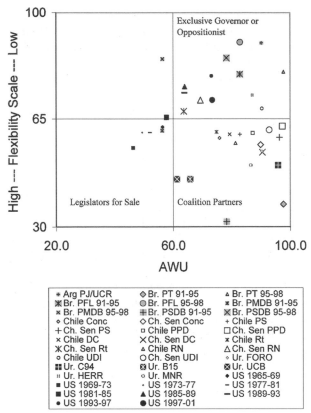

FIGURE 7.1. A comparison of agent types. Average weighted unity scores for Argentina and the United States are averages of the two main parties.

extreme of that scale. But, because it did side with various factions of the presidents' parties and of the other traditional party, its position is unclear. As a result, the graph just places the Colorado and Blanco factions, based on interactions between factions of these colors.[1] A flexible Blanco faction, thus, is one that frequently voted with Colorado factions.

I argued in Chapter 1 that agents could fit into three of the four quadrants of this type of graph, and here no agents are in the top left part of the graph, though the arbitrary cut-offs put US 1981–85 and Br. PMDB 95–8 just inside the top left box. In the lower right "coalition partners" box are the Chilean legislative agents because they maintained reasonably high levels of unity and a willingness to cross alliance borders. With the prominent exception of the Herreristas, the president's faction, the Uruguayan factions also fit into the coalitional corner. The Herreristas placement in the top right box,

---

[1] The graph also ignores the 1985–90 period.

however, suggests an important level of executive-legislative conflict. Next, because the PT and PSDB sided together frequently in the 1991–5 period, they too fall into the lower right box. But, for the 1995–8 period, the Brazilian parties score much lower on the flexibility scale because there were very few controversial votes in which a majority of the PT voted with the PMDB, PSDB, or PFL. This earns the Brazilian parties exclusive or oppositionist labels. The latter group of parties are differentiated by their AWU scores, with the PMDB so low that labeling it an inflexible party is a bit problematic. The Argentine parties fit in the top right box as well, as a result of the infrequent cross-party agreements (at least on roll-call votes).

Drawing a comparison between the United States and the countries of Latin America was an important motivator of this study, in part because of the common assumption that the U.S. agent system has helped the U.S. democracy survive in spite of presidentialism. The graph does show important distinctions. First, though a single party has always controlled a majority of seats in the U.S. House (and Senate), until the 1990s the majorities of the two parties in the United States showed a greater propensity to join together than either Argentina's parties or Chile's alliances. But, the U.S. parties also showed much weaker unity than these other cases. The U.S. distinction, however, has been eroding. The parties have left their unique position in the extreme bottom left box and have steadily moved toward the top right, crossing into the top right box in the 1980s and reaching an apex during the 1993–7 period. Though I have argued that increased unity aids representation and accountability, it would be difficult to portray the country's move toward the positions occupied by the Brazilian and Argentine parties in a positive light.

As other measures of flexibility and identifiability are available, the graph does not tell the whole story. In particular, other measures of flexibility (e.g., the number of relatively unanimous votes in the legislature) and identifiability (e.g., the number of relatively unanimous votes of an agent) can put a more positive light on either of these traits for any particular agent or the full legislature. Changing the indicators of either axis, however, would not have much effect on the relative positions of the agents. The Chilean legislature, for example, would still show much more flexibility than the Brazilian legislature of 1995–8 by almost any measure. It is also doubtful that other measures of identifiability could boost the United States' low score such that they would overtake the positions of the other countries.

I have argued in this book that electoral institutions and ideology have very important roles in explaining the general shape of the agent system and the patterns of voting in the legislature. Somewhat hidden within these general patterns, however, are important details that the statistical techniques cannot easily uncover. Further, other variables that are more difficult to quantify can play determinant roles in explaining both the trends and the aberrations from them. For example, while the experience with dictatorships surely encouraged today's agents to compromise amongst one another, it is not easy to evaluate how different legislators weigh this issue when making their voting decisions. Similarly, I have attempted to differentiate the agents based only on how they might position themselves for elections in terms of whether they were part of the In- or Out-group but not more detailed electoral strategies that might change their view of the value on unity or the strategic value of an opposition stance. These and other contextual variables, however, cannot be overlooked in explaining the particularities of a given agent's behavior. This issue is evident in the differences that the figure exhibits for the Brazilian and Chilean agents. A full explanation of this difference goes beyond the scope of this conclusion, but a few observations are in order.

First, the electoral system apparently has played a key role in supporting the high levels of identifiability and flexibility in Chile, but it does not fully explain the Brazilian traits. Three features distinguish the Chilean electoral system. First, Chilean voters directly choose among coalitions on their ballots. This promotes accountability at the coalition level. The system also encourages the accountability of the parties, since voters choose among a limited number of parties within their favored alliance in the general election. This collective responsibility encourages unity at both the party and alliance levels, at least on core issues.

Accountability in Chile is furthered by the second trait, the system features that push the multiple parties into two stable alliances. This congealing, as argued in Chapter 3, is the result of the two-member districts in conjunction with the arcane seat distribution system that encourages the different parties to remain within the alliances.

While these first two traits encourage unity and accountability of the two alliances, the final trait, intraagent (usually alliance) competition, allows multipartism to continue and discourages such great unity within the alliances as to preclude interalliance deals. In particular, by allowing each alliance to run two candidates in each district (usually from two different parties), the system fosters intraalliance rivalries. This, as argued in Chapter 4, encourages the alliance partners to seek out their own identities, which implies that they must seek cross-alliance policy partners at times.

While these three factors seem to explain much of the Chilean agent system, the electoral system does not do a good job of accounting for either the high unity of some of the Brazilian parties or their low levels of flexibility. In Brazil, voters choose candidates and parties, but not (generally) among alliances.[2] This, plus the intraparty competition, explains why the unity rates of some of the parties are low. But, the electoral system fails to explain why, in spite of multipartism and intraparty competition, majorities of the Brazilian

---

[2] Alliances can and do form among some parties for Brazilian elections, but the system rules do not push the parties into just two competing alliances.

parties tend to vote in exclusive blocs to a much greater extent than in Chile. In sum, however important, the electoral system does not seem a sufficient explanation for the distinction between Brazil and Chile because it would predict higher flexibility for Brazil than the data reveals. Other variables suffer from a similar fate, also explaining one case better than the other.

I showed in Chapter 6 that ideological vicinity and to a lesser extent cabinet membership play important roles in determining policy coalitions. These variables do a good job of explaining which agents in the two countries generally form coalitions, but they too fail to explain why Chilean agents are much more prone to also include cross-alliance agents in the policy coalitions than are the Brazilians. First, while there are sharp ideological differences between the PT and the other Brazilian parties, according to the Salamanca surveys the differences between the PS and the RN or UDI was even greater (Table 7.1). For Brazil, in the survey of 1996, the PT members rated their party at 1.9 on the left–right scale, and the nearest of these other parties was the PMDB at 4.6, though the distance when legislators ranked other parties rather than their own was a bit greater (3.4 versus 2.7). In a survey done in 1999, where party elites were asked to rank other parties, the PT was placed at 1.2 and the PMDB at 5.7. This difference of 4.5 is rather large, but it is still significantly less than the distance between the PS and the RN or UDI. In

TABLE 7.1. *Ideological Placement of Agents in Brazil and Chile*

	1996		1999	
Agent	Avg. self-placement of legislators	Avg. placement by other legislators	Avg. self-placement of party elites	Avg. placement by other party elites
Brazil				
PT	1.9	2.6	3.3	1.2
PMDB	4.6	6.1	6.5	5.7
PSDB	4.2	6.2	5.2	6.8
PFL	5.1	8.3	8.3	8.9
Chile				
Concertación	4.0			
PS	2.9	2.6	2.8	2.2
PPD	3.6	4.2	3.9	3.9
DC	4.5	4.7	4.7	4.9
Right	6.5			
RN	6.7	7.5	6.2	8.1
UDI	6.5	8.9	7.5	9.4

Note: Statistics from the 1999 survey were taken from Marenghi (2002). Statistics for 1996 were calculated from the Salamanca surveys (and those of column I are also reported in Appendix 5.2). The statistics for Chile differ slightly from those reported by Marenghi, and she does not report statistics for Brazil (see note 9 in Chapter 5).

the 1996 Salamanca survey, the PS self-placement of legislators was 2.9 and the rightist parties were at about 6.5. When legislators ranked other parties in 1996, the PS was placed at 2.6, and the RN and UDI were moved to 7.5 and 8.9, respectively. For the survey of party elites of 1999–2000, the RN and UDI were moved even further to the right.[3]

The possibility that the extremist position of the PS is moderated by its membership in the Concertación, which has been dominated by the centrist Christian Democrats, is also an insufficient explanation. The DC scored a 4.4 on the 1996 survey of legislators, and the party elites placed themselves further to the right (4.8 and 4.7) in the subsequent surveys. The other parties ranked the DC about the same, or a bit more toward the center. This places it about 2.0 points from the RN in the three surveys, although the distance is over 3 if the placements perceived by other legislators or agent leaders are considered. This distance still suggests that the breach between the DC and the rightist parties is similar to that between the PT and the PMDB in Brazil. In terms of the placements perceived by others, the distance between these sets of parties is greater in Brazil (3.2 versus 4.3), but the difference does not seem significant enough to explain the very different results.

Next, it would be difficult to argue that the agents' electoral hopes were determining factors because the PT, UDI, and PS have all been serious contenders for the president's office. The PT's leader, Luis Inácio "Lula" da Silva, has been a serious presidential candidate in every election since 1989, finally winning in 2002. In Chile, the left wing of the Concertación overcame the dominance of the Christian Democrats, and with the active support of the PS, Ricardo Lagos of the PPD (and ex-PS member) won the presidency in 2000. In that election, however, the UDI also showed its electoral strength, coming within a whisker of winning the presidential contest over Lagos. The UDI then more than doubled its representation in both houses of Congress in the election of 2001, not only overtaking the RN as the leading party in the rightist coalition, but dwarfing their partner's delegation (cf. Table 3.9).

Finally, the totality of the agent system in the lower house is not a sufficient explanation because both countries have multiagent systems. Perhaps the most significant difference between the systems is external to the agents in question: the balance of power in the Senate. In Brazil, the PT can be excluded from legislative decisions without threat to the passage of a given policy. But, in Chile, if the UDI or RN is excluded in the House, the Concertación runs the risk of blockage in the Senate, where the rightist parties, if joined by the institutionals, control the majority. Thus in Chile, the minority veto appears to have served its purpose of encouraging cross-alliance coalitions (which may also explain the large number of interparty deals in the U.S.

---

[3] Data for this paragraph comes from the two different Salamanca surveys, Elites Parlamentarias en América Latina and Partidos Políticos y Gobernabilidad en América Latina. Some of the data used in this paragraph was compiled in Marenghi (2002).

Senate). The movement to end the system of institutional senators (on the grounds that they are an undemocratic remnant of Pinochet's constitution) thus runs the risk of increasing interalliance tensions. Moreover, though the rightists have shown themselves to be legitimate contenders for the presidential office and majority control of Congress, if they were to fall back to their traditional support levels without the prospect of preventing distasteful legislation, their interest in working within the democratic system might also erode. At the same time, a conclusion that veto gates will bring about harmonious democratic compromises must be tempered with the Linzian view regarding the dangers of gridlock. This suggests, in sum, that while the system of electoral competition, ideological beliefs, cabinet membership, and veto gates condition the political decisions of the agents and their leaders, the value that the politicians put on democratic compromise and sustainability must also enter the equations.

In this book, I have not tried to gather the many ad hoc and intangible factors to explain each of these idiosyncratic behaviors. My goal, instead, has been to identify the specific voting patterns for each agent and explore the variables that explain general trends. While this strategy, I hope, has been fruitful, it, of course, leaves important questions about the impact of these different patterns on policy and democracy for future research.

THE NEXT STEPS

The main purpose of this study has been to explore two key aspects of legislative politics: the unity and coalitional relationships among legislative agents. These phenomena are interesting in their own right, but I have here tried to justify my interest in them by discussing how they affect representation, the policy process, and ultimately democratic sustainability. These issues are ripe for further study, and this final section notes some areas where the agent system framework could contribute to studies of these topics.

First, while I have asserted that unity allows voters and watchdog groups to hold legislators accountable, future studies should test this proposition. Studies of the accountability of legislators in the United States have led to a rich literature that is concerned with the very high reelection rates in the United States (Mayhew, 1974; Fiorina, 1977a; 1977b; Jacobson, 1987). The concern there is that if legislators are reelected with a very high probability, then they may not be responsive to voter demands. These and other studies have therefore raised important questions about how legislators protect their hold on electoral offices. Fiorina, for example, argues about the relation between the growing bureaucracy and legislators' desire to solve constituent demands. Fenno (1978) looks at the ways in which legislators develop relationships with their constituents. Other implications could include the impact of money in campaigns, the role of interest groups, and the revolving door between the bureaucracy, interest groups and government contractors, and the legislature.

Studies of Latin American politics have only just begun to test questions about accountability. Further, the first steps toward these types of studies have focused only on the presidents. In her work on economic voting, Stokes and her co-contributors (1996; 2001a) ask why voters have returned; for example, Fujimori and Menem were reelected to office after these candidates took radically different courses than they promised in their electoral campaigns. These are very interesting and useful studies that should provide a starting point for studies of legislative accountability.

Of course, legislative accountability is more complicated because it involves multiple legislators who are not as readily identifiable with policy outcomes as chief executives. The framework that I have suggested here could give future researchers a direction for study. We might expect, for example, that unified agents would be more susceptible to voters angered over broad policy outcomes. Agents that lack such unity may be more insulated. This, perhaps, would help dampen swings from one agent to another (i.e., volatility).

Another strain of hypotheses could examine the factors that affect an agent's electoral performance and the impact of common electoral interests on policy. I showed in Chapter 5 that when the vote totals of all members of an agent experience a common rise or fall in their electoral returns, the members' unity increases. For the United States, Stokes (1965; 1967) and Cox and McCubbins (1993) argue that common fates should help orient the agents toward national policy concerns. Future studies should test this proposition.

A second question in this vein regards the electoral strategies of agents based on different levels of unity. A full answer to this question cannot simply bifurcate the unified and nonunified agents, assuming that the former relies on national orientations and the latter on pork or clientelism. Nationally oriented agents must still be responsive to local constituencies and could, perhaps, develop reputations based on provision of particularistic goods. On the other hand, even agents with very low levels of unity may have at least some programmatic or ideological bases. Further, even if the agents do work to provide pork to their hungry districts, studies such as Samuels (2002) and Ames (1995), which focus on budget amendments, can be quite illuminating in showing how legislators are fulfilling their electoral mandates.

Another area that this study has suggested for future research is the relationship between agent systems, representation, and democratic sustainability. While it is clear that there is a relation among these three concepts, the specific nature of that relation is murky. The theory of democracy is based on the concept of representation, and thus the absence of representation implies the end of democracy. But, representation is not a linear concept; different agent systems imply different forms of representation, none of which is clearly better or worse than another. For example, it is not clear where to draw the line in the tradeoff between unified agents that are likely to be attuned to national issues and agents with low levels of unity that are likely to be more concerned with district interests. As noted in Chapter 1, the downfall of Chilean democracy was blamed in part on constitutional changes that limited the legislature's focus on local issues. Among other problems, Venezuela's upheaval in the 1990s has been blamed on the parties' lack of ties to district concerns. Still, the other extreme, too much concern with pork and not enough concern with raising national welfare, would not be a favorable mix. Thus a first issue that deals with democratic sustainability is how different forms of representation relate to the types of policies a system produces and the implied impacts on economic development.

This discussion also bears on the question of voters' support for the democracy and Sartori's (1976) concern about the permanent exclusion of an agent. In this current democratic period, I have shown that there are no pariah agents, as all are participating in policy coalitions. This should increase the value that the constituents put on democracy, since even relatively extremist agents are winning something from the system. An interesting question is whether the legislators and/or the constituents perceive this value.

In addition to broad and difficult questions about representation and democratic sustainability, the agent framework could help inform studies of particular policy outcomes. The data I have explored in this book are largely devoid of policy content. An important next step in developing our understanding of the Latin American legislatures must be to analyze the particular policies that they produce. Use of the agent system framework to conceptualize the policy coalitional patterns will greatly aid this analysis.

This type of study will require a more detailed coding of the roll-call data for issue content and an analysis of the relationship between issues and the shape of policy coalitions. Are the leftist agents, for example, included in bills that deal with trade and economic development, education and poverty issues, the environment, procedural issues, or other types of bills? Are the rightist agents intransigent on labor and environmental issues, or are they more conciliatory? On what issues do centrist agents base their appeals and separate themselves from others that lie to their right or their left?

These questions have important normative foundations and theoretical implications. Normatively these are important issues since they address which policies actually make it through the political process. The theoretical value would be in explaining how the agent system affects which questions generate support.

Last, an element of dynamism should be brought into the analysis. While history has shown that the U.S. system can survive, my review of the voting records in the U.S. Congress turned up a surprising move toward higher levels of polarization and party unity. Previous periods of polarization (e.g., the lead up to the Civil War, the Depression era, and the 1960s) have signaled important partisan realignments, if not social upheaval. The current move may not suggest that the U.S. system has reached a critical point, but it is very curious that the post–Cold War era has opened a wider gap between the parties in the United States at the same time that agents in Latin America have apparently converged.

Changing patterns of identifiability and flexibility have not been a focus of the book because only the United States has sustained a democracy long enough (and utilized roll-call voting long enough) to support a cross-temporal explanation. As a result, this study has provided primarily static descriptions and explanations of the different agent systems across Latin America. Still, as Smith (1969; 1974) showed for Argentina in the first part of the twentieth century, and Poole and Rosenthal (1997) show for the history of the United States, agent systems are dynamic structures that both reflect and affect changing divisions within a polity. These changes are evident in the patterns of legislative voting; thus, as the countries continue to take roll calls and analysts continue to scrutinize them, our understanding of Latin American democracy will continue to improve.

Bibliography

Alcántara Sáez, Manuel, and Flavia Freidenberg, eds. 2002. *Partidos Políticos de América Latina*. Salamanca: Ediciones Universidad Salamanca.

Aldrich, John H. 1995. *Why Parties? The Origin and Transformation of Political Parties in America*. Chicago: The University of Chicago Press.

Aldrich, John H., and David W. Rohde. 1997–98. "The Transition to Republican Rule in the House: Implications for Theories of Congressional Politics." *Political Science Quarterly* 112,4:1–27.

Aldrich, John H., and David W. Rohde. 1998. "Measuring Conditional Party Government." Paper presented at the annual meeting of the Midwest Political Science Association, Chicago.

Aldrich, John H., and David W. Rohde. 2001. "The Logic of Conditional Party Government." In Lawrence Dodd and Bruce Oppenheimer, eds. *Congress Reconsidered*. Washington, DC: CQ Press.

Altman, David. 1998a. "Cooperation under Multiparty Presidential Regimes: Building and Sustaining Coalitions in Uruguay 1985–1997." Paper presented at Latin American Studies Association, Chicago.

Altman, David. 1998b. "The Politics of Coalition Formation and Survival in Multiparty Presidential Democracies: Building a Rational Choice and Neo-Institutionalist Theory." Paper presented at American Political Science Association, Boston.

Altman, David. 2000a. "Politics of Coalition Formation and Survival in Multiparty Presidential Democracies: Uruguay 1989–1999." *Party Politics* 6,3:259–83.

Altman, David. 2000b. "Executive Coalitions in Nine Latin American Multiparty Presidential Democracies." Paper presented at Latin American Studies Association, Miami.

American Political Science Association, Committee on Political Parties. 1950. *Toward a More Responsible Two-Party System*. New York: Rinehart and Company, p. 18.

Ames, Barry. 1995. "Electoral Strategy Under Open-List Proportional Representation." *American Journal of Political Science* 39,2:324–43.

Ames, Barry. 2001. *The Deadlock of Democracy in Brazil*. Ann Arbor: University of Michigan Press.

Ames, Barry. 2002. "Party Discipline in Brazil's Chamber of Deputies." In Scott Morgenstern and Benito Nacif, eds. *Legislative Politics in Latin America*. Cambridge: Cambridge University Press.

Amorim Neto, Octavio. 1998. "Of Presidents, Parties, and Ministers: Cabinet Formation and Legislative Decision-Making Under Separation of Powers." Unpublished Ph.D. dissertation, University of California, San Diego.

Amorim Neto, Octavio. 2002. "Presidential Cabinets, Electoral Cycles, and Coalition Discipline in Brazil." In Scott Morgenstern and Benito Nacif, eds. *Legislative Politics in Latin America*. Cambridge: Cambridge University Press.

Amorim Neto, Octavio, Gary W. Cox, and Mathew McCubbins. 1999. "The Cartel Model in Comparative Perspective: The Case of Brazil." Prepared for presentation at the annual meeting of the American Political Science Association, Washington, DC, August 31–September 3, 2000.

Amorim Neto, Octavio, and Fabiano Santos, 2001. "The Executive Connection: Presidentially Defined Factions and Party Discipline in Brazil." *Party Politics* 7,2:213–34.

Aronoff, Myron. 1993. *Power and Ritual in the Israel Labour Party: A Study in Political Anthropology*. Armonk, NY: M. E. Sharpe.

Axelrod Robert M. 1984. *The Evolution of Cooperation*. New York: Basic Books.

Barahona, Elena Martínez. 2002. "Uruguay." In Manuel Alcántara Sáez and Flavia Freidenberg, eds. *Partidos Políticos de América Latina*. Salamanca: Ediciones Universidad Salamanca.

Beck, Nathaniel, and Jonathan N. Katz. 1995. "What to do (and not to do) with Time-Series Cross-Section Data." *The American Political Science Review*, 89,3 (Sep): pp. 634–47.

Beck, Paul Allen, and Frank J. Sorauf. 1992. *Party Politics in America*. 7th ed. New York: HarperCollins Publishers.

Belloni, Frank P., and Dennis C. Beller, eds. 1978. *Faction Politics: Political Parties and Factionalism in Comparative Perspective*. Santa Barbara, CA: ABC-Clio.

Berger, Mark. 2000. "Impact of a Multi-Faceted Party on Senate Roll Call Votes: An Illustration of Conditional Party Government." Paper presented at Midwest Political Science Association, Chicago.

Buquet, Daniel, Daniel Chasquetti, and Juan Andrés Moraes. 1998. "Fragmentación Política y Gobierno en Uruguay: ¿Un Enfermo Imaginario?" Montevideo: Instituto de Ciencia Politítica, Universidad de la Republica.

Burke, Edmund. [1774] 1949. *Burke's Politics*. Edited by Ross J. S. Hoffman and Paul Levack. New York: Alfred A. Knopf.

Cain, Bruce, John Ferejohn, and Morris Fiorina. 1987. *The Personal Vote: Constituency Service and Electoral Independence*. Cambridge, MA: Harvard University Press.

Caramani, Daniele. 2000. *Elections in Western Europe since 1815: Electoral Results by Constituencies*. London: Macmillan Reference.

Carey, John M. 1996. *Term Limits and Legislative Representation*. Cambridge: Cambridge University Press.

Carey, John M. 2000. "Party Unity in Legislative Voting." Paper presented at American Political Science Association.

Carey, John M. 2002. "Parties, Coalitions, and the Chilean Congress in the 1990s." In Scott Morgenstern and Benito Nacif, eds. *Legislative Politics in Latin America*. Cambridge: Cambridge University Press.

Carey, John M. forthcoming. "Discipline, Accountability, and Legislative Voting in Latin America." *Comparative Politics*.

Carey, John, and Matthew S. Shugart. 1995. "Incentives to Cultivate a Personal Vote: A Rank Ordering of Electoral Formulas." *Electoral Studies* 14,4:417–39.

del Castillo, Pilar, and Daniel Zovatto G., eds. 1998. *La Financiación de la Política en Iberoamérica*. San José, Costa Rica: Instituto Interamericano de Derechos Humanos.

Chalmers, Douglas A., Maria do Carmo Campello de Souza, and Atilio A. Boron, eds. 1992. *The Right and Democracy in Latin America*. New York: Praeger.

Chasquetti, Daniel, 2000. "Democracia, Multipartidismo y Coaliciones: Evaluando la Difícil Combinación." Paper presented at Latin America Studies Association, Miami.

Cohen, Youssef. 1994. *Radicals, Reformers, and Reactionaries: The Prisoner's Dilemma and the Collapse of Democracy in Latin America*. Chicago: University of Chicago Press.

Cooper, Joseph, David Brady, and Patricia A. Hurley. 1977. "The Electoral Basis of Party Voting: Patterns and Trends in the U.S. House of Representatives." In Louis Maisel and Joseph Cooper, eds. *The Impact of the Electoral Process*. Beverly Hills, CA: Sage.

Coppedge, Michael. 1994. *Strong Parties and Lame Ducks: Presidential Partyarchy and Factionalism in Venezuela*. Stanford, CA: Stanford University Press.

Coppedge, Michael. 1998. "The Dynamic Diversity of Latin American Party Systems." *Party Politics* 4,4 (October).547–68.

Cox, Gary W., and Mathew D. McCubbins. 1993. *Legislative Leviathan: Party Government in the House*. Berkeley: University of California Press.

Cox, Gary W., and Scott Morgenstern, 2001. "Latin America's Reactive Assemblies and Proactive Presidents." *Comparative Politics* 33,2:171–89.

Cox, Gary W., and Emerson Niou. 1994. "Seat Bonuses Under the Single Non-Transferable Vote System: Evidence from Japan and Taiwan." *Comparative Politics* 26,2:221–236.

Cox, Gary W., and Frances Rosenbluth. 1993. "The Electoral Fortunes of Legislative Factions in Japan." *American Political Science Review* 87:577–89.

Cox, Gary W., and Frances Rosenbluth. 1994. "Reducing Nomination Errors: Factional Competition and Party Strategy in Japan." *Electoral Studies* 13,1:4–16.

Cox, Gary W., and Frances M. Rosenbluth 1995. "The Structural Determinants of Electoral Cohesiveness: England, Japan, and the United States." In Peter F. Cowhey and Mathew D. McCubbins, eds. *Structure and Policy in Japan and the United States*. Cambridge: Cambridge University Press.

Cox, Gary W., and Frances Rosenbluth. 1996. "Factional Competition for the Party Endorsement: The Case of Japan's Liberal Democratic Party." *British Journal of Political Science* 26:259–97.

Cox, Gary W., and Matthew Shugart. 1995. "In the Absence of Vote Pooling: Nominations and Vote Allocation Errors in Colombia." *Electoral Studies* 14:441–60.

Crisp, Brian. 1997. "Presidential Behavior in a System with Strong Parties: Venezuela, 1958–1995." In Scott Mainwaring and Matthew S. Shugart, eds. *Presidentialism and Democracy in Latin America*. Cambridge: Cambridge University Press.

Crisp, Brian. 2000. *Democratic Institutional Design: The Powers and Incentives of Venezuelan Politicians and Interest Groups*. Stanford, CA: Stanford University Press.

Czudnowski, Moshe. 1975. "Political Recruitment." In Fred I. Greenstein and Nelson W. Polsby, eds. *Handbook of Political Science*. Reading, MA: Addison-Wesley.

D'Amato, Luigi, 1965. *Correnti di Partido di Correnti*. Milan: Giuffre.

Deheza, Grace Ivana. 1997. *Gobiernos de Coalición en el Sistema Presidential: America del Sur*. Doctoral Thesis, Instituto Universitario Europeo.

de la Garza, Rudolf. 1972. *The Mexican Chamber of Deputies and the Mexican Political System*. Dissertation, University of Arizona.

Desposato, Scott W. 2002. "The Impact of Federalism on National Political Parties in Brazil." Working Paper. University of Arizona.

Dix, Robert H. 1984. "Incumbency and Electoral Turnover in Latin America." *Journal of Interamerican Studies and World Affairs* 26:435–48.

Dix, Robert H. 1992. "Democratization and Institutionalization of Latin American Political Parties." *Comparative Political Studies* 26:488–511.

Downs, Anthony. 1957. *An Economic Theory of Democracy*. New York: Harper.

Drake, Paul W., and Iván Jaksic. 1991. *The Struggle for Democracy in Chile: 1982–1990*. Lincoln: University of Nebraska Press.

Druckman, James. 1996. "Party Factionalism and Cabinet Durability." *Party Politics* 3:397–407.

Duverger, Maurice. 1954. *Political Parties: Their Organization and Activity in the Modern State*. Translated by Barbara and Robert North. New York: Wiley.

Eaton, Kent. 2002. "Fiscal Policy Making in the Argentine Legislature." In Scott Morgenstern and Benito Nacif, eds. *Legislative Politics in Latin America*. Cambridge: Cambridge University Press.

Epstein, Leon D. 1967. *Political Parties in Western Democracies*. New York: Praeger.

The Economist. July 29, 2000. "Peru, Unrest Surrounding Alberto Fujimori's Inauguration."

Fenno, Richard F. 1978. *Home Style: House Members in Their Districts*. Boston: Little Brown.

Ferreira Rubio, Delia, and Matteo Goretti. 1998. "When the President Governs Alone: The Decretazo in Argentina, 1989–93." In John M. Carey and Matthew Soberg Shugart, eds. *Executive Decree Authority*. Cambridge: Cambridge University Press.

Figueiredo, Argelina, and Fernando Limongi. 1995. "Partidos Políticos na Camara dos Deputados: 1989–1994." *Dados* 38:497–524.

Figueiredo, Argelina Cheibub, and Fernando Limongi. 2000. "Presidential Power, Legislative Organization, and Party Behavior in Brazil." *Comparative Politics* 32, 2:151–70.

Fiorina, Morris. 1977a. *Congress, Keystone of the Washington Establishment*. New Haven, CT: Yale University Press.

Fiorina, Morris. 1977b. "The Case of the Vanishing Marginals: The Bureaucracy Did It." *American Political Science Review.* 71 (March):177–81.

Foweraker, Joe. 1998. "Institutional Design, Party Systems and Governability – Differentiating the Presidential Regimes of Latin America." *British Journal of Political Science*, 28:651–76.

Gallagher, Michael. 1988. "Introduction." In Michael Gallagher and Michael Marsh, eds. *Candidate Selection in Comparative Perspective: The Secret Garden of Politics.* London: Sage.

Gallagher, Michael, and Michael Marsh, eds. 1988. *Candidate Selection in Comparative Perspective: The Secret Garden of Politics.* London: Sage.

Garretón, Manuel Antonio. 1989. *The Chilean Political Process.* Boston: Unwin Hyman.

Gillespie, Charles Guy. 1991. *Negotiating Democracy: Politicians and Generals in Uruguay.* Cambridge: Cambridge University Press.

González, Luis E. 1991. *Political Structures and Democracy in Uruguay.* South Bend, IN: Notre Dame Press.

González, Luis Eduardo. 1993. *Estructuras Políticas y Democracia en Uruguay.* Montevideo: Fundación de Cultura Universitaria and Instituto de Ciencia Política.

González, Luis E. 1995. "Continuity and Change in the Uruguayan Party System." In Scott Mainwaring and Timothy R. Scully, eds. *Building Democratic Institutions: Party Systems in Latin America.* Stanford, CA: Stanford University Press.

Heller, William. 2001. "Making Policy Stick: Why the Government Gets What It Wants in Multiparty Parliaments." *American Journal of Political Science.* 45,4 (October):780–98.

Hinich, Melvin, and Michael Munger. 1994. *Ideology and the Theory of Political Choice.* Ann Arbor: University of Michigan Press.

Hinich, Melvin, and Michael Munger. 1997. *Analytical Politics.* Cambridge: Cambridge University Press.

Huber, John D. 1996. *Rationalizing Parliament: Legislative Institutions and Party Politics in France.* Cambridge: Cambridge University Press.

Huneeus, Carlos. 1998. "El Financiamiento de los Partidos Políticos y las Campañas Electorales en Chile." In Pilar del Castillo and Daniel Zovatto G., eds. *La Financiación de la Política en Iberoamérica.* San José, Costa Rica: Instituto Interamericano de Derechos Humanos.

Huntington, Samuel. 1968. *Political Order in Changing Societies.* New Haven, CT: Yale University Press.

Jackson, John E., and John W. Kingdon, 1992. "Ideology, Interest Group Scores, and Legislative Votes." *American Journal of Political Science.* 36,3:805–23.

Jacobson, Gary J. 1987. "Running Scared: Elections and Congressional Politics in the 1980s." In Mathew D. McCubbins and Terry Sullivan, eds. *Congress: Structure and Policy.* Cambridge: Cambridge University Press.

Jones, Mark. 1995. *Electoral Laws and the Survival of Presidential Democracy.* Notre Dame, IN: University of Notre Dame Press.

Jones, Mark. 1997. "Evaluating Argentina's Presidential Democracy, 1983–1995." In Scott Mainwaring and Matthew S. Shugart, eds. *Presidentialism and Democracy in Latin America.* Cambridge: Cambridge University Press.

Jones, Mark. 2002. "Explaining the High Level of Party Discipline in the Argentine Congress." In Scott Morgenstern and Benito Nacif, eds. *Legislative Politics in Latin America*. Cambridge: Cambridge University Press.

Jones, Mark P., and Scott Mainwaring. 2003. "The Nationalization of Parties and Party Systems: An Empirical Measure and an Application to the Americas," *Party Politics* 9:2.

Katz, Richard S. 1973. "The Attribution of Variance in Electoral Returns: An Alternative Measurement Technique." *American Political Science Review* 67,3:817–28.

Katz, Richard S. 1986. "Intraparty Preference Voting." In Bernard Grofman and Arend Lijphart, eds. *Electoral Laws and Their Political Consequences*. New York: Agathon Press.

Kawato, Sadafumi. 1987. "Nationalization and Partisan Realignment in Congressional Elections." *American Political Science Review* 81:1235–50.

Kiewiet, D. Roderick, and Mathew D. McCubbins. 1991. *The Logic of Delegation: Congressional Parties and the Appropriations Process*. Chicago: The University of Chicago Press.

King, Gary, Robert O. Keohane, and Sidney Verba. 1994. *Designing Social Inquiry: Scientific Inference in Qualitative Research*. Princeton, NJ: Princeton University Press.

Krehbiel, Keith. 1991. *Information and Legislative Organization*. Ann Arbor: University of Michigan Press.

Krehbiel, Keith. 1993. "Where's the Party?" *British Journal of Political Science* 23: 235–66.

Krehbiel, Keith. 2000. "Party Discipline and Measures of Partisanship." *American Journal of Political Science* 44,2:212–27.

Lanzaro, Jorge Luis. 2000. *La 'Segunda Transición' en Uruguay*. Montevideo: Instituto de Ciencia Politica.

LaPalombara, Joseph. 1987. *Democracy Italian Style*. New Haven, CT: Yale University Press.

Laurnaga, Maria Elena. 1993. "Fraccionamiento Partidario y Disciplina Politica en el Gobierno del Partido Nacional." *Revista Uruguaya de Ciencia Politica* 6: 57–80.

Laver, Michael, and Norman Schofield. 1990. "Coalitions and Cabinet Government." *American Political Science Review* 84,3:873–90.

Laver, Michael, and Kenneth A. Shepsle. 1990. "Coalitions and Cabinet Government." *American Political Science Review* 84:873–90.

Laver, Michael, and Kenneth A. Shepsle. 1996. *Making and Breaking Governments: Cabinets and Legislatures in Parliamentary Democracies*. Cambridge: Cambridge University Press.

Lijphart, Arend. 1984. *Democracies: Patterns of Majoritarian and Consensus Government in Twenty-One Countries*. New Haven, CT: Yale University Press.

Lijphart, Arend. 1994. *Electoral Systems and Party Systems: A Study of Twenty-Seven Democracies 1945–1990*. New York: Oxford University Press.

Lindahl, Goran G. 1962. *Uruguay's New Path: A Study of Politics During the First Colegiado, 1919–33*. Stockholm: Library and Institute of Ibero-American Studies.

Linz, Juan J. 1990. "The Perils of Presidentialism." *Journal of Democracy* 1:51–69.

Linz, Juan J. 1994. "Presidential or Parliamentary Democracy: Does It Make a Difference?" In Juan Linz and Arturo Valenzuela, eds. *The Failure of Presidential Democracy*. Baltimore: The Johns Hopkins University Press.

Linz, Juan J., and Alfred Stepan. 1996. *Problems of Democratic Transition and Consolidation*. Baltimore: The Johns Hopkins University Press.

Londregan, John. 2000. *Legislative Institutions and Ideology in Chile*. Cambridge: Cambridge University Press.

Londregan, John. 2002. "Appointment, Reelection, and Autonomy in the Senate of Chile." In Scott Morgenstern and Benito Nacif, eds. *Legislative Politics in Latin America*. Cambridge: Cambridge University Press.

Luebbert, Gregory M. 1986. *Comparative Democracy: Policymaking and Governing Coalitions in Europe and Israel*. New York: Columbia University Press.

Lyne, Mona M. 1999. "Party Behavior and Electoral Law in Brazil: Is the Tail Wagging the Dog?" Paper prepared for Southwestern Social Science Association, San Antonio, TX.

Mainwaring, Scott. 1993. "Presidentialism, Multipartism, and Democracy: The Difficult Combination." *Comparative Political Studies* 2:198–228.

Mainwaring, Scott. 1995. "Brazil: Weak Parties, Feckless Democracy." In Scott Mainwaring and Timothy R. Scully, eds. *Building Democratic Institutions: Party Systems in Latin America*. Stanford, CA: Stanford University Press.

Mainwaring, Scott. 1997. "Multipartism, Robust Federalism, and Presidentialism in Brazil." In Scott Mainwaring and Matthew S. Shugart, eds. *Presidentialism and Democracy in Latin America*. Cambridge: Cambridge University Press.

Mainwaring, Scott P. 1999. *Rethinking Party Systems in the Third Wave of Democratization*. Stanford, CA: Stanford University Press.

Mainwaring, Scott P., and Aníbal Pérez Liñán. 1997. "Party Discipline in the Brazilian Constitutional Congress." *Legislative Studies Quarterly*, XXII,4:453–83.

Mainwaring, Scott, and Matthew S. Shugart, 1997. "Conclusion: Presidentialism and the Party System." In Scott Mainwaring and Matthew S. Shugart, eds. *Presidentialism and Democracy in Latin America*. Cambridge: Cambridge University Press.

Mainwaring, Scott, and Timothy R. Scully, eds. 1995. *Building Democratic Institutions: Party Systems in Latin America*. Stanford, CA: Stanford University Press.

Maira, Luis. 1979. "The Strategy and Tactics of the Chilean Conterrevolution in the Area of Political Institutions." In Federico G. Gil, Ricardo Lagos, and Henry A. Landsberger, eds. *Chile at the Turning Point: Lessons of the Socialist Years, 1970–1973*. Philadelphia: Institute for the Study of Human Issues.

Marconi Nicolau, Jairo (org). 1998. *Dados Eleitorais do Brasil (1982–1996)*. Editora Revan: IUPERJ.

Marenghi, Patricia. 2002. "Organización de Los Partidos Políticos del Cono Sur: Dimensiones Comparadas." In Manuel Alcántara and Flavia Freidenberg, eds. *Partidos Políticos de América Latina: Cono Sur*. Salamanca: University of Salamanca.

Martz, John. 1988. "The Malaise of Venezuelan Political Parties: Is Democracy Endangered?" In Donald Herman, ed. *Democracy in Latin America: Colombia and Venezuela*. New York: Praeger.

Mayer, Fredrick. 1998. *Interpreting NAFTA: The Science and Art of Political Analysis*. New York: Columbia University Press.

Mayhew, David R. 1974. "Congressional Elections: The Case of the Vanishing Marginals." _Polity_ 6:295–317.

McDonald, Ronald H. 1978. "Party Factions and Modernization: A Comparative Analysis of Colombia and Uruguay." In Frank P. Belloni and Dennis C. Beller, eds. _Faction Politics: Political Parties and Factionalism in Comparative Perspective._ Santa Barbara, CA: ABC-Clio.

McDonald, Ronald H., and J. Mark Ruhl. 1989. _Party Politics and Elections in Latin America._ Boulder, CO: Westview Press.

McGuire, James W. 1995. "Political Parties and Democracy in Argentina." In Scott Mainwaring and Timothy R. Scully, eds. _Building Democratic Institutions: Party Systems in Latin America._ Stanford, CA: Stanford University Press.

Mezey, Michael L. 1979. _Comparative Legislatures._ Durham, NC: Duke University Press.

Michels, Robert. 1915. _Political Parties: A Sociological Study of Oligarchical Tendencies in Modern Democracy._ Translated by Eden and Cedar Paul. Glencoe, IL: Free Press.

Middlebrook, Kevin. 2000. "Conservative Parties, Elite Representation, and Democracy in Latin America." In Kevin Middlebrook, ed. _Conservative Parties, the Right, and Democracy in Latin America._ Baltimore: The Johns Hopkins University Press.

Molina Armas, Pilar. 1993. "RN-UDI: La Gran Batalla." _El Mercurio,_ Santiago, Chile: 12/31/93: D1, D11–12.

Molinelli, N. Guillermo. 1995. "President-Congress Relations in Argentina: 1983–1995." Paper presented at Latin American Studies Association, Washington, DC.

Molinelli, N. Guillermo, M. Valeria Palanza, and Gisela Sin. 1999. _Congreso, Presidencia y Justicia en Argentina: Materiales Para su Estudio._ Buenos Aires: CEDI.

Morgenstern, Scott. 2001. "Organized Factions and Disorganized Parties: Electoral Incentives in Uruguay." _Party Politics_ 7,2:235–56.

Morgenstern, Scott, and Luigi Manzetti. Forthcoming. "Legislative Oversight: Interests and Institutions in the United States and Argentina." In Scott Mainwaring and Guillermo O'Donnell, ed. _Institutions, Accountability, and Democratic Governance in Latin America._ Oxford: Oxford University Press.

Morgenstern, Scott, and Benito Nacif, eds. 2002. _Legislative Politics in Latin America._ Cambridge: Cambridge University Press.

Morgenstern, Scott, and Richard F. Potthoff. 2003. "The Components of Elections: District Heterogeneity, District-Time Effects, and Volatility." Working Paper. Barcelona: Institut de Ciències Politiques i Socials.

Mustapic, Ana María. 2002. "Oscillating Relations: President and Congress in Argentina." In Scott Morgenstern and Benito Nacif, eds. _Legislative Politics in Latin America._ Cambridge: Cambridge University Press.

Mustapic, Ana María, and Natalia Ferretti. 1995. "El Veto Presidencial Bajo los Gobiernos de Alfonsin y Menem (1983–1993)." Working Paper 14. Buenos Aires: Instituto Torcuato di Tella.

Nohlen, Dieter, ed. 1993. _Enciclopedia Electoral Latinoamericana y del Caribe._ San José, Costa Rica: Instituto Interamericano de Derechos Humanos.

O'Donnell, Guillermo A. 1973. _Modernization and Bureaucratic Authoritarianism._ Berkeley: University of California Press.

O'Donnell, Guillermo. 1992. "Substantive or Procedural Consensus? Notes on the Latin American Bourgeoisie." In Douglas A. Chalmers, Maria do Carmo Campello de Souza, and Atilio A. Borón, eds. *The Right and Democracy in Latin America.* New York: Praeger.

O'Donnell, Guillermo. 1994. "Delegative Democracy." *Journal of Democracy* 5,1: 55–69.

Olson, Mancur. 1993. "Dictatorship, Democracy, and Development." *American Political Science Review* 87,3:567–76.

Özbudun, Ergun. 1970. *Party Cohesion in Western Democracies: A Causal Analysis.* Beverly Hills, CA: Sage.

Packenham, Robert. 1970. "Legislatures in Political Development." In Allan Kornberg and Lloyd D. Musolf, eds. *Legislatures in Developmental Perspective.* Durham, NC: Duke University Press.

Panebianco, Angelo. 1988. *Political Parties: Organization and Power.* Translated by Marc Silver. Cambridge: Cambridge University Press.

Pasquino, G. 1990. "Party Elites and Democratic Consolidations: Cross-national Comparison of Southern European Experience." In Geoffrey Pridham, ed. *Securing Democracy: Political Parties and Democratic Consolidation in Southern Europe.* London: Routledge.

Pedersen, Mogens. 1979. "The Dynamics of European Party Systems: Changing Patterns of Electoral Volatility." *European Journal of Political Research* 7,1:1–26.

Peeler, John. 1998. *Building Democracy in Latin America.* Boulder, CO: Lynne Rienner Publishers.

Pivel Devoto, Juan E. 1956. *Historia de los Partidos e Ideas Políticas en el Uruguay, Tomo II.* Monetvideo: Universidad de la Republica Oriental del Uruguay.

Polsby, Nelson W. 1968. "The Institutionalization of the U.S. House of Representatives." *American Political Science Review* 62,2:144–68.

Poole, Keith T., and Howard Rosenthal. 1985. "A Spatial Model for Legislative Roll Call Analysis." *American Journal of Political Science* 29:357–84.

Poole, Keith T., and Howard Rosenthal. 1991. "Patterns of Congressional Voting." *American Journal of Political Science* 35,1:228–78.

Poole, Keith T., and Howard Rosenthal. 1997. *Congress: A Political-Economic History of Roll Call Voting.* New York: Oxford University Press.

Powell, G. Bingham. 1999. *Elections as Instruments of Democracy: Majoritarian and Proportional Visions.* New Haven, CT: Yale University Press.

Pridham, Geoffrey, ed. 1995. *Transitions to Democracy: Comparative Perspectives from Southern Europe, Latin America, and Eastern Europe.* Brookfield, VT: Dartmouth.

Przeworski, Adam. 1995. *Sustainable Democracy.* Cambridge: Cambridge University Press.

Ragin, Charles C. 1987. *The Comparative Method: Moving Beyond Qualitative and Quantitative Strategies.* Berkeley: University of California Press.

Ranney, Austin, and Willmoore Kendall. 1956. *Democracy and the American Party System.* Westport, CT: Greenwood Press.

Rial, Juan. 1998. "La Financiación de los Partidos Políticos en Uruguay." In Pilar del Castillo and Daniel Zovatto G., eds. *La Financiación de la Política en Iberoamérica*. San José, Costa Rica: Instituto Interamericano de Derechos Humanos.

Rice, Stuart A. (1925). "The Behavior of Legislative Groups." *Political Science Quarterly* 40:60–72.

Riker, William H. 1959. "A Method for Determining the Significance of Roll Calls in Voting Bodies." In John C. Wilkie and Heinz Eulau, eds. *Legislative Behavior: A Reader in Theory and Practice*. Glencoe, IL: The Free Press: 377–84.

Riker, William. 1962. *The Theory of Political Coalitions*. New Haven, CT: Yale University Press.

Roberts, Kenneth M., and Erik Wibbels. 1999. "Party Systems and Electoral Volatility in Latin America: A Test of Economic, Institutional, and Structural Explanations." *American Political Science Review*. 93,3:575–90.

Rohde, David. 1991. *Parties and Leaders in the Postreform House*. Chicago: University of Chicago Press.

Sabsay, Daniel. 1998. "El Financiamiento de los Partidos Políticos en Argentina." In Pilar del Castillo and Daniel Zovatto G., eds. *La Financiación de la Política en Iberoamérica*. San José, Costa Rica: Instituto Interamericano de Derechos Humanos.

Samuels, David J. 2000. "The Gubernatorial Coattails Effect: Federalism and Congressional Elections in Brazil." *Journal of Politics* 62,1: 240–53.

Samuels, David J. 2002. "Progressive Ambition, Federalism, and Pork-Barreling in Brazil." In Scott Morgenstern and Benito Nacif, eds. *Legislative Politics in Latin America*. Cambridge: Cambridge University Press.

Samuels, David J. 2003. *Ambassadors of the States: Political Ambition, Federalism, and Congressional Politics in Brazil*. Cambridge: Cambridge University Press.

Sani, Giacomo, and Giovanni Sartori. 1983. "Polarization, Competition, and Fragmentation in Western Democracies." In Hans Daalder and Peter Mair, eds. *Western European Party Systems: Continuity and Change*. Beverly Hills, CA: Sage: 307–40.

Sartori, Giovanni. 1976. *Parties and Party Systems: A Framework for Analysis*. Cambridge: Cambridge University Press.

Schattschneider, E. E. 1942. *Party Government*. New York: Rinehart.

Schattschneider, E. E. 1960. *The Semisovereign People*. New York: Rinehart.

Scheiner, Ethan. 1999. "Urban Outfitters: City-Based Strategies and Success in Postwar Japanese Politics." *Electoral Studies* 18:179–98.

Schlesinger, Joseph A. 1991. *Political Parties and the Winning of Office*. Ann Arbor: University of Michigan Press.

Scully, Roger, and Samuel C. Patterson. 2001. "Ideology, Partisanship, and Decision-Making in a Contemporary American Legislature." *Party Politics* 7,2:131–55.

Scully, Timothy R. 1995. "Reconstituting Party Politics in Chile." In Scott Mainwaring and Timothy R. Scully, eds. *Building Democratic Institutions: Party Systems in Latin America*. Stanford, CA: Stanford University Press.

Shalev, Michael. 1998. "Limits of and Alternatives to Multiple Regression in Macro-Comparative Research." http://micro3.mscc.huji.ac.il/~method/Papers/Stockholm.htm. Prepared for Second Conference on the Welfare State at the Crossroads, Stockholm.

———. 1988. "Japan: Localism, Factionalism, and Personalism." In Michael Gallagher and Michael Marsh, eds. *Candidate Selection in Comparative Perspective: The Secret Garden of Politics*. London: Sage.

Shugart, Matthew S., and John Carey. 1992. *Presidents and Assemblies*. Cambridge: Cambridge University Press.

Siavelis, Peter M. 2000. *The President and the Congress in Post-Authoritarian Chile: Institutional Constraints to Democratic Consolidation*. University Park: University of Pennsylvania Press.

———. 2002. "Exaggerated Presidentialism and Moderate Presidents: Executive/Legislative Relations in Chile." In Scott Morgenstern and Benito Nacif, eds. *Legislative Politics in Latin America*. Cambridge: Cambridge University Press.

Smith, Peter. 1969. *Politics and Beef in Argentina*. New York: Columbia University Press.

Smith, Peter H. 1974. *Argentina and the Failure of Democracy: Conflict among Political Elites, 1904–1955*. Madison: University of Wisconsin Press.

Smith, Peter H. 1979. *Labyrinths of Power*. Princeton, NJ: Princeton University Press.

Solari, Aldo. 1991. *Uruguay: Partidos Politicos y Sistema Electoral*. Montevideo: Fundación De Cultura.

———. 1965. "A Variance Components Model of Political Effects." In John M. Claunch, ed. *Mathematical Applications in Political Science*. Dallas: Southern Methodist University.

Stokes, Donald. 1967. "Parties and the Nationalization of Electoral Forces." In William N. Chambers and Walter D. Burnham, eds. *The American Party Systems: States of Political Development*. New York: Oxford University Press.

Stokes, Susan. 1996. "Public Opinion and Market Reform: The Limits of Economic Voting." *Comparative Political Studies*. 29:499–519.

Stokes, Susan C., ed. 2001a. *Public Support for Market Reforms in New Democracies*. Cambridge: Cambridge University Press.

Stokes, Susan C. 2001b. "Introduction: Public Opinion of Market Reforms: A Framework." In Susan C. Stokes, ed. *Public Support for Market Reforms in New Democracies*. Cambridge: Cambridge University Press.

Strom, Kaare. 1990. "A Behavioral Theory of Competitive Political Parties." *American Journal of Political Science* 34:565–98.

Strom, Kaare. 1994. "The Presthus Debacle: Intraparty Politics and Bargaining Failure in Norway." *American Political Science Review* 88:112–27.

Swindle, Stephen M. 2002. "Supply and Demand of the Personal Vote: Theoretical Considerations and Empirical Implications of Collective Electoral Incentives." *Party Politics* 8,3:279–300.

Taylor, Philip B. 1963. "Interests and Institutional Dysfunction in Uruguay." *The American Political Science Review* 57,1:62–74.

Taylor, Philip B. 1985. "Uruguay: The Costs of Inept Political Corporatism." In Howard J. Wiarda and Harvey F. Kline, eds. *Latin American Politics and Development*. Boulder, CO: Westview Press.

Tezanos, Jose Felix, Ramon Cotarelo, and Andres de Blas, eds. 1989. *La Transición Democrática Española*. Madrid: Editorial Sistema.

Thayer, Nathaniel. 1969. *How the Conservatives Rule Japan.* Princeton, NJ: Princeton University Press.

Thies, Michael Fredrick. 1994. *Majority Party Decision Making and Policy Change: The Liberal Democratic Party and Japanese Fiscal Policy.* Dissertation, University of California, San Diego.

Thies, Michael F. 1998. "When Will Pork Leave the Farm? Institutional Bias in Japan and the United States." *Legislative Studies Quarterly* 23,4:467–92.

Tsebelis, George. 1995. "Decision Making in Political Systems: Veto Players in Presidentialism, Parliamentarism, Multicameralism, and Multipartyism." *British Journal of Political Science* 25:289–326.

Valen, Henry. 1988. "Norway: Decentralization and Group Representation." In Michael Gallagher and Michael Marsh, eds. *Candidate Selection in Comparative Perspective: The Secret Garden of Politics.* London. Sage.

Valenzuela, Arturo. 1978. *The Breakdown of Democratic Regimes: Chile.* Baltimore: The Johns Hopkins University Press.

Valenzuela, Arturo. 1994. "Party Politics and the Crisis of Presidentialism in Chile: A Proposal for a Parliamentary Form of Government." In Juan Linz and Arturo Valenzuela, eds. *The Failure of Presidential Democracy.* Baltimore: Johns Hopkins University Press.

Valverde Loya, Miguel Ángel. 1997. "Vinculación entre Política Interna y Política Exterior in los Estados Unidos: La Negociación del Tratado de Libre Comercio en América del Norte." *Politica y Gobierno* IV,2:377–406.

Von Neumann, John, and Oskar Morgenstern. 1944. *The Theory of Games and Economic Behavior.* Princeton, NJ: Princeton University Press.

Weingast, Barry, and William Marshall. 1988. "The Industrial Organization of Congress; or, Why Legislatures, Like Firms, Are Not Organized as Markets." *Journal of Political Economy* 96:132–63.

Weldon, Jeffrey A. 2000. "Voting in Mexico's Chamber of Deputies, 1998–1999." Paper presented at Latin American Studies Association, Miami.

Weldon, Jeffrey. 2002. "Legislative Delegation and the Budget Process in Mexico." In Scott Morgenstern and Benito Nacif, eds. *Legislative Politics in Latin America.* Cambridge: Cambridge University Press.

Wells, Henry. 1980. "The Conduct of Venezuelan Elections: Rules and Practice." In Howard R. Penniman, ed. *Venezuela at the Polls.* Washington, DC: American Enterprise Institute.

Zariski, Raphael, 1978. "Party Factions and Comparative Politics: Some Empirical Findings." In Frank P. Belloni and Dennis C. Beller, eds. *Faction Politics: Political Parties and Factionalism in Comparative Perspective.* Santa Barbara, CA: ABC-Clio.

Zovatto, Daniel G. 1998. "La Financiación Política en Iberoamérica: Una Visión Preliminar Comprada." In Pilar del Castillo and Daniel Zovatto G., eds. *La Financiación de la Política en Iberoamérica.* San José, Costa Rica: Instituto Interamericano de Derechos Humanos.

Zuckerman, Alan S. 1979. *The Politics of Faction: Christian Democratic Rule in Italy.* New Haven, CT: Yale University Press.

Subject Index

215

Author Index